STORIES OF THE STATES

GEORGIA HISTORY STORIES

BY

J. HARRIS CHAPPELL, Ph.D
PRESIDENT OF THE GEORGIA NORMAL
AND INDUSTRIAL COLLEGE.

ILLUSTRATED

SILVER, BURDETT AND COMPANY
NEW YORK   ATLANTA   BOSTON   DALLAS   CHICAGO

609925
C

Copyright, 1905, by
SILVER, BURDETT AND COMPANY.

This scarce antiquarian book is included in our special *Legacy Reprint Series*. In the interest of creating a more extensive selection of rare historical book reprints, we have chosen to reproduce this title even though it may possibly have occasional imperfections such as missing and blurred pages, missing text, poor pictures, markings, dark backgrounds and other reproduction issues beyond our control. Because this work is culturally important, we have made it available as a part of our commitment to protecting, preserving and promoting the world's literature. Thank you for your understanding.

To My Mother
Mrs. Loretto Lamar Chappell

A native and life-long Georgian, now in her eighty-seventh year, this little book about the State and the people she loves so well is affectionately dedicated.

PREFACE.

In this book the author has undertaken to relate what seemed to him to be the most interesting events in the history of Georgia, from the planting of the colony in 1733 to the years immediately preceding the War of Secession. The narrative, as a rule, is adapted to children from twelve to fifteen years of age; however, the author believes that it will be interesting reading for grown people, and for youths of some maturity. In several instances the author has found that the subjects treated could not be well presented in the form of children's stories. Such is especially the case with nearly all that is contained in Part III, the Development Period.

In preparing this volume the author has read and studied with the utmost care a great many books bearing on Georgia's history. He has also done much original investigation. His aim above all things has been to make his work authentic and reliable. While he has tried to write in an attractive style, he has refrained from trifling with his subject—a fault too common with many writers of the so-called history stories of the day.

The following are the principal sources from which

the facts and information contained in this volume are derived:

History of Georgia to 1798. By Rev. W. B. Stevens. 2 vols. Philadelphia, 1859.

History of Georgia to end of American Revolution. By C. C. Jones. 2 vols. Boston, 1883.

James Oglethorpe. By Henry Bruce. New York, 1890.

History of Alabama. By Albert J. Pickett. Charleston, 1851.

Miscellanies of Georgia. By Absalom H. Chappell. Columbus, 1874.

Story of Georgia and the Georgia People. By Rev. G. G. Smith. Macon, 1900.

Historical Collections of Georgia. By Rev. George White. New York, 1854.

The Salzburgers. By P. A. Strobel. Baltimore, 1855.

Tomo-chi-chi, Mico of the Yamacraws. By C. C. Jones. Savannah, 1876.

Dead Towns of Georgia. By C. C. Jones. Savannah, 1878.

School History of Georgia. By Lawton B. Evans. New York, 1898.

School History of Georgia. By Charles H. Smith. Boston, 1896.

Stories of Georgia. By Joel Chandler Harris. New York, 1896.

Life of Gen. James Jackson. By Thomas M. P. Charlton. Augusta, 1809.

Life of George M. Troup. By E. J. Harden. Savannah, 1840.

Case of the Cherokee Indians Against the State of Georgia. By Richard Peters. Philadelphia, 1831.

Georgia and State Rights. By Ulrich B. Phillips. Washington, 1902.

Preface. vii

Memories of Fifty Years. By W. H. Sparks. Philadelphia, 1870.

Recollections of a Georgia Loyalist. By Elizabeth L. Johnstone. New York, 1901.

Historical Sketches of Colonial Florida. By Richard L. Campbell. Cleveland, 1892.

Historical Record of Savannah. By F. D. Lee and J. L. Agnew. Savannah, 1869.

American State Papers (numerous volumes).

Old Pamphlets on Georgia Colonial history.

The author is also indebted to that scholarly gentleman, Mr. Otis Ashmore, Superintendent of Schools, Savannah, for valuable aid; to Mrs. J. J. Wilder, Savannah, President of the Society of Colonial Dames of Georgia, and Mrs. R. E. Park, Atlanta, Ex-Regent of the Georgia Daughters of the American Revolution, for information on particular points; and to numerous persons in different parts of Georgia for their prompt and satisfactory answers to special questions addressed to them.

The author hopes his book will prove instructive and interesting both to the youth and to the adults of Georgia, and that it may be found valuable as a supplementary reader in the schools of the State.

J. HARRIS CHAPPELL.

Milledgeville, Ga., September, 1904.

CONTENTS.

PART I.—COLONIAL PERIOD.

Page.

CHAPTER I. JAMES OGLETHORPE.
   I. Oglethorpe's Early Career 1
   II. Oglethorpe's Georgia Colony Enterprise 7

CHAPTER II. FOUNDING OF SAVANNAH.
   I. Seeking a Location 13
   II. Planting the Colony 19

CHAPTER III. TOMO-CHI-CHI, MICO OF THE YAMACRAWS.
   I. Tomo-chi-chi's Treaty with Oglethorpe 27
   II. Tomo-chi-chi's Visit to England 33
   III. Tomo-chi-chi's Religious Views 39
   IV. Tomo-chi-chi's Florida Expedition 42
   V. Tomo-chi-chi's Death and Burial 49

CHAPTER IV. THE SALZBURGERS.
   I. Persecution in Austria 54
   II. Emigration to Georgia 57
   III. Old Ebenezer 61
   IV. New Ebenezer 64

CHAPTER V. THE HIGHLANDERS 74

CHAPTER VI. FREDERICA 79

CHAPTER VII. THE SPANISH WAR.
   I. Preparations for the War 87
   II. Siege of St. Augustine 92
   III. Battle of St. Simon's Sound 98
   IV. Bloody Marsh 102

CHAPTER VIII. "NON SIBI SED ALIIS" 109

Contents.

Part II.—REVOLUTIONARY PERIOD.

		Page.
Chapter IX. The Stamp Act in Georgia		119

Chapter X. Capture of Savannah.

    I. Arrival of the British Fleet 131
   II. Quash Dolly and the Flank Movement 137

Chapter XI. Three Georgia Tories.

    I. Thomas Brown 145
   II. Daniel McGirth 151
  III. Colonel Grierson 155

Chapter XII. Three Georgia Patriots.

    I. Elijah Clarke 157
   II. James Jackson 164
  III. John Twiggs 172

Chapter XIII. Siege of Savannah.

    I. D'Estaing Outwitted 173
   II. The Bombardment 176
  III. The Assault and Pulaski's Death 178
  IV. Death of Sergeant Jasper 185

Chapter XIV.—Nancy Hart 192

Part III.—DEVELOPMENT PERIOD.

Chapter XV. Alexander McGillivray.

    I. McGillivray's Pedigree and Early Career 204
   II. McGillivray in the Revolution 207
  III. The Oconee War 210
  IV. The Treaty of New York 218
   V. William Augustus Bowles 225
  VI. Passing of McGillivray 231

Contents.

CHAPTER XVI. THE YAZOO FRAUD.

		Page.
I.	The Yazoo Country and the Speculators	235
II.	"The Yazooists" and Their Scheme	237
III.	Passage of the Yazoo Act	241
IV.	James Jackson and the Day of Wrath	244
V.	Repeal of the Yazoo Act	248

CHAPTER XVII. TROUP AND THE TREATY.

I.	Status of Indian Affairs in Georgia in 1823	251
II.	The Indian Spring Treaty	255
III.	Murder of McIntosh	261
IV.	Troup's Altercation with Major Andrews and General Gaines	226
V.	Troup's Controversy with the Federal Government	271
VI.	Declaration of War	277
VII.	"All's Well that Ends Well"	279
VIII.	Last Days of Troup	282

CHAPTER XVIII. GEORGIA AND THE CHEROKEES.

I.	Early Relations	285
II.	Civilizing of the Cherokees	288
III.	Political Status of the Cherokees	291
IV.	Georgia and the Cherokees Lock Horns	294
V.	Georgia and the Gold Diggers	298
VI.	The Cherokee Nation *vs.* The State of Georgia	300
VII.	Worcester and Butler *vs.* The State of Georgia	304
VIII.	Georgia's Aggressions	308
IX.	Treaty Factions	310
X.	Expulsion of the Cherokees	314
XI.	Assassination of the Treaty Chiefs	320

CHAPTER XIX. EXPANSION OF GEORGIA.

I.	Georgia at the Close of the Revolution	322
II.	First Expansion: From the Ogeechee to the Oconee	326

Contents.

		Page
III.	Second Expansion: From the Oconee to the Ocmulgee	333
IV.	Third Expansion: From the Ocmulgee to the Flint	340
V.	Fourth Expansion: South Georgia and Its Slow Development	344
VI.	Fifth Expansion: From the Flint to the Chattahoochee	346
VII.	Sixth Expansion: The Cherokee Country	349

CHAPTER XX. GEORGIA AND GEORGIANS OF 1840.

I.	The Mountains	353
II.	The Up Country	356
III.	The Cotton Belt	357
IV.	The Sea-Coast	364
V.	South Georgia	369

ILLUSTRATIONS AND MAPS.

	Page.
James Oglethorpe. (*Portrait and Autograph*) . .	Frontispiece.
The Duke of Marlborough	3
Prince Eugene of Savoy	4
The Houses of Parliament	5
A Philanthropist Visiting the Debtors' Prison	7
King George II	9
The River at Savannah as It Appears To-day	15
The Colony of Georgia	25
Tomo-chi-chi and Toonahowi	37
John Wesley Teaching the Indians	40
Map Showing Settlements	43
Mouth of the St. John's River as It Appears To-day . . .	45
George Whitfield Preaching	50
Tomo-chi-chi's Grave	53
Queen Caroline	68
Jerusalem Church at Ebenezer	70
A Highland Officer	75
Wesley Oak at Frederica	84
Ruins of the Old Fort at Frederica	85
The Old Spanish Gate at St. Augustine	94
St. Mark's Castle, St. Augustine	97
Map of St. Simon's Island	100

xiv   *Illustrations and Maps.*

	Page.
Oglethorpe at the Age of Ninety-two	115
English Stamps for America	119
King George III	122
Colonists Burning the Stamp Seller in Effigy	123
William Pitt	129
George Walton	133
Button Gwinnett	134
Lyman Hall	134
Lachlan McIntosh	135
Noble Jones	136
Joseph Habersham	136
General Robert Howe	137
Residence of George Walton at Augusta	148
Colonel Andrew Pickens	158
"Light Horse Harry" Lee	161
James Jackson	165
General Benjamin Lincoln	167
Lee's Cavalry Skirmishing	169
General Anthony Wayne	171
Count d'Estaing	173
Count Pulaski	175
Monument to Pulaski	184
Sergeant Jasper at Fort Moultrie	186
Monument to Sergeant Jasper	190
Indians Plundering Cattle on a Frontier Plantation	213
George Washington	218
Stone or Rock Mountain	220
William Augustus Bowles	226
General Nathaniel Greene	238

Illustrations and Maps. xv

	Page.
William McIntosh	254
Governor George M. Troup	255
President Monroe	257
Chiefs of the Creek Nation and a Georgia Squatter	261
President John Quincy Adams	266
General Edmund P. Gaines	269
State House at Milledgeville	278
Major Ridge	289
John Ridge	289
Governor George M. Gilmer	296
William Wirt	302
John Marshall	303
President Jackson	307
Governor Wilson Lumpkin	308
President Van Buren	316
General Winfield Scott	317
The Walton-Hall-Gwinnett Monument at Augusta	323
Map Showing Expansion of Georgia	325
A Block-House	328
Family of a Pioneer in the Interior of Georgia	329
Emigrants and Plantation Wagon	330
Oglethorpe University	336
The University of Georgia	337
Picking Cotton on a Georgia Plantation	339
Scene on a Cotton Plantation	343
Columbus, as It Appeared When First Settled	348
Cabin of a Mountain Settler	354
A Mountaineer	355
Mountaineer Mother and Daughter	355

	Page.
City Hall at Augusta	358
Medical College, Augusta	358
A Black Mammy and Her Charge	361
Type of Middle Georgia Slave: Family Cook	362
Type of Middle Georgia Slave: Mulatto House-Maid	363
A Mountaineer and His Wood Cart	364
A Piny Woodsman and His Splinter Cart	364

PART I.
COLONIAL PERIOD

CHAPTER I.
JAMES OGLETHORPE.

I. OGLETHORPE'S EARLY CAREER.

James Oglethorpe was born at Westminster, England, on June 1st, 1689. While he was yet a babe in the cradle it might have been expected that he would become a great man, for he came of a family of great people. Six hundred years before he was born, one of his ancestors, Sheriff Oglethorpe, was a high officer in the English army and was killed in the famous Battle of Hastings while bravely fighting for his country against the invader, William the Conqueror. This brave soldier had many distinguished descendants, the greatest of whom was James Oglethorpe.

James's father, Sir Theophilus Oglethorpe, also was a noted officer in the English army. He fought with great valor in many battles and rose to the high rank of Major-General. When he was forty years old, he retired from the army and settled down in an elegant home in the little country town of Godalming, about thirty miles from London. He lived in great affluence with his family, and his children had the best educational advantages that could be obtained in Europe in that day. James's mother was a Scotch-Irish lady of fine family and of good education. She was counted one of the cleverest and shrewdest English women of her day. She was one of the Ladies of the Court to "Good Queen Anne" and was a leader in society and a power in politics. She was a woman of strong will and no doubt had great influence in forming the character of her distinguished son.

James grew to be a tall, lithe, handsome youth, quiet mannered, good natured, and high spirited. Here is a story that illustrates both his good nature and his high spirits: When a youth of seventeen, while on a visit to Paris, he was invited to dine in company with a number of distinguished military men. He sat at the table by the side of the Prince of Wurtemberg, an officer of high rank and a noted society man. The prince, thinking to have some fun at young Oglethorpe's expense, by a dexterous twirl of his glass flipped some drops of wine into his face. The prank was noticed by the company, and a smile went round the table. Young Oglethorpe did not relish being made a butt of ridicule, even by so great a man as the Prince of Wurtemberg, but he kept his temper. With a smile on his lips he said, in polite French, "Well done, prince; but we do it even better than that in England," whereupon he dashed a whole glass of wine full into the prince's face. The prince flushed with rage and it looked as if the affair would end in a serious difficulty, but an old officer on the other side of the table quickly exclaimed, "Come now, prince, don't get angry; it was rightly done by the youngster; *you* started it!" Then the prince joined the others in a hearty laugh and the incident passed off pleasantly.

The Duke of Marlborough.

Oglethorpe was educated at a military school, and before he was twenty he joined the English army. He served with the rank of ensign under the great Duke of Marlborough in the Flanders War. After the war was over, he withdrew from the army and attended college for a year or two, but he was a born soldier and did not like the "weak, piping times of peace." As England had no wars to fight at that time, he went over to the Continent and joined the Austrian army, which was then engaged in a war with the Turks. The leader of the Austrian army was Prince Eugene of Savoy, the most

Prince Eugene of Savoy.

brilliant soldier of his day. He was a small man but a great general, "a bright little soul with a flash in him as of heaven's own lightning," as Carlyle, the famous English writer, said of him. Prince Eugene took a very decided liking to young Oglethorpe and made him his aide-de-camp, with the rank of Captain. By the side of this "bright little soul with a flash in him as of heaven's own lightning," Oglethorpe thoroughly learned the soldier's trade and fought with dashing valor in many desperate battles. These were his romantic days, and he always loved to talk about them. When he was an old, old man, nearly a hundred years old, he would charm brilliant company with his vivid descriptions of the battles in which he had fought by the side of Prince Eugene.

When the Turkish war was over, he returned to England and settled down to ways of peace. His father and elder brothers died, and he inherited the family estates. He was now a very rich man, but he lived a simple and sober life. He was elected to Parliament and served as a member for many years. While he was in Parliament, an event occurred that

The Houses of Parliament.

turned his attention toward America and caused him to become the founder of Georgia. This is how it happened:

There was a cruel law in England at that time by which a person in debt might be thrown into prison by his creditors and kept there until his debts were somehow paid. Many poor, unfortunate people, innocent of any crime, languished in these debtors' prisons. Oglethorpe had a dear friend, a Mr. Robert Castell, who was a scholar and an artist. He wrote a fine book on architecture, which he illustrated with splendid pictures drawn by his own hand. He was so much taken up with writing the book that he neglected his business affairs, and when the book was published instead of making money for him it brought him heavily in debt, and he was condemned to be cast into the debtors' prison. In the prison to which he was assigned, smallpox was at that time raging, and he had never had the disease. He begged the prison keeper, a heartless wretch by the name of Bambridge, to let him lie in the common jail until the prison should be freed of the smallpox or until his friends could arrange to pay his debts for him, which he was sure would be done in the course of a few months. Bambridge agreed to do so if Castell would pay him down in cash a certain sum of money as a bribe, but poor Castell had not the money, so he was thrown into the smallpox-infested prison, where he soon contracted the disease; and after a few days' suffering he died an awful death, leaving his wife and little children poverty stricken and helpless.

When Oglethorpe heard of this outrage his blood

boiled with indignation. He at once introduced a bill in Parliament to have a committee appointed to examine the prisons of England and bring about a reform in their management. The bill was passed, Oglethorpe was made Chairman of the Committee, and, with the other members, he spent several months visit-

A Philanthropist Visiting the Debtors' Prison.

ing the prisons. He found in them many practices of shocking cruelty, all of which were immediately abolished.

II. OGLETHORPE'S GEORGIA COLONY ENTERPRISE.

If Oglethorpe had done nothing more than bring about this reform, he would deserve the lasting gratitude of humanity, but he did not stop at this. While visiting the prisons his sympathies were deeply aroused for the poor debtors whom he found languishing behind iron bars, though innocent of any crime. He determined to try to do something to help them out of their sad condition. By his earnest appeals he got Parliament to pass a law by which they might be set free, provided they would agree to go to America and establish there for England a new colony on a broad strip of unsettled country already claimed by her, south of the Savannah River. It lay next to Florida, which then belonged to Spain and had been colonized by her. The Spaniards were at that time one of the most powerful and warlike nations in the world, and in their hearts they were very hostile to the English, although not openly at war with them. The Spanish soldiers were bold, skillful, and heartless; so much so that some one said of them, "A Spanish soldier is a machine of steel with the devil inside of it!"

Fortunately for Oglethorpe's enterprise, King George II of England was anxious to plant colonies in his unoccupied possessions south of the Savannah River as a protection for South Carolina against the bold and unscrupulous Spaniards of Florida. So he gladly granted to Oglethorpe "for the use of debtors and other poor persons" all the country between the Savannah and the Altamaha Rivers, and as far westward as they might choose to go.

This strip of country was named Georgia in honor of King George. A Board of Trustees, consisting of thirty-six members, among whom were some of the

King George II.

most distinguished men in England, was appointed by the King to have entire charge of planting, establishing, and governing the new colony. They were to serve without pay or compensation of any sort. It must be purely a labor of love with them. The good and great

Lord Perceval was president of the Board, and Oglethorpe was one of the members. The Trustees set about raising money to pay the cost of establishing the colony, for the poor people who were to go were not able to pay any part of their own expenses. Parliament made quite a liberal appropriation for the purpose, and a larger amount still was raised by public subscription from benevolent people in all parts of England. Altogether, the Trustees soon had in hand $150,000, which was sufficient to establish a small colony.

At one of the meetings of the Trustees it was suggested that some member of the Board, a man of education and ability, should go over to America with the first colonists as their Governor and live in Georgia with them until they were well and thoroughly established. Oglethorpe nobly volunteered to go, and the Trustees were delighted. In undertaking this trying service, Oglethorpe would have to give up his luxurious home, the pleasures of refined society, and the splendid public career that was fast opening to him in England and would have to endure untold hardships, privations, and dangers; and from it all he had nothing, in a worldly sense, to gain for himself. The Trustees had chosen as the official seal of the Board a group of silk worms spinning their cocoons and, written underneath, the noble motto, "Non sibi sed aliis!"* "Not for themselves but for others!" As those of you who have studied Latin know, the word *sibi* may also be correctly translated *himself.* The motto truly expressed the spirit of Oglethorpe in volunteering to go on this trying expedition, *"Non sibi sed aliis!"* "Not for himself but for others!" He was at this time forty-three years old and was yet unmarried. So far as we know, he had never had a sweetheart. Perhaps he was so busy that he had never had time to fall in love!

When it was known that the great and good Oglethorpe himself would accompany the expedition, hundreds and hundreds of poor people, debtors and others, were anxious to go; but only a few could be taken. Out of the hundreds of applicants, the Trustees carefully selected forty strong, healthy men of good morals and with small families. All together, men, women, and children, the party consisted of one hundred and twenty souls. Many poor wretches who begged to go had to be turned away with tears in their eyes and bitter disappointment in their hearts.

The good ship *Anne,* a sailing vessel of two hundred

---

* The original of this famous seal is in the British Museum, London. A few years ago a wax impression of it was obtained from the curator of the Museum by the Oglethorpe Chapter, Daughters of the American Revolution, at Columbus. It is the only copy extant in America.

tons burden, was chartered to take the emigrants across the ocean to America. In her hold, as she lay moored to the wharf at Gravesend, were stored provisions and all kinds of tools and implements for the journey and for getting the colony well established in Georgia. Everything was then ready for the voyage.

CHAPTER II.

FOUNDING OF SAVANNAH.

I. SEEKING A LOCATION.

At high noon on the 16th of November, in the year 1732, the good ship *Anne* spread her white sails and, like some great canvas-winged bird of the sea, flew from the shores of England westward over the Atlantic, bearing in her kindly bosom James Oglethorpe and his one hundred and twenty emigrants. She did not sail straight for Georgia, but for Charleston, South Carolina, where Oglethorpe wished to get the advice and help of the Governor of that province in settling his colony. She reached Charleston on the 13th of January, 1733, and cast anchor just outside the harbor bar. Oglethorpe, leaving his people on board, was rowed to shore in an open boat, and was received with great honor by Governor Johnson and the Legislature of South Carolina, which was then in session.

The Governor had been notified several weeks before that Oglethorpe was coming and he was prepared to extend to him a hearty welcome. The people of South Carolina were very glad that an English colony was to be planted in Georgia, for well they knew that it would be a protection for them against the fierce Spaniards of Florida. Governor Johnson offered to do anything in his power to help Oglethorpe. He appointed Colonel Bull, one of the most prominent men in South Carolina, to act as Oglethorpe's guide and assistant in settling his colony in Georgia and offered to take care of the emigrants until a suitable location could be found for them.

The good ship *Anne* was taken down to Port Royal Bay where it was safely moored in the harbor. At the head of the bay was the little town of Beaufort, where there was a fort garrisoned by a hundred South Carolina soldiers. A new barracks building had just been erected for the soldiers, but they had not yet moved into it. Governor Johnson turned this building over to the use of the emigrants, and here they were comfortably housed until Oglethorpe could locate a permanent home for them.

Having seen his people thus comfortably provided for, Oglethorpe started out in search of some favorable spot on Georgia soil on which to plant his little colony. From study of the maps, he had already decided to locate the settlement somewhere on the banks of the Savannah River, that broad and beautiful stream which, coming down from the northwest, flows for one

Founding of Savannah.

hundred and fifty miles as a boundary line between South Carolina and Georgia, and then, as it nears the sea, turns to the left in a graceful scythe-like curve and pours its wealth of waters into the great Atlantic Ocean.

On the 16th of January, Oglethorpe, accompanied

Copyright, 1901, by the Detroit Photographic Company.
The River at Savannah, as It Appears To-day.

by Colonel Bull, left Port Royal in a little vessel lent to him by Governor Johnson and manned by four sailors. He sailed down the South Carolina coast and entered the Savannah River where Tybee Island juts out as a headland into the ocean. As he ascended the river, he passed many low-lying barren islands and flat salt marshes covered with rank sea-grass. It was an ugly country, and perhaps Oglethorpe's brave heart sank within him as he surveyed the dreary prospect. But, about eighteen miles up the river, the lowlands on the south bank suddenly rose into a bold, forest-covered bluff forty-five feet high. Here the little vessel was stopped, and Oglethorpe and Colonel Bull climbed up the bluff. On top they beheld an extensive level plain covered, as far as the eye could see, with a great woods of majestic pines interspersed with broad, spreading live-oaks. For several moments Oglethorpe stood enraptured and then exclaimed, "Surely a merciful God has designed this glorious spot as a restful home for my poor, persecuted people!"

Colonel Bull, who had visited this region before, told Oglethorpe that at the other end of the bluff, about three miles from where they stood, there was a small, isolated Indian tribe called the *Yamacraws,* and that they were the only Indians within forty miles. Oglethorpe knew that it was important that he should gain the good-will of these savages before making his settlement; so, accompanied by Colonel Bull, he went in search of the Indians. He found their little town of thirty wigwams scattered about under the trees, in a beautiful spot on the edge of the bluff, in full view of the river. The chief, or mico, of the tribe was a wonderful old savage named *Tomo-chi-chi.** He was ninety years old, but was still strong and robust in body and mind. He was over six feet tall and stood straight as the great pine tree under which his wigwam was pitched. His immediate family consisted of his wife Seenawki and his nephew Toonahowi, a boy thirteen years old whom he had adopted as his son. He had no living children of his own.

On reaching the village Oglethorpe called for Tomo-chi-chi, and the old savage stepped forth like a king. He was not surprised to see the white men. He had often seen white people before, for he had once gone to Charleston, where he spent several days while making a treaty with the Governor and the Legislature; moreover, English and Spanish traders had frequently visited his village. Indeed, at this very time there stood out in the woods, a few hundred yards from his wigwam, a log hut occupied as an English "trading post" by a white man, named John Musgrove. Musgrove's wife, Mary Musgrove, was a half-breed Indian woman who had been reared and educated among the whites in South Carolina and could speak both the Indian and the English language fluently. On the occasion of

* Pronounced *Tŏmō-chĭ-chĭ.*

Tomo-chi-chi's visit to Charleston, she had acted as his interpreter; and he sent for her now. In a little while she came, and the interview began.

Oglethorpe told Tomo-chi-chi that he wished to settle with his colony in the woods near by, but that they would not interfere in any way with the Yama-craws; that they would do no harm but only good to the Indians, would give them blankets, hatchets, guns, and other things, and would help them in many ways. He hoped they might always be good friends and live as peaceful neighbors. Oglethorpe's noble countenance, kind manner, and fine promises completely won old Tomo-chi-chi's heart, and he said: "There is plenty of room here for both red men and white men. Bring your people on to our woods. As soon as they get settled, we will call to welcome them." Tomo-chi-chi was a wise statesman. He knew that the whites might be of great benefit to the Indians, and that to make enemies of them would bring certain ruin to the Indians. Such was the first meeting between these two remarkable men who afterwards became such fast friends, and who worked together so harmoniously for the founding of Georgia. Though one was a cultured gentleman and the other a benighted savage, in character they were strikingly alike.

Oglethorpe and Colonel Bull spent several days in surveying the surrounding country. Accompanied by two or three Yamacraw Indian guides, they would tramp all day long through the deep, dark, beautiful woods, returning at night to sleep in their little boat at the foot of the bluff. The more Oglethorpe saw of the country, the better he liked it. The high bluff extended more than a mile along the river bank and stretched back from the stream five miles in a level plain. Standing on the edge of the bluff, he could see the broad sweep of the Savannah River for miles above and below, as it flowed onward toward the sea. The water under the bluff was so deep that big ships could come right up to the bank.

II. PLANTING THE COLONY.

On the 5th of February, Oglethorpe, having finished his survey, got aboard his little vessel and sailed back to Port Royal. He found that during his ten days' absence his colonists had been most kindly treated by the soldiers and the people of Beaufort. Many of the folk from the surrounding country, too, had called to see them and had brought them presents of fat pigs, fowls, eggs, butter, and home-made bread. They were in good health and fine spirits; and no wonder, for they had been treated like heroes and had lived on the "fat of the land." On the night after his return, Oglethorpe got them together and described to them the beautiful spot in Georgia that he had selected for their home and told them about the Yamacraw Indians. He instructed them to be ready, bag and baggage, to start for *Savannah* (as he had already named the place) early on the next Monday morning.

On the Sunday morning before leaving South Carolina, the colonists held a special thanksgiving service. After the service, Oglethorpe gave, at his own expense, a grand dining, to which, in the name of the colonists, he invited the soldiers and all the good South Carolina people that had been so kind to them. More than three hundred people partook of the feast, at which was served, as we are told by one who was present, four fat hogs, two fine English beeves, eight turkeys, one hundred chickens and ducks, a hogshead of rum punch, a hogshead of beer, and a barrel of wine. Notwithstanding the large quantity of liquor consumed, not a man got drunk and perfect order was preserved. This was the first Georgia barbecue; for, though spread in South Carolina, it was given by the first Georgian and was served in that abundant and generous way that has since made Georgia barbecues the most famous of feasts.

The morning following, the colonists boarded four little vessels and sailed away for Georgia. On the afternoon of February 12th, 1733, they landed at the high bluff on the Savannah River. By sunset, they had spread under the tall pine trees four big, white tents; and in these the whole colony, one hundred and twenty souls—men, women, and children—were stored away "as snug as a bug in a rug." Thus they spent their first night on Georgia soil. Oglethorpe occupied by himself a little tent pitched under a group of three tall pine trees.

Early the next morning, the colonists were assembled in front of Oglethorpe's tent for prayers, which were conducted by the Chaplain, Rev. Henry Herbert. After prayers Oglethorpe gave them a kind, fatherly talk and some good advice; and then they went about their work, the men unloading the boats and the women putting their household goods in order.

About eleven o'clock, while they were busy about their tasks, they were startled by hearing in the distance strange shouting of voices and the beating of some instrument like a drum. Looking in the direction of the sound, they saw far away through the level pine forest a band of Indians approaching them. The people were much frightened and began gathering around Oglethorpe's tent, the men with guns in their hands; but he soon calmed their fears, for he knew that it was only old Tomo-chi-chi and his followers coming to fulfill his promise, "As soon as your people get settled, we will come to welcome them."

In front of the band of visitors marched the Yamacraw priest, or "medicine man" as the Indians call him. He was dressed in gaudy and grotesque style; his face and the upper part of his body were painted red, blue, yellow, and black; on the top of his head were the antlers of a young stag, and over his shoulders was thrown the skin of a fawn. In each hand he carried an outspread fan of eagle's feathers attached to a long handle which was strung from top to bottom with little jingling bells. As he approached, he cut all sorts of queer but graceful antics, now crouching low down to the ground, then straightening up to his full height, and every now and then leaping high into the air, all the time jingling his bells and keeping up a mighty jabber in the Indian language, while those marching behind him uttered a strange grunting sound, "Ugh, ugh!"

As the procession drew near, Oglethorpe stepped a few paces in front of his tent to meet them. Suddenly they all stopped still except the "medicine man," who advanced, walked slowly, with a stately stride, around

Oglethorpe, and, stroking him from head to foot with the outspread fans, said, or rather chanted, over and over again in the Indian language, "May there be eternal peace between your people and our people!" After this ceremony was over, old Tomo-chi-chi, taking a buffalo robe from one of his attendants, stepped forward and said to Oglethorpe:

"We have come to welcome you as I promised. I have brought you a present. This is the skin of a buffalo, which is the strongest of all beasts; in the inside you see painted the head and feathers of an eagle, which is the swiftest and farthest flying of all birds. So the English are the strongest of all people, and nothing can withstand them; and they have a swift and far flight like the eagle, seeing that they have flown hither from the uttermost parts of the earth, over the vast seas. The eagle's feathers are soft and signify love; the buffalo's robe is warm and signifies protection; therefore love and protect our little families."

As he made the speech, Mary Musgrove stood by his side and interpreted what he said, sentence by sentence. Oglethorpe was deeply touched. He made a kind, noble speech in reply, while the colonists—men, women, and children—stood behind him looking on in wonder at this strange, impressive scene.

Oglethorpe invited his visitors to stay to dinner, and they readily accepted. The women of the colony bestirred themselves mightily to get up a "company dinner" for their distinguished and unexpected guests, and they managed to prepare a fine repast. By two o'clock it was ready. In the meantime, the men had no difficulty in entertaining the Indians by showing them the many wonderful things they had brought from England. After dinner, as the guests were leaving, Oglethorpe made each of them a present: a scarlet shawl with a heavy fringe to Tomo-chi-chi; a blanket and a hatchet to each of the other men; and to each of the three women of the party, a string of beads and a looking-glass. Then he bade them good-by and asked them to call again. Such was the first "state dining" ever given in Georgia.

For more than a year Oglethorpe continued to live in his little tent under the three great pine trees overlooking the river, while he directed the work of the colonists, all of whose hardships and privations he shared. He laid off in the great forest the plan of the town that was to be builded there. That plan is perfectly preserved in the city of Savannah of to-day, though, of course, the original streets have been lengthened, and many new streets and squares have been added. Oglethorpe's six streets—Bull, Bryan, Drayton, Abercorn, St. Julian, and Whitaker—are still the principal thoroughfares of the city. Bull street, he named for that Colonel Bull who so greatly helped him in planting his colony; and the others he named for benevolent persons in England and South Carolina who

From an old print. The Colony of Georgia.

had helped the colony by contributions in money and in other ways.

In the mighty work of clearing the forests, building homes, erecting forts, and cultivating gardens, the colonists were greatly aided during the first year by the generous South Carolinians, who furnished many laborers and mechanics free of charge. The Legislature of South Carolina also gave to them a herd of one hundred and five cows and a drove of eighty hogs, and private citizens of the same colony presented them with flocks of sheep and a number of horses.

From time to time new emigrants, sent over by the Trustees, arrived; so that by the end of the first year the colony numbered about six hundred people, all under the fatherly care of James Oglethorpe.

Such is the story of the founding of the beautiful city of Savannah and the beginning of the great State of Georgia.

CHAPTER I.
TOMO-CHI-CHI

1. TOMO-CHI-CHI'S TREATY WITH OGLETHORPE.

Tomo-chi-chi, mico, or chief, of the Yamacraws, although a savage, was a truly great man. When Oglethorpe first met him he was ninety years old.* For one so aged, he was wonderfully vigorous in body and mind. His figure was still erect, his step light and spry, his faculties bright, and his eye undimmed. He was over six feet tall and had a noble and commanding countenance. Anywhere in the world people looking on him would have felt, "He is a great man!"

Georgia at this time was inhabited mainly by a nation of Indians known as the Creeks. They were divided into the Upper Creeks and the Lower Creeks. The Upper Creeks lived chiefly in what is now Alabama, and the Lower Creeks in what is now middle and lower Georgia. The Lower Creeks were divided into nine different tribes, and the smallest and weakest of these tribes were the Yamacraws of which old Tomo-chi-chi was chief or mico.

*This was Tomo-chi-chi's reputed age, but it is not entirely authentic. It seems hardly credible that one so aged could have possessed such wonderful physical and mental vigor. At any rate he was a very old man.

Tomo-chi-chi had spent most of his life in middle Georgia, where he was a member of one of the most powerful tribes of the Creek Nation, and he was regarded as one of their greatest men and most valiant warriors; but in his old age, for some reason that we do not know, he withdrew from his people and wandered through the wilderness far to the east, where at length he settled on a high bluff on the banks of the Savannah River. Here he was joined by a number of devoted followers whom he organized into a tribe called the Yamacraws, and here Oglethorpe found them when he came to Georgia in 1733.

You have learned how Tomo-chi-chi and the Yamacraws allowed Oglethorpe and his colony to settle peacefully in the woods near them and how they became their strong friends. But Tomo-chi-chi had no right to give this land to Oglethorpe, for it belonged not only to the Yamacraws but to the whole Lower Creek Nation. Oglethorpe suspected this, and Tomo-chi-chi knew it well. He was an honest and frank man, so one day he went to Oglethorpe and said: "The Yamacraws will never molest you, but other tribes of the Creeks may do so. They may come at any time and kill you all or drive you away. They are stronger than we are, and we cannot defend you from them. You had better make friends with them. I will send messengers to all of the tribes to tell their chiefs and big warriors to meet here on a certain day to hold a great council. You can have a big talk with them and make a treaty with them. I will do my best to make them your friends just as I am your friend." Oglethorpe was glad to do this, for he knew that his little colony was in constant danger of attack from hostile tribes of the Lower Creeks, and he had felt very uneasy about it.

So Tomo-chi-chi sent messengers, or "runners" as he called them, to all of the tribes of the Lower Creeks to ask their chiefs to meet at Savannah on a certain day to have a "big talk" with the English, and he was careful at the same time to send them word that the English were good people and would be a great help to the Indians. The Lower Creeks consisted of nine tribes, which were widely scattered over middle and southern Georgia at great distances apart. They were the Cowetas, Cussetas, Osweechees, Chehaws, Echetas, Pallachucolas, Oconas, Eufaulas, and Yamacraws. The chiefs of all these tribes, attended by a number of warriors, responded to the call of Tomo-chi-chi and came to the "big talk" at Savannah. A few of them came down the rivers and up the rivers in their canoes; but most of them came on foot, for the Indians of that time had no other means of traveling through the country. Many of them walked hundreds of miles and none of them less than fifty miles to attend the meeting.

The council was held on the 21st of May, 1733. In all, chiefs and warriors, there were fifty-six Indians present. Not one of them, we are told, was under six feet tall, and they stood as straight and stately as the great pine trees under which they had been born and bred. They were dressed in full Indian costume. Their long, jet-black hair was adorned with eagle's feathers standing high over their foreheads and falling in a festoon down their backs. Their faces and the naked upper part of their bodies were painted red, blue, and yellow. They had rings in their ears and, around their necks, beads made of shells or of the teeth of wild animals. From the waist down, they wore a skirt of buckskin ornamented with paintings and falling just below the knees with a heavy fringe; their legs were encased in buckskin stockings, and they were shod in buckskin sandals called "moccasins." Savages though they were, these "lords of the forest" made a splendid looking assembly.

The meeting was held in the largest house then in Savannah. The Indians, according to their custom, sat flat on the floor, arranged in semi-circles. In the front row sat the nine chiefs, and back of them the warriors. Oglethorpe, clad in the full dress of an English gentleman, stood facing them; and with him were the principal men of the colony and two white interpreters, John Musgrove and Mr. Wiggan. Oglethorpe was glad to see that the Indians had a pleasant expression on their faces, or at least as pleasant as Indians can have. Tomo-chi-chi had given them a good talk and had done his best to gain their favor for the English. He had a powerful influence over them, for they esteemed him as one of the best and wisest men of the Creek Nation.

Oglethorpe rapped on the table in front of him and declared the council to be opened. He asked to hear from the Indians. The first speaker was Weekachumpa, chief of the Oconas. He was a very tall old man with white hair and a wrinkled face, but he stood straight as an arrow while in a pleasant voice and with graceful gestures he made his speech. It was a long speech but honest and straightforward. The substance of it all was this:

"We are glad you have come to our country. The Great Spirit who dwells in heaven and all around, and who has given breath to all men, has sent you here to help us; for we need help. The Lower Creeks own all the country from the Savannah River down to the line of Florida where the Spaniards live. You may settle in our country anywhere you please, for here we have many times more land than we can use. But you must not disturb us in our homes and our hunting grounds. You must protect us from our powerful enemies and from your own bad men, if you have any such. You must not trade with any red men but us. You must not let your traders cheat us. You must teach us wise things and instruct our children. You must do all you can to help us in every way. You must let us keep St. Catharine's, Ossabaw, and Sapelo islands forever as our own for hunting grounds and bathing places."

All the other chiefs, one after another, made short speeches in which they agreed to what Weekachumpa had said. Tomo-chi-chi was the last speaker; and no doubt he made the best speech of all, for he was a born orator. Oglethorpe replied to them in a talk full of kindness, wisdom, and good promises that he meant to keep and that he always did keep. He won their hearts completely. They trusted him perfectly, as well they might. The treaty was drawn up in writing and properly signed, and for many years it was faithfully kept by both sides. In no other part of America, in those early days, did the white man and the red man live together so peacefully and pleasantly as in the colony of Georgia. The credit and the thanks for this happy state of affairs were due mainly to Tomo-chi-chi, for it was his powerful influence that brought the two races so happily together. A word from him might have turned the Creek Nation against the whites and caused the destruction of Oglethorpe's little colony with much bloodshed and suffering afterward. But Tomo-chi-chi was a wise and good old man; he raised his voice for peace and not for war. This was much the better, not only for the whites but for the Indians, too.

II. TOMO-CHI-CHI'S VISIT TO ENGLAND.

About a year after the treaty, Oglethorpe decided to go to England on a visit; and he was anxious to take Tomo-chi-chi and a number of other Indians with him. Tomo-chi-chi gladly accepted the invitation for himself, his wife, Seenawki, and his nephew, Toona-howi. Every Indian in the tribe was eager to go, but Oglethorpe could take only a few; so he carefully selected six big warriors and several attendants. These with two white interpreters made up the party.

On the 7th of April, 1734, they set sail for England. Never before had these "lords of the woods" been out on the vast ocean. How wonderful it must have seemed to them! The weather was delightful, and they had a smooth and prosperous voyage. We can fancy that old Neptune, the god of the sea, pleased at the sight of these strange, new visitors to his watery realm, greeted them with smiles that beamed over the ocean and made it calm and serene. They reached England early in June. Oglethorpe took them first to his own beautiful country home where he entertained them as his guests for several days. Then they were conveyed to London where comfortable quarters had been provided for them in the Georgia Building. The news of their arrival soon spread throughout the great city, and hundreds of people flocked to see them, treating them with the utmost respect and bringing them many presents.

The king, George II, sent them an invitation to visit him on a certain day at Kensington Palace, and they accepted with great delight. They knew that this visit would be an important event in their lives, and they were greatly excited over it. When the appointed day arrived, they spent several hours dressing for the occasion. They wished to go, as they always did on state occasions at home, with the upper part of their bodies naked, but Oglethorpe would not permit this. He induced them to wear shawls over their shoulders, pinned at the throat; and as the shawls were dyed a brilliant blue, they were quite reconciled. In other respects they were clad in full Indian costume; paint, beads, feathers, and all. Old Tomo-chi-chi wore a scarlet mantle of rich velvet trimmed with gold lace; and his wife, Seenawki, wore a crimson dress of the finest silk, made as nearly in the Indian style as was admissible in polite English society.

The king sent three magnificent royal coaches, each drawn by six horses, to convey them to the palace. People by thousands thronged the streets and windows to see them pass. At the palace gates, they were welcomed by the king's bodyguard standing at "present arms." At the palace door, they were received by the Lord High Chamberlain and ushered into the presence of the king, who was seated on his throne with the queen—good Queen Caroline—seated by his side. Tomo-chi-chi had prepared a set speech for the occasion and had practiced it over and over again to his interpreter, so he made it to the king smoothly and without a blunder. He held in his hand a bunch of eagle's feathers as a present to the king, and at the close of his speech he said: "These are the feathers of the eagle, which is the swiftest of birds, and which flieth all around our nation. These feathers signify peace in our land and have been carried from town to town there, and we have brought them over to leave them with you, O great king, as a sign of everlasting peace between your people and our people!" He made also this pretty little speech to the queen: "I am glad to see this day, and I am glad to see you who are the good mother of this great people. As our people are now joined to your people, we hope you will also be the mother of us and of our children." Both king and queen made gracious replies and gave a rich present to each of the visitors.

Tomo-chi-chi and his party spent four months in England. During the whole time everything possible was done for their comfort and enjoyment. They were shown the great sights of London and of other parts of the kingdom. Wherever they went, crowds of people flocked to see them and to shake hands with them. Even the nobility gave them elegant entertainments, which were attended by the finest ladies and gentlemen in the land. Tomo-chi-chi met nearly all of the leading men of the country and conversed with them through his interpreter. His dignified manner, good sense, shrewd observations, and high-toned character filled them with surprise and admiration. They had no idea that an American savage could be so noble a man. He had several long talks with the Trustees of the Georgia

From the original London portrait.

Tomo-chi-chi and Toonahowi.

Colony, in which he showed his good business sense by getting them to pass a number of important measures for the benefit of the Creek Indians in Georgia. While he was in London, the Trustees had a fine portrait made of him with Toonahowi standing by his side holding an American eagle in his arms. It was done by a famous portrait painter and was considered a splendid likeness. It hung for many years in the Georgia Building, and a great many copies have been made of it. It shows a stately figure and a noble countenance, worthy of a king.

At times Tomo-chi-chi seemed very sad when he saw the contrast between the power, intelligence, and wealth of the English and the weakness, ignorance, and poverty of his own race. He was wise enough to know that the red men would be perfectly helpless against the whites and that it would never do to arouse their enmity. He once said: "The Great Spirit has given to the English mighty wisdom and power and great wealth, and they want nothing but more land; to the Indians He has given vast quantities of land, more than they can use, but they want everything else; so Indians must give lands to the English, and the English will give Indians things that they want."

In October, Tomo-chi-chi and his party left England to return to Georgia. They carried back four thousand dollars' worth of useful and beautiful presents that their English friends had given them. Among these presents was a fine gold watch that the king's young son, Prince William, Duke of Cumberland, had given to Toonahowi, saying to him: "Whenever you look at this watch to see the time of day, remember me and call on the name of Jesus, the blessed Saviour of us all!" On reaching Georgia, Tomo-chi-chi gave his people a full account of what he had seen and experienced on his wonderful journey, and he distributed among them nearly all of the rich gifts he had received in England, for he was a generous hearted, unselfish man.

Oglethorpe did not return to Georgia with the Indians, but remained in England nearly two years longer, all the time busy getting money, supplies, and new emigrants to go over to the colony in Georgia.

III. TOMO-CHI-CHI'S RELIGIOUS VIEWS.

When Oglethorpe returned to Georgia in February, 1736, he brought over on the ship with him, as a missionary to the Indians, a young English clergyman named John Wesley, who afterward became a very famous man. Tomo-chi-chi met the party at the ship and was overjoyed to welcome his good friend Oglethorpe back to Georgia again. "While you were gone, I did moult like the eagle," he said. When Oglethorpe introduced John Wesley to him and explained the purpose of his coming to America, the old savage welcomed the young preacher in these remarkable words: "I am glad you have come to speak the *great word* to us. I will do my best to get our people to listen to you well. But we don't want to be made Christians as the

John Wesley Teaching the Indians.

Spaniards make them. They put water on Indian's head and say, 'You are Christian,' but we want you first to explain the great word to us so that we can understand it; then we will be baptized and be real Christians." As soon as Wesley was settled in his quarters, kind-hearted Seenawki brought him as a present a jar of honey and a jar of milk, saying: "The honey signifies our feelings and disposition toward you; the milk signifies the needs of our children; so please come and teach them." But John Wesley, though a great and good man, was an utter failure as a missionary to the savages. He lacked the power of winning their hearts and of teaching the "great word" in the simple way they needed. He didn't even try to learn the Indian language, but preached to them entirely through an interpreter and explained the Christian religion to them in such a learned way that the poor savages could not understand him. Tomo-chi-chi seemed to take a dislike to him from the first and would have little to do with him.

Tomo-chi-chi had deep religious instincts. He used to go himself every Sunday to Oglethorpe's church in Savannah, and, as we have just seen, he was anxious to have the "great word" preached to his people. But after a while he lost all interest in the Christian religion. The reason of this came out one day when some one asked him: "Tomo-chi-chi, why don't you become a Christian?" With flashing eye and scorn in his voice the old man replied: "The people at Savannah are Christians, the people at Frederica are Christians, but they are no good; they get drunk, they tell lies, they fight, they beat weak people, they cheat poor Indians. *Devil* Christian, *me* no Christian!" He had made the mistake that many people make, of judging religion by the lives of the worst and most hypocritical of its professed followers.

IV. TOMO-CHI-CHI'S FLORIDA EXPEDITION.

Not long after Oglethorpe's return from England, Tomo-chi-chi said to him: "Before I die I want you to go down the coast with me and let me show you the dividing line between the Creek country and Florida. While I was in England, some Spaniards and Florida Indians crossed over into our hunting grounds and killed some of our warriors. You must build forts down there to protect our country and your country." Oglethorpe was glad to go on such an expedition, for he had long wished to settle the boundary line between Georgia and Florida. Two months before, he had sent Major Richards with an escort of six men down to St. Augustine with a message to the Spanish governor of Florida asking for a conference on this subject; but the party had never returned, and Oglethorpe was uneasy about them and wished to go down and see what had become of them.

So on April 16th, 1736, Oglethorpe started from St. Simon's Island down the coast on this important expedition. He was accompanied by Tomo-chi-chi and several gentlemen from Savannah. They had, as an escort, forty Indian warriors and thirty Highland soldiers from the little town of Darien, which had just been settled on the Altamaha River by a party of Scotch emigrants. They were all fully armed and furnished with implements for building forts. They embarked in four large boats propelled partly by oars and partly by sails, and in each boat there were two or three small canoes. A few miles south of St. Simon's, they came to a beautiful island where they camped that night and to which Oglethorpe gave the name of Jekyl Island, after

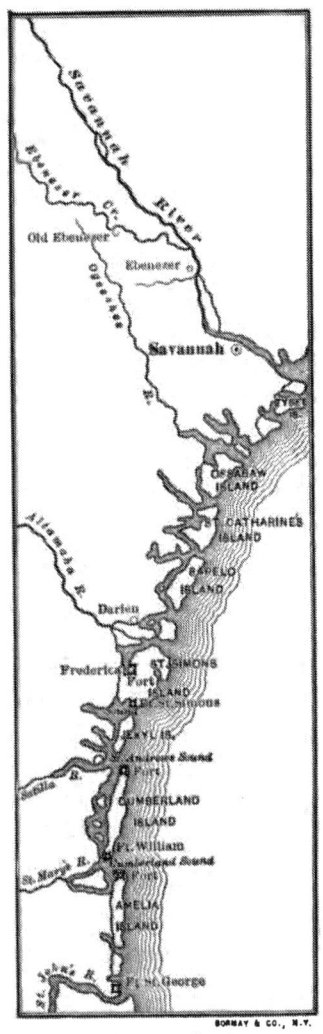

Map Showing Settlements.

his friend Sir Joseph Jekyl, of England. This island is now owned by the "Jekyl Club," composed of northern millionaires, who use it as a winter resort and have erected many costly houses there.

The next day, going further down the coast, they discovered a very large and beautiful island of which Oglethorpe had never even heard before. It had a high bluff on the western side and was covered with a grand forest of pines and live-oaks, from whose boughs hung festoons of long, gray moss. The Indians called it Wisso Island, or, in English, Sassafras Island, because many sassafras bushes grew there; but Oglethorpe changed its name to Cumberland, after the king's young son, William, Duke of Cumberland, the same who had given Toonahowi the fine gold watch. It is said that Oglethorpe gave it this name at the request of Toonahowi himself, who was with the party and had with him the much-prized watch. On the high bluff on the northwestern side of the island, Oglethorpe marked out the plan of a fort; and at the southern end, he marked out the plan of another fort. Both of these forts were afterward built good and strong. A little below Cumberland they came to a small island that looked like the Garden of Eden, so covered was it with flower-bearing trees and shrubbery, in full bloom.

Oglethorpe named it Amelia Island. On the northern end of this island now stands the Florida town of Fernandina, for the island belongs to Florida now though it was then a part of Georgia.

Oglethorpe's party continued to sail slowly down the coast for two days longer. On the afternoon of the second day they came to a high, rocky promontory jutting out from the mainland a little distance into

Mouth of the St. John's River as It Appears To-day.

the sea. The whole party climbed to the top of these high rocks; and looking to the southward they saw two miles away a great river emptying into the ocean, and on the high banks on the other side a lonely log house that looked like a small fort. The river was the St. John's. Tomo-chi-chi, pointing with his outstretched arm, said: "That river is the dividing line. All on this side we hunt; all on the other side they hunt. That house is the Spanish fort where there are soldiers to keep us from crossing to their side. But while I was in England some Spaniards and Florida Indians crossed over to our side and killed some of our warriors; so to-night when they are all asleep in that house we will creep up and kill *them*," making a gesture as if braining a man with a hatchet. The old mico spoke with great excitement and was in dead earnest. The Indian instinct glared fiercely in his eye. He was no longer the mild man of peace. He was nothing now but a ferocious, bloodthirsty savage gloating over an opportunity for revenge. The other Indians were equally excited, like hounds that see their prey! It was all that Oglethorpe could do to restrain them from making a secret midnight attack on the Spanish soldiers supposed to be in the lonely house on the river bank. He knew that such an attack would bring disaster to his colony, for it would give the Spaniards an excuse for invading Georgia with a hostile army, a thing that they were only too anxious to do. At length he succeeded in getting Tomo-chi-chi to take his warriors back to their camp in a palmetto grove several miles up the coast, and the night passed without further adventure.

Early the next morning Oglethorpe, attended by a few men, took a boat and rowed up the St. John's River to the Spanish fort, but he found not a living soul there; he rowed some miles further up the stream to another fort, but that also was unoccupied. He then returned to the camp in the palmetto grove, where he found that during his absence Tomo-chi-chi had slipped away with two boat-loads of Indians. Whither he had gone, no one could say. Oglethorpe feared that the old man was up to mischief, but it was night now and he could not well go in search of him.

About ten o'clock that night a canoe containing four Indians rowed up to shore opposite the palmetto grove camp, and the Indians sprang out and rushed up to the camp fire, exclaiming to Oglethorpe: "Tomo-chi-chi has found enemies! They have a big fire on a hill. When they go to sleep, he is going to creep up with his braves and kill them. He sent us back to take care of you, but we want to be at the killing. Please let us go back and help about the killing!" They were terribly excited; they brandished their hatchets and uttered the war whoop and foamed at the mouth and jumped about like men beside themselves, all the time begging Oglethorpe to let them go back and "help about the killing." Quickly Oglethorpe took the whole party, gentlemen, Highlanders, and Indians, in the large boat and hurried down the coast in search of Tomo-chi-chi. Four miles down he found the old man and his warriors hiding in the black darkness behind some thick bushes, like wild beasts crouching to spring upon their prey. On a hill a mile away could be seen the expiring flames of a big camp fire. "I crept up close there," said Tomo-chi-chi, "and counted seven Spaniards. I know there are Florida Indians there too, back in the woods. As soon as the Spaniards get good asleep, we will steal up and kill them with our hatchets as they lie; then we will attack the Indians with their guns. When I was in England, they killed our men and now we must kill them. I will take Toonahowi with me and teach him to be big warrior!"

Oglethorpe found it even more difficult than the day before to hold the savages back from this mad and bloody deed. In spite of his utmost remonstrances and persuasions, they were actually starting for the camp fire, when, placing his hands on Tomo-chi-chi's shoulder, he said with great earnestness: "It will be cowardly to attack the men while they are asleep; and you are not cowards; you are brave Creek warriors! Wait until to-morrow morning, and I will go with you!" Then old Tomo-chi-chi sat down with a grunt of disappointment and called the others back. Before daybreak Oglethorpe slipped away from the others and went alone to the camp fire on the hill. He found the men to be his own long-lost messenger Major Richards and his escort, on their way back from St. Augustine. Major Richards explained that a wrecked boat and other accidents had detained him. When the truth was made known to Tomo-chi-chi and his warriors, they seemed much ashamed that in their rage they were about to kill men without knowing who they were.

The next day Oglethorpe and his party started back on their return voyage. They reached Frederica, on St. Simon's Island, safe and sound, after being absent just one week on this important expedition. As long as Tomo-chi-chi lived, he continued to be a faithful friend to the English colonists and to help them greatly in many ways. This he did not mainly from love for the whites but because he was wise enough to know that it would be for the good of his own people in the present and in future generations. He was a true patriot.

V. TOMO-CHI-CHI'S DEATH AND BURIAL.

Tomo-chi-chi had lived nearly a hundred years, and through them all he had been wonderfully strong and robust; but now, at last, he began to feel in his brain and in his heart and through all the marrow of his bones the strange, benumbing chill of old age. One day he started to walk with Toonahowi from his village to Savannah, a distance of three miles, but before he had proceeded far he felt so tired that he had to turn and go back. Soon afterward he took to his bed, from which he never rose again. There for days and weeks he lay as helpless as a new-born babe. He knew that his end was very near, so he called his family and the leading men of his little tribe around him and exhorted them to continue their friendship to the English, and asked that he might be buried in the settlement of Savannah that he loved and among the people that had always been so kind to him.

One day John Wesley called on him, but he seemed too feeble to talk, and not a word did Wesley get from him. Perhaps he would not try to talk to Wesley; for, as we know, the heart of the old savage had never warmed to this great divine. A few days later George Whitfield, one of the most famous preachers that ever lived, came to see him. He found him lying on a blanket under the shade of a great live-oak tree, while his faithful old wife, Seenawki, sat by his side fanning him with a snow-white fan made of crane's feathers. Whitfield took his

George Whitfield Preaching.

hand and (not knowing what else to say, I suppose) asked him: "How long do you think you have to live?" "I do not know," replied Tomo-chi-chi; which was a sensible answer to a foolish question. "Where do you expect to go when you die?" pursued Whitfield. "To heaven!" answered Tomo-chi-chi, in simple faith. Maybe that was the last word he ever spoke; for a few hours after Whitfield left, the old mico died, aged ninety-seven years.

For ninety years he had wandered through the gloomy, primeval forests of America, in intellectual and spiritual darkness. Many, no doubt, were his adventures, valiant deeds, and hair-breadth escapes, for we know that the Creeks counted him as one of the greatest hunters and warriors of their nation; but in blackest oblivion lies all that part of his life. It was only during the last few of his many years on earth that he came out into the open where history could take note of him, like a star that has made its journey across the firmament under clouds but emerges for a little while just before its setting, to shine on the world! History tells us that he was honest and truthful, bright of mind, generous of heart, earnest of purpose, strong of will, eager for improvement, anxious for the uplifting and betterment of his race, a sincere believer in Almighty

God, and hopeful of a purer and nobler life in the world to come; and these are qualities that go to make a great man, whether they be embodied in a rude savage like Tomo-chi-chi or in a fine gentleman like James Oglethorpe.

In accordance with his dying request, Tomo-chi-chi was buried in Savannah. His body was borne to the grave by six of the most distinguished citizens and soldiers of Georgia. James Oglethorpe followed his coffin as chief mourner. During the funeral services minute guns were fired from the fort near by, and a company of militia discharged three volleys of musketry over his grave after the coffin was lowered. The whole tribe of Yamacraws and many visiting Indians and nearly all of the people of Savannah—men, women and children—attended the solemn ceremonies.

Oglethorpe planned to have a suitable monument placed over the grave, but for some reason it was not done. For more than a hundred years the last resting place of the old mico was unmarked, though the exact spot, or very nearly the exact spot, was preserved in the memories of people by tradition from generation to generation. Finally, in the year 1899, that fine society of women, the Colonial Dames of Georgia, had a great, rugged granite boulder brought from middle Georgia, where Tomo-chi-chi had spent most of his life, and placed it, just as it came from the hands of nature, without chiseling or polish, on the grave of the old savage—a most fitting monument to him who was one of nature's own rugged and unpolished noblemen. To the stone is affixed a circular bronze tablet bearing an appropriate

Tomo-chi-chi's Grave.

inscription and symbolic figures. The grave is in Johnson Square in the very heart of the city of Savannah. May we not say, without exaggeration, that there sleeps to-day beneath Georgia's sod no nobler man, no truer patriot than Tomo-chi-chi, the grand old mico of the little tribe of Yamacraws!

CHAPTER IV.

THE SALZBURGERS.

I. PERSECUTION IN AUSTRIA.

If you will look on the map of Europe, you will find located in the extreme western part of Austria a town by the name of Salzburg. It is situated on the Salza River and is surrounded by smooth green valleys, rocky mountains, and clear, swift-running streams. Two hundred years ago this town and the surrounding green valleys and mountain gorges were inhabited by a simple, honest German folk known as the Salzburgers. They were chiefly poor people, and they dressed in plain clothes and wore big slouch hats with broad brims and peaked crowns. Those in the town were makers of famous wooden clocks that were known all over Europe, and those in the country earned their living as farmers and herdsmen. In religion most of these people were Protestants and belonged to what is called the Lutheran Church. Austria and Germany were at that time Roman Catholic countries, and by the law of the land no other form of religion was allowed, and Protestants were bitterly persecuted. In some way, however, it happened that these quiet Salzburgers in their remote mountain fastnesses were for many years not molested in their religion but were allowed to worship God in their own way. Perhaps the rulers of the country thought, "The poor creatures are so quiet and harmless away off there that we will let them alone." Still they did not dare to build churches or to have regular preachers. Out of doors in the thickly wooded mountain gorges they held their services and poured out their devout souls in worship to that God who "prefers before all temples the upright heart and pure!"

But after a while their days of peace came to an end. In the year 1729, a new Archbishop was put in charge of Salzburg. His name was Leopold, Count Firmian, and he was feudal lord of the district as well as an official of the Roman Catholic Church. He immediately began a cruel persecution of the poor Protestant Salzburgers. He made his sheriffs and bailiffs enter their houses and break open their chests and take their Lutheran Bibles and hymn-books out and burn them in bonfires in the streets. He had their leading men arrested and brought before him, and said to them: "I will throw you into prison, confiscate your property, and destroy your homes if you do not abandon your Protestant religion." "We cannot, your reverence, must not, dare not," bravely answered the poor men. "Then you shall suffer for it," yelled Leopold. "Pray, let us sell our possessions and emigrate," pleaded they. "No, I will keep you here until I stamp that devilish heresy out of you," shrieked Leopold. Then he threw them into prison and confiscated their property. He tore little children from the arms of their mothers and placed them in convents to be brought up in the Roman Catholic religion by priests and nuns.

When the news of this bitter persecution reached the ears of the Emperor, Frederick William, he felt that he must interfere, although he himself was a Roman Catholic. He sent Leopold word to stop his cruelties to the Salzburgers and let them emigrate, as under the law they had a right to do. Leopold had to obey the Emperor, so he said: "Emigrate, then, you Lutheran dogs, and be quick about it!" "How about our property and our goods and chattels?" asked they. "You shall take nothing with you. Be thankful you have kept your skins. Emigrate, I say," cried the cruel Leopold.

So in the course of two years, from 1730 to 1732, many thousands of poor Salzburgers were driven from their homes and from their country, carrying scarcely anything with them but the clothes on their backs. The whole Protestant world opened its arms to receive them.

In the Free Towns of Germany and Prussia, in Holland and in England they found kind friends to help them in their dire distress; but in all the world they had no truer friend than James Oglethorpe, the great Englishman. His heart burned within him as he heard and read of their wrongs, and one of his objects in founding the colony of Georgia was to provide a home for them.

II. EMIGRATION TO GEORGIA.

As soon, therefore, as Oglethorpe got his English colony well settled at Savannah, he turned his attention toward the Salzburgers. By correspondence with their ministers in Germany he found out that hundreds of them would be glad to emigrate to Georgia and become subjects of the British Government, but were utterly poverty stricken and had not the means for this costly move. The Trustees of Georgia were able at that time to pay the expenses of only a few of them. So a select party was made up, composed of seventy-eight persons, forty-two of whom were strong, stalwart men and the rest women and children. The Trustees agreed to pay their expenses over to Georgia and to give to each family fifty acres of land and a year's support until they could clear the lands and make a crop.

They assembled in the town of Berschtalgaden, Bavaria, to make ready for the emigration. The good Protestants of that town furnished them with three wagons, each drawn by two horses, for the long, overland journey through the German Empire to the sea. In two of the wagons they placed all of their earthly goods and chattels, and in the third wagon they seated the feeble women and the little children. The men and the stronger women and children walked. A noble band of martyrs marshaled under no flag save the banner of the cross, carrying no weapons but their Bibles and prayer-books, following no general except the Great Captain of Salvation, they trudged patiently for hundreds of miles through the German Empire northwestward toward the sea. Most of their way lay through Roman Catholic countries where they were subjected to many indignities and insults, but ever and anon they would come to a Protestant town where they received the utmost kindness and love.

About the middle of November they reached the Protestant town of Frankfort-on-the-Main, which was the end of their long, wearisome foot journey. The people of Frankfort turned out in great crowds to welcome them and to minister to their wants. In this beautiful city, among these kind people, they rested for several days; and then, embarking in a vessel that had been provided for them, they sailed down the River Main to the Rhine and down the Rhine toward the sea. As they glided down this beautiful river between the castellated crags, the vineyards, and the white-walled cities that adorn its banks, they poured out their hearts in joyous songs to the living God. They were fine singers, for from childhood they had been taught singing as a part of their religion; and for beauty and melody their hymns have never been surpassed.

On the 27th of November they reached Rotterdam, where the Rhine pours its waters into the North Sea. Here they were joined by Rev. John Martin Bolzius and Rev. Israel Christian Gronau, distinguished and cultured men, who were to accompany them to Georgia as their chosen pastors and teachers. From Rotterdam they made a tempestuous passage across the channel and through the strait to Dover, England. On the 28th of December they at last embarked from Dover on their long voyage to the new home that awaited them in Georgia. Born and bred in the interior of Europe among the peaks and gorges of the Alps Mountains, not one of them, except Bolzius and Gronau, had ever before looked upon the grandeur of the mighty ocean. It was a great wonder to them and inspired their devout souls with religious awe. No sooner did the shores of England vanish from their sight than they broke forth into psalms of glory to Him "Who measures the waters in the hollow of His hand!"

On the 11th day of March, 1734, having stopped several days at Charleston (S. C.), they reached Savannah. Here is the account of the landing, given by Rev. Bolzius himself:

"On the 11th day of March we lay at anchor off the banks of our dear Georgia, in a very lovely calm, and heard the birds singing sweetly. It was really edifying to us that we came to the borders of the promised land on this our 'Reminiscere Sunday,' when, as we are taught by the gospel, Jesus came to the sea coast after He had endured persecution and rejection by His countrymen. At the place of our landing almost all the inhabitants of Savannah were gathered together. They fired off some cannon and cried 'Huzzah!' which was answered by our sailors and other English people in our ship in the same manner. We were received with all possible demonstrations of joy, friendship, and civility. Even the Indians reached their hands to us as a testimony of their joy for our arrival. A good dinner was prepared for us."

III. OLD EBENEZER.

To the Salzburgers the generous Oglethorpe said: "You may select for your homes any place in Georgia that is not already reserved by my English colonists or by the Indians." Some of the English advised them to go to the south of Savannah and settle on the sea coast. "No," said they, "we are told that to the south live the warlike and meddlesome Spaniards. We are a peaceful folk and want to keep away from them. Besides, we are not used to the sea coast and flat lands. We should like to settle in the interior where there are mountains, or hills like those which we had at home."

So Oglethorpe, accompanied by Baron Von Rek, a notable man and leader of the emigrants, and several other Salzburgers and three Indian guides, started from Savannah and journeyed through the woods to the northwest in search of a place for the Salzburgers to settle. About twenty-five miles from Savannah they came to a spot that seemed to strike the fancy of Von Rek and the others, possibly because it reminded them in some way of their homes in Austria. It was situated on a big creek that flowed in a winding, tortuous channel toward the Savannah River. The country was undulating, rising and falling in alternate hills and plains, and was watered by a number of little streams that flowed into the big creek. It was rather thinly wooded with tall pines and small oaks, cypress and myrtle trees, and quantities of sassafras bushes. It was located in what is now Effingham County, six miles west of the Savannah River and about four miles from the present town of Springfield. "This suits us exactly," said Von Rek and the others; "we will build our town here, and we will call it Ebenezer, 'the stone of help,' for truly 'Hitherto the Lord hath helped us!'" The party remained in the locality for several days and, under the direction of Oglethorpe, carefully laid out the future town; then they made their way back to Savannah through the woods, taking care to "blaze" the trees as they went so that they might easily find their way to the spot again when they returned with the colonists.

Several weeks later, early in the month of April, the whole body of Salzburgers, guided through the forest by the "blazed" trees, moved from Savannah to Ebenezer. They made the journey on foot, their household goods being carried in packs on the backs of the few horses that could be had. The strong men carried the babies and the little children in their arms. Kind-hearted Oglethorpe accompanied them on horseback, though he really walked nearly all the way, lending his horse turn about to the weakly women of the party. It was a toilsome and trying journey; for there was no road to travel in, much of the way lay through swamps and jungles, and the streams had to be crossed on fallen trees. But the Salzburgers were strong of limb and stout of heart, and as they trudged cheerily along they often made the great forest ring with songs of praise to God. Although the distance was less than thirty miles it took them two or three days to reach their destination.

On the 10th day of April they reached Ebenezer. A gang of eight stout men, who had been sent ten days ahead of them, had already erected rude bush arbor tents for them, and in these they were made fairly comfortable until they could build better homes. Oglethorpe carefully divided out the land among them. To each family he gave a two-acre lot in town and a farm of fifty acres in the suburbs. They went to work with a will, clearing the lands, building houses, and planting crops. The good people of Savannah sent them a present of ten cows and calves which furnished an abundance of milk for the little colony of seventy-eight persons. In the hollow of a big tree they found a great quantity of honey which the wild bees had made. The friendly Indians near by supplied them with venison, their huntsmen killed wild turkeys and partridges in the woods, and from the clear waters of the tortuous Ebenezer Creek they caught perch and "channel cats," and some one taught them how to brew a very good beer made of molasses, sassafras, and pine tops. So, as far as the table was concerned, our good Salzburgers lived "on the fat of the land." In a few months they were joined by another party of sixty or more brother Salzburgers, who had just come over from Germany, and the town of Ebenezer now contained about one hundred and fifty inhabitants.

Here in the wilderness of Georgia, far distant from the land of their birth and the graves of their fathers, these poor exiles found at least a sheltering home of sympathy and love.

IV. NEW EBENEZER.

But the trials and tribulations of the Salzburgers were not yet over. Baron Von Rek, as it turned out, was a very poor judge of land, or at least of Georgia land. The region around Ebenezer, instead of being "rich and fat," as he supposed, proved to be thin and sterile. The Salzburgers with their hardest labor could not dig a living out of it, and had to depend largely on the charity of the Trustees for a support. Furthermore, the big Ebenezer Creek which Von Rek had described as "a noble river, twelve foot deep, and navi-

The Salzburgers.   65

gable for large boats," proved to be entirely useless for commercial purposes. Its channel was so crooked and tortuous that no boat of considerable size could make the sharp bends or approach within six miles of Ebenezer. The little streams that emptied into the big creek, when swollen by the heavy rains of winter and spring, overflowed their banks and flooded the country: but during the droughts of summer they dried up into stagnant pools and ponds that filled the air with malaria. This caused a great deal of sickness among the people, and many of them died.

Separated from the rest of the world in the depths of the wilderness, toiling like slaves and yet unable to make a living, sorely stricken with sickness and death, no wonder the poor Salzburgers, patient people though they were, became dissatisfied and disheartened.

Early in the spring of 1736, John Martin Bolzius and Israel Christian Gronau, the two good pastors of the Salzburgers, appeared at Savannah as representatives of their people to ask Oglethorpe to let them move to a better locality. Kind-hearted Oglethorpe, finding that the entire colony was heartily in favor of it, gave his consent to the move. Then the whole colony of Salzburgers packed up bag and baggage and, abandoning their farms and houses, upon which they had wasted two years of hard toil, moved for six miles through the trackless forests to the place selected for their new settlement. This place was a beautiful and romantic spot on the banks of the Savannah River. It was known as Red Bluff on account of the color of the soil. To the east, at the foot of the bluff, rolled the broad waters of the Savannah; to the south flowed a small stream now known as Lockner's Creek; while to the north Ebenezer Creek, their old friend, came zigzagging to pour its tribute waters into the Savannah.

Here they had all the hard work of clearing the forest and building homes to do over again; but they went at it with strong arms and brave hearts, and in two years their new town had risen like magic. Clinging with affection to the old name, they called the place New Ebenezer. In the meantime Old Ebenezer went to rack and ruin.

God blessed the Salzburgers in their new homes. At last, after years of persecution, exile, wandering, and misfortune, these simple, honest people found peace and happiness "under their own vine and fig tree." For some years they were the most prosperous people in Georgia. Other Salzburgers came over from the fatherland to join them. In all, about fifteen hundred Salzburgers emigrated to Georgia. Some of these settled in Savannah and Frederica, but most of them made their home in New Ebenezer and the surrounding country. They worked hard, and the soil yielded them abundant harvests. For a number of years they paid much attention to raising silk. In this industry they were greatly encouraged by Oglethorpe and the Trustees, who had a notion that Georgia could be made one of the greatest silk-growing countries in the world.

The leaves of the white mulberry tree are the natural food of the silk worm, and great quantities of these trees were brought from Italy and planted in the country around Ebenezer. From first to last many thousands of dollars were made by the Salzburgers by the silk culture industry; but later on other employments were found more profitable, and the raising of silk was entirely abandoned in Georgia. Good Queen Caroline of England had a dress made of Georgia silk, which she used to wear on state occasions and of which she was very proud.

The Salzburgers all belonged to the Lutheran Church. In this faith they were born and bred, and for their devotion to it they had suffered cruel persecution and exile from their native land. They were served for many years by the three good pastors, Revs. Bolzius and Gronau, who came to Georgia with them, and Rev.

Rabenhorst, who came over later. They were not only the pastors but also the principal governors and rulers of the colony. Three better or more saintly men never lived on earth. For many years after coming to Georgia

Queen Caroline.

the people adhered strictly to their mother tongue, the German language, and they would not encourage their children to learn English. This, in the long run, proved a great disadvantage to them, as it cut them off, in a

The Salzburgers.

large measure, from intercourse and commerce with the other colonies in Georgia.

Thus in the beautiful wilderness of Georgia on the banks of the broad Savannah River and its tributary creeks, these good people lived for many years in peace, prosperity, and happiness.

"Far from the madding crowd's ignoble strife,
 Their sober wishes never learned to stray;
 Along the cool, sequestered vale of life
 They kept the noiseless tenor of their way."

Still their life was not without its sorrows and its tragedies. In January, 1745, their good pastor, Israel Gronau, died after a long sickness. His mind was strong and bright to the last but his body was very weak. As his brethren gathered around his dying bed, he said to one of them, "Friend, raise my arms for me"; then clasping his thin, uplifted hands he cried in a clear, sweet voice, "Come, Lord Jesus, come!" and his pure spirit took its flight to that other world where supernal beauty dwells and the rainbow never fades. His death was felt as a keen personal grief by every member of the colony. A Rev. Mr. Lembke was called from Germany soon afterward to take his place and proved to be a worthy successor.

Some years later the saintly John Martin Bolzius

also ended his mission on earth and was gathered to his fathers. His death turned out to be not only a deep sorrow but a great calamity to the little colony. The Lutheran Council in Germany sent over to Georgia to take his place a Mr. Triebner. He was a highly educated, talented, energetic young man; but he was self-centered, imperious, and bad hearted. He was a great mischief maker, and immediately set about stirring up trouble. He soon had the peaceful and harmonious Salzburgers divided into two violent factions that strove against each other with great bitterness, causing deep spiritual wounds that were many years in healing. During his ministration of ten years he did much harm, and was a constant "thorn in the flesh" to the best people of the colony.

Jerusalem Church at Ebenezer.

About 1744, the devout souls of the Salzburgers were made happy by the erection of a fine new brick church at Ebenezer. It cost over two thousand dollars and most of the money was contributed by their kind

Lutheran friends in Germany. It would be considered a plain little church now; but to these poor exiles in the Georgia wilderness it seemed a magnificent edifice, and they were very proud of it. It was surmounted by a neat belfry, on the spire of which appeared the figure of a swan made of shining brass; for the swan was the "coat of arms" of Martin Luther, the great founder of the Lutheran Church. It was built good and strong and stands there to-day as sound as when it was erected one hundred and sixty years ago.

Few people in Georgia suffered more from the Revolutionary War than did the gentle Salzburgers. Most of them were true to the patriot cause, but Preacher Triebner, who might always be counted on to be on the wrong side, was a rank Tory and led a number of the people off with him. As soon as the British had captured Savannah in 1779, this odious Mr. Triebner mounted his horse and galloped to that plantation where he called on Colonel Campbell, the British commander, and advised him to send a detachment of soldiers at once to Ebenezer. He was even mean enough to lead these soldiers himself against his own town and his own people.

During all of the rest of the war a British garrison was kept at Ebenezer, and armies of British soldiers were constantly marching back and forth through the place. They treated the patriot inhabitants so badly that most of them abandoned their homes and moved away, and the houses of many of them were burned by the British and the Tories. The soldiers desecrated Jerusalem Church most shamefully. They destroyed the precious church records, cut up the benches and the pulpit for firewood, and used the church itself as a stable for their cavalry horses. When the refugee Salzburgers returned to Ebenezer after the war was over, they found their dear town in ruins and they had it nearly all to build over again.

When the British army returned to England after the war, Preacher Triebner went with them, for well he knew that he would not be tolerated in America any longer. The Salzburgers never saw his hateful face again.

As the children and the grandchildren of the pilgrim Salzburgers grew up, most of them moved away from the quiet place to seek their fortunes in other parts of Georgia and in other states. By the year 1820 the town was completely deserted and fell into decay and oblivion. Nothing is left of it now except old Jerusalem Church, which still stands on the bluff by the river with the brass swan glistening on its lofty spire. Near by is the grave-yard where rest the bones of the saintly preachers, Bolzius, Gronau, Lembke, and Rabenhorst, and many other good Salzburgers of that olden time.

Hundreds of the descendants of the Salzburgers still live in different parts of Georgia, mainly in Savannah and in Lowndes, Liberty, and Effingham counties. They are among the most substantial citizens of the State; some of them have become wealthy as merchants and farmers, but not many of them seem to have ever attained to any great distinction in the professions or in public life.

CHAPTER V.

THE HIGHLANDERS.

The Spaniards down in Florida were dangerous neighbors for the Georgia settlers. There had been a long dispute between Spain and England concerning the territory claimed by the two countries in America. Spain declared that both Georgia and South Carolina belonged by rights to her, and she was constantly threatening to invade the country and take it away from the English. To guard against this threatened invasion, Oglethorpe determined to plant colonies and build forts along the sea coast and on the sea coast islands south of Savannah, as far down as the mouth of the St. John's River, which was then considered the boundary line between Georgia and Florida. He began to cast about to see where he could find people to send down into this dangerous region, and he was very fortunate in finding them.

In the year 1736 there emigrated to Georgia a splendid body of Highlanders from the hills and mountains of Scotland. The company consisted of one hundred and fifty men and fifty women and children. They were not paupers, like the debtors who settled in Savan-

The Highlanders.

nah, nor impoverished exiles like the Salzburgers who settled Ebenezer, but brave, sturdy, independent folk, whose spirit had never been broken by poverty or persecution. They belonged to the farming class of people in Scotland, and were accustomed to hard work out in the open air. The men had all been trained, too, to military service. They were tall, broad-shouldered, stalwart fellows; and dressed in their plaids, with their broadswords, targets, and fire-arms, they made a superb body of soldiers. Altogether they were the finest lot of emigrants that had yet come to Georgia. They were the very people that Oglethorpe needed to guard the dangerous southern frontier.

Oglethorpe had selected as their home a place on the banks of the Altamaha River, near its mouth, sixty

A Highland Officer.

miles below Savannah, right where the little town of Darien now stands. They called the place New Inverness, after the city of Inverness in Scotland, from the neighborhood of which most of them had come; but the name was afterward changed to Darien.

While the emigrants were in Savannah, some meddlesome Carolinians tried to frighten them from going south by telling them, "The spot that Oglethorpe has selected for your home is so situated that the Spaniards can shoot you from the houses in their fort." "Why, then, we will beat them out of their fort, and shall have houses ready built to live in!" answered the brave Highlanders.

New Inverness was beautifully located on a high bluff on the river bank, in a grove of broad spreading live-oaks, while all around for many miles stretched the vast, level pine forests of southern Georgia. In this great wilderness the hardy Highlanders went to work in high spirits and with intelligent industry, and it is wonderful what they accomplished. In a few months under their busy hands a strong fort was built on the banks of the river, and a pretty little town arose with many houses surrounded by well-cultivated gardens and outlying fields. The soil was very thin and poorly adapted to agriculture; but for a few years while it was yet fresh and enriched with the decayed leaves of centuries, it yielded abundant harvests. Well might it be said of these good Scotch emigrants, in the beautiful language of the Bible, "The wilderness and the solitary places shall be glad for them, and the desert shall rejoice and blossom as the rose!"

The Highlanders were great favorites with Oglethorpe. His soldier heart was completely won by their energy, heroism, and fine military bearing. Soon after they had settled at New Inverness, and before they had yet built their houses, he paid them a visit of several days. While he was there, in order to please them, he wore the Highland costume. Captain Mackay, the leader of the colony, offered him the use of his own comfortable tent and warm bed, the only one in the settlement that was furnished with sheets, but Oglethorpe declined the offer and slept out of doors by the camp fire wrapped in his Scotch plaid. While he remained, he cheerfully shared all the hardships of the people, and by his kindness and genial manners made himself greatly beloved by them.

All the other colonists of Georgia felt grateful to the Highlanders, for well they knew that these doughty men stood as a bulwark and a protection between them and the dreaded Spaniards. In the Spanish war that came a few years later, the valiant Highlanders, as we shall see in the next chapter, were Oglethorpe's mainstay. They fought with reckless bravery, and it was mainly through them that the colony of Georgia was saved from destruction. Many of them were slain, and in all ways they bore the brunt of the conflict and were the chief sufferers of the war.

This gallant band of emigrants suffered dreadfully from the Spanish war. Many of them were killed in battle, many taken prisoners, and the colony was broken up and scattered. Altogether they had a hard time in America. Their story was a short, brave, sad one. Their little town of New Inverness passed into other hands, and its name was changed to Darien. No body of emigrants that crossed the great waters in those early days to make their home in the New World was more interesting and picturesque than the doughty Highlanders who settled on the banks of the Altamaha in the somber piny woods of Georgia.

CHAPTER VI.

FREDERICA.

Having seen his Highlanders well settled at New Inverness, Oglethorpe went ahead with great energy to carry out his plan of establishing forts along the southern coast of Georgia as a protection against the Spaniards. With his fine military eye he saw that the first and most important of these forts should be located on St. Simon's Island near the mouth of the Altamaha River. St. Simon's is separated from the mainland by a narrow strip of water which is really an arm of the Altamaha. It is a narrow stream, but the water is very deep and navigable for the largest boats. Oglethorpe knew that if the Spaniards should ever invade Georgia, their fleet would be sure to come up this stream; and for this reason he determined to place a strong fort on the west side of the island by the river's edge. He also thought it best to plant a colony back of the fort and establish a sort of military town there.

St. Simon's was a beautiful island; and at that time it was covered with a grand primeval forest of live-oak, water-oak, laurel, bay, cedar, sweet gum, and pines. The trees were festooned with long gray moss; and from many of them hung vines bearing muscadines, purple fox-grapes, and fragrant yellow jasmine. The ground beneath them was covered with palmettoes and bushes of azaleas, white, pink, and scarlet honeysuckles, and all manner of beautiful wild flowers. The woods abounded with deer, rabbits, raccoons, opossums, squirrels, wild turkeys, turtle doves, mocking birds, and great droves of rice birds; while the adjacent marshes were frequented by wild geese, herons, cranes, and marsh hens; and the waters teemed with fishes, crabs, shrimps, and oysters. The soil was fertile, the climate healthful, and the air delightful, the temperature being neither very warm nor very cold. Surely it was a choice place for the habitation of man!

On the northwest side of the island there was a cleared spot about forty acres in extent where an Indian town and cornfields had once stood, but which was now deserted. On this spot Oglethorpe determined to plant his colony and build his fort. For this purpose he brought over from England a shipload of two hundred emigrants. Some were German Lutherans, like the Salzburgers; a few, perhaps, were Scotch Highlanders; but most of them were English people. They landed at Savannah in February, 1736. Oglethorpe took thirty of the strongest men of the company and one hundred other workmen and a number of Indians and sailed down to St. Simon's to begin the building of the town and the fort.

Arriving at the island, he immediately put his laborers to work, and under his energetic supervision they worked like beavers. The town was soon laid off and the land cleared. There was in the company a shrewd Jew, who had lived in Brazil and who knew how to make houses out of palmetto leaves. This plant fortunately grew in great abundance on the island. So under the skilful direction of the Jew many palmetto booths or bowers were erected. Each one was thirty feet long and twenty feet wide. They made a pretty appearance as they stood in rows like soldiers' tents, only much further apart. They were so well constructed that they kept perfectly dry inside, even during the hardest and most driving rain; and they served finely as a temporary abode for the colonists until more substantial houses could be built. To the town thus started, Oglethorpe gave the name of Frederica, after Frederick, Prince of Wales, eldest son of King George II of England.

While the Jew was attending to the erection of the palmetto houses, Oglethorpe was directing the building of the fort; and a great fort he made of it. There is no rock or stone in that part of Georgia, so Oglethorpe made his fort of a sort of artificial stone called tabby, composed of crushed shells and cement, a composition almost as enduring as granite. The fort was built at the water's edge and commanded the full sweep of the river, so that no hostile ship could pass it. Back in the woods several hundred yards from the fort, he erected a large storehouse and barracks building, also made of tabby and possessing considerable architectural beauty.

Besides this great fort Oglethorpe built a number of others down the southern coast of Georgia; one at the south end of St. Simon's Island, two on Cumberland Island,—one at the north and the other at the south end,—one on Amelia Island, and one on St. George Island at the mouth of the St. John's River. In each of these forts he placed cannon and a small garrison of soldiers. This pushing of his forts and his soldiers down to the very edge of the Spanish country was a very bold, audacious step on Oglethorpe's part. It was what the gamblers call "playing a bluff game"; that is, putting on the appearance of being stronger and more confident than he really was. It had the intended effect: it frightened the Spaniards and deterred them for several years from making the invasion they so much desired.

Early in March, the palmetto houses being finished, the colonists, who had been waiting at Savannah for a month, were brought down to Frederica. They came in broad, open rowboats called periaguas. It was a trying voyage for them, exposed, as they were, to the chill March winds. When at last beautiful St. Simon's was reached, it looked like Paradise to them. The women went cheerily to housekeeping in their cozy palmetto bowers, while the men cleared the lands and erected more permanent homes. The people were all charmed with their new home, as well they might be.

Frederica grew and flourished mightily. When at its best it numbered, including the soldiers, more than a thousand inhabitants; and, except Savannah, it was the largest and most important town in Georgia. It was a favorite place with Oglethorpe. He made his home there from the time the town was founded until his departure for England. The only house he ever owned in America was there, and the spot on which it stood can still be pointed out. He always spoke of the place with great affection; and yet while he lived there he had no end of worry and trouble with insubordinate officers, mutinous soldiers, Spanish spies, unjust critics, and all sorts of cranky and mean people. Charles Wesley, the famous younger brother of the still more famous John Wesley, also lived at Frederica. The great live-oak under which he preached his first sermon is still standing in its green old age, and is pointed out to visitors as an object of sacred interest.*

After the Spanish Colonial War was over, Frederica declined rapidly, because there was no longer any reason for its existence. During the Revolutionary War, what remained of it was almost completely destroyed by the British army. Afterwards, mighty and patriotic efforts were made to revive it and to restore it to its old glory, but all in vain. It had finished its mission and must pass away. By the year 1820 it was entirely deserted. In recent years three or four modern

Wesley Oak at Frederica.

---

* The short life of this island town was full of tragedies and comi-tragedies, but we have not space to relate them here. You may find a full and interesting account of them in Bishop Stevens's and C. C. Jones's big and good histories of Georgia. The extremely important part that the town played in the Spanish Colonial War and why historians call it "The Thermopylæ of Georgia," you will soon learn in another chapter of this book.

houses have been erected on the ground where the town stood, but Frederica itself is no more. Like Ebenezer, it is one of the dead towns of Georgia.

A fragment of the old fort with one of its iron cannon still stands by the water's edge;* and out in the

Ruins of the Old Fort at Frederica.

woods near by, the arched and castellated front of the barracks building rises "grand, gloomy, and peculiar," among the green trees—and a handsome piece of architecture it is, too, in its gray and neglected old age.

* Since these lines were written the Colonial Dames of Georgia have had the old fort restored, as nearly as practicable, as it stood in 1735. The unveiling of the tablet took place April 11, 1904.

Still further back in the woods is the colonial graveyard, where, under moss-covered trees centuries old, good people of the vanished town have been sweetly sleeping for one hundred and sixty years. That is all that is left of Frederica. *"Sic transit gloria mundi!"*

CHAPTER VII.

THE SPANISH WAR.

I. PREPARATIONS FOR THE WAR.

One day in the latter part of the year 1736, a Spanish officer, one Captain Don Antonio Arredondo, came from St. Augustine to Frederica with this message for Oglethorpe: "The King of Spain demands that the English evacuate all towns and forts south of St. Helena Sound as being located on the dominions of Spain!" Oglethorpe replied, "We refuse to evacuate these towns and forts, for they belong to the King of England and not to the King of Spain!" Having received this answer the messenger returned to St. Augustine.

Soon after this, Oglethorpe was informed that a large fleet of ships and a big army had been sent by the Spanish Government from Havana to St. Augustine. What could this mean but preparation for the invasion of Georgia? Oglethorpe saw the danger and acted with his usual promptness and vigor. He at once got aboard a ship and sailed for England, where he laid the whole situation before the king. The king and parliament made him general of all the forces in

South Carolina and Georgia, with orders to protect these provinces from the Spaniards "to the last extremity." They also furnished him with a splendid regiment of English soldiers to aid in the defense and sent them over on a vessel to Frederica. Having accomplished this much, Oglethorpe got aboard his ship and hastened back to Georgia. On reaching Savannah he found that the Spaniards had been up to mischief while he was gone. They had sent emissaries, or secret agents, to all the tribes of the Creek Indians to try to turn them against the English, and to induce them by bribes and fair promises to join the side of Spain. The Indians at this time really had some just ground of complaint against the English, on account of the bad way in which they had been treated by dishonest English traders. The Spaniards made the most of this grievance and caused the Indians to take a greatly exaggerated view of it. It looked as if they might succeed in winning nearly the whole Creek Nation over to their side, which would have been ruinous to Georgia.

Chiefs of several of the tribes, stanch friends of Oglethorpe, came to Savannah to tell him of these things and to warn him of the danger. They also told him that during the coming summer the chiefs of all the tribes of the Creeks and of several other Indian nations would assemble in their yearly council at Coweta Town on the Chattahoochee River; and they urged him to attend this meeting, so that he might confer with the chiefs and fix their loyalty to him. Oglethorpe determined so to do, though it would be a most arduous and perilous expedition; but when duty called, Oglethorpe was always indifferent to hardship and reckless of danger. He sent word to the chiefs of the various tribes that he would meet them in the big council at Coweta Town.

Coweta Town was situated on the west side of the Chattahoochee River a few miles below the present city of Columbus, and on the spot where now stands the little village of Fort Mitchell, Alabama. It was, of course, an Indian town, and few if any white men had ever seen the place. It was two hundred and fifty miles in a bee line from Savannah, but by the zigzag route that Oglethorpe would have to pursue it was four hundred miles.

Oglethorpe's party consisted of three white attendants, two white interpreters, and three Indian guides. They were mounted on horses, and there were several pack horses besides to carry their baggage. With this little retinue Oglethorpe, starting from Savannah, plunged into the wilderness, with which nearly the whole state of Georgia was then covered. Over swamps, through tangled thickets, along ravines, past rivers that had to be crossed on rafts or by swimming, he pushed his way to the westward. At night he slept on the ground by the watch-fires, giving up to his attendants the two little tents that were brought on the pack horses. He was guided through the wilderness by the "blazed trees" of traders or by the narrow Indian trails that he struck now and then, or frequently by nothing but his pocket compass. For over two hundred miles he journeyed without meeting a human being, for Georgia was very thinly settled by Indians; their towns and villages were few and far between.

When forty miles from Coweta Town, he was met by a number of Indian chiefs who had come to escort him and bring him supplies of provisions. He crossed the Chattahoochee River in a canoe at the point where the city of Columbus now stands. The exact place on the river bank from which he embarked on the Georgia side is still pointed out and has been marked with a suitable stone and inscription by the Oglethorpe Chapter of the Daughters of the American Revolution. Proceeding a few miles further to the southwest, he reached Coweta Town, where the chiefs were holding their big council. The Indians were overjoyed to see him, for he held a very deep place in their affections.

For days he listened patiently to their long, tiresome "talks," as they called their public speeches. At night he witnessed their wild, satyr-like dances in the lurid glare of the big bonfires. He was lulled to sleep by their weird incantations and the dreary beating of the "tom tom." He assured them that their grievances against the dishonest traders should be adjusted and that they should be cheated no more. He convinced them that the English were still their best friends. He easily induced them to make a solemn promise that they would continue to stand by him and that they would aid the English in any trouble that might arise between them and the Spaniards. No other white man that ever came to America, not even the great William Penn himself, had such a powerful and wholesome influence over the Indians as did James Oglethorpe!

Having fully accomplished his purpose in coming to Coweta Town, Oglethorpe turned his face eastward and again plunged into the great wilderness. His return trip was even more toilsome than his coming, for the weather was bad and men and horses were jaded. He reached Augusta on September 7th, 1739, and for three weeks he was prostrated by fever brought on by fatigue and exposure. In this wild and wonderful journey he had taken his life in his hands. Aside from other perils, he was in daily danger of assassination by some treacherous Indian; for there was not a red man in all the Creek Nation that did not know he would receive a princely reward from the Spaniards for James Oglethorpe's scalp.

As soon as he had recovered from the fever, he went to Charleston to see what aid South Carolina would extend in case of a struggle with Spain. He had some trouble with the authorities of that selfish colony; but at last they made him fair promises, which they never kept. He had now done everything in his power to get ready for the threatened conflict with Spain; and, as it turned out, that conflict was very near at hand.

II. SIEGE OF ST. AUGUSTINE.

About the middle of November, 1739, a party of Spaniards landed on Amelia Island during the night and concealed themselves among the palmetto bushes. At daybreak next morning, they shot to death two unarmed Highland soldiers who had come out of the fort to gather fuel, and cut off their heads and mutilated their bodies horribly. Their purpose was to push on and capture the little fort; but Captain Francis Brooks, who commanded an English scout boat, hearing the firing that killed the Highlanders, came quickly up and drove the Spaniards away. The murder of these two Highlanders was the first bloodshed of the Spanish War.

When Oglethorpe, at Frederica, heard of this outrage, he determined not to wait for the Spaniards to invade Georgia, but to take the initiative himself and invade Florida and capture St. Augustine. This was a bold step, but Oglethorpe felt that he must continue to play a bluff game with the Spaniards. He was greatly delayed in his preparations by the conduct of South Carolina. That colony at first refused to render any assistance, but at last consented and furnished a considerable contingent for the war, though not nearly so large a one as was rightly due from her. The Creek Indians did much better. Mindful of the promise they had made to Oglethorpe at Coweta Town, they readily furnished him with all the warriors he called for—nearly one thousand in number. By the last of May, 1740, he had everything ready to start on the great invasion. His army numbered over two thousand men, nearly one thousand of whom were Indians, the rest being made up of the five hundred regulars that had been sent from England, of Scotch Highlanders, and of South Carolina and Georgia militia. He also had a considerable fleet of ships that was to operate against St. Augustine from the water side. The land army was transported in vessels to the mouth of the St. John's River, where it disembarked.

Starting from the mouth of the St. John's, Oglethorpe swept southward, capturing with little trouble all Spanish forts and outposts up to the very gates of St.

The Old Spanish Gate at St. Augustine.

Augustine; but there he was completely checkmated. St. Augustine was splendidly protected by walls, forts and entrenchments, well built and skilfully arranged. Its army of defense consisted of 1,400 veteran Spanish soldiers under a very able commander, General Manuel de Monteano. On the ocean side it was so well guarded by Spanish warships that the English fleet could not approach near enough to render much assistance to the

The Spanish War.

land army. Oglethorpe was greatly astonished to find the city so strongly protected. He soon saw that he could not take it by storm, as he had fully expected to do. He must try to take it by siege and the "starving out" plan.

He completely surrounded the city with his army and his ships, so that no provisions or reinforcements could be brought in. For a while this plan worked admirably, but it soon failed through the disobedience of one of Oglethorpe's officers. To the west several roads led from the city out into the country. On one of these roads, two miles from the town, was Fort Moosa, which Oglethorpe had taken from the Spaniards. He appointed Colonel Palmer with a force of ninety-five Highlanders and forty Indians to guard these roads, saying to him, "Patrol the roads night and day. See that not a soul passes over them into the city. Make your headquarters at Fort Moosa, but don't stay there or anywhere else any two nights in succession; move constantly about from place to place, lest the Spaniards capture you by a surprise attack." For a while Colonel Palmer obeyed these orders strictly, but he soon grew careless. He spent three nights in succession in Fort Moosa. It was so much more comfortable there than lying out in the woods! On the third night, June 24th, the great iron gate of St. Augustine opened and out marched a body of three hundred Spanish soldiers, picked men, the very flower of the army. Stealthily they crept near the fort and hid in the bushes. Just before day, when men are wont to sleep most soundly, they made the attack. The Highlanders were taken completely by surprise, but they fought like tigers. Although awakened from sound sleep by this terrific attack they were not panic stricken, but seized their broadswords and slashed the Spaniards right and left. Spanish blood flowed like water. Many of the Highlanders, too, fell under Spanish bullets and bayonets. Among the first to fall was the disobedient but brave Colonel Palmer. Perhaps he sought death, feeling keenly that this disaster was all his fault. Twenty-two brave Highlanders were killed. The Indians fled panic-stricken in the early part of the fight. More than a hundred Spanish soldiers lay dead; only a few of them were shot; nearly all were killed by the terrible broadswords of the Highlanders. But the Spaniards had gained a great victory. Colonel Palmer's command was utterly destroyed, Fort Moosa was recaptured, the roads were opened, and provisions came pouring into St. Augustine for the pent-up garrison!

Oglethorpe's starving-out plan had failed, but he

The Spanish War.

still held the city in siege, hoping that he might force a surrender with his cannon balls. For days and days, all day long, his cannon boomed and boomed away at St. Augustine, while, in reply, the Spanish cannon thundered forth; but the distance between the two was too great, the shots mostly fell short, and with all the booming not much damage was done on either side. Midsummer had now come. The heat of the tropical sun was terrible to Oglethorpe's poor soldiers in their open camps, unaccustomed as they were to such a climate. Many of them sickened and died; and the rest had their lives almost tormented out of them by the terrible heat, sand flies and mosquitoes. The Indians, who can never stand a waiting fight, became restless, and deserted by hundreds. The South Carolina soldiers became mutinous and threatened to disband and go home.

St. Mark's Castle, St. Augustine.

At last Oglethorpe, finding that with all his cannonading he could do no great hurt to the Spaniards, gave up the whole thing as a hopeless undertaking. So on the 20th day of July he ordered the siege to be raised.

He marched his weary and bedraggled Georgia soldiers back to Frederica, while the South Carolina contingent sailed for Charleston. The whole expedition had been a dismal failure. Poor Oglethorpe was most severely and unjustly criticized by all America and all England.

III. BATTLE OF ST. SIMON'S SOUND.

Oglethorpe's unsuccessful attack on St. Augustine proved, after all, to be of great benefit to Georgia. The boldness of the attempt so frightened Spain that she deferred for many months her proposed invasion of Georgia and South Carolina. For nearly two years there was a lull in the war and almost a complete cessation of active hostilities. Oglethorpe spent the time preparing with great energy for the terrific storm that he knew would, sooner or later, burst upon him. He greatly strengthened the defences around Frederica; he built a new fort at the other end of St. Simon's Island, nine miles from Frederica; he withdrew the forces from St. George's Island, Amelia Island, and Fort St. Andrew and used them to strengthen the garrison at Fort William; he reinforced his army as far as possible and drilled the soldiers constantly. Scarcely were these preparations completed before the storm burst upon him.

In May, 1742, a Spanish armada consisting of fifty-

The Spanish War. 99

four warships and seven thousand soldiers left Havana for St. Augustine. Its avowed purpose was to sweep up the Atlantic coast and wipe the English colonies out of Georgia and South Carolina and add those provinces to the possessions of Spain. When Oglethorpe received this alarming news he dispatched a messenger to Charleston to call on South Carolina to send to him at once her quota of soldiers and ships for the common defence, but much to Oglethorpe's chagrin South Carolina refused to give any assistance. So the brave Oglethorpe, with his little army of less than a thousand men, whites and Indians, and only three warships, was left to meet alone the dreadful war storm that was gathering to the south. But his heroic spirit rose with the danger, and his noble language was, "We are resolved not to suffer defeat; we will rather die like Leonidas and his Spartans, if we can but protect Georgia and Carolina and the rest of the Americans from desolation!"

On the 21st of June, a Spanish fleet of fourteen warships appeared off the south end of Cumberland Island and tried to pass between the island and the mainland, but was driven off by a cannonading from Fort William, aided by one of Oglethorpe's warships that was patrolling in the sound. Six days later, on the

28th day of June, the same fleet, reinforced to thirty-six warships and carrying five thousand soldiers, having sailed up along the east side of Cumberland and Jekyl, made its appearance just outside St. Simon's Sound, as the strip of water between Jekyl and St. Simon's is called. There for several days it rode back and forth, waiting for a favorable wind to take it through the sound and up the narrow river to Frederica.

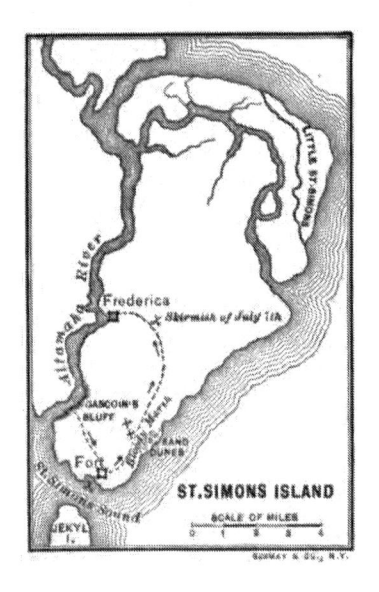

All was now energy and activity on St. Simon's, preparing for the life-and-death struggle that was so near at hand. Oglethorpe and his little band of eight hundred must defend Frederica to the last gasp against this overwhelming Spanish armada; for if the enemy should succeed in taking this stronghold, they could sweep almost without resistance over the whole of Georgia and South Carolina. Frederica being lost, all would be lost. The situation was not unlike Leonidas and his Spartans facing Xerxes and his mighty host at the Pass of Thermopylæ. Oglethorpe drew his soldiers up on parade ground and made them an inspiring speech that fired their hearts with heroism.

The first resistance was to be made down at Fort St. Simon's, on the south end of the island. The fort stood at the water's edge overlooking the sound, just where a great lighthouse stands at this day. At this point Oglethorpe concentrated nearly all of his forces. Besides the fort, he had in the sound three battleships and eight small sloops moored close against the shore, each sloop having on board a little cannon and one man to fire it.

On July 5th, a favorable wind sprang up, and at the same time the high spring tide came in and raised the waters in the sound and in the river; so the Spanish ships spread their sails and, forming in line of battle, started through the sound. It was a grand and appalling spectacle! Just as they turned northward to go up the narrow river, the fort, the three English battleships, and all the little sloops opened fire on them. A terrific naval battle ensued. It lasted three hours, during which more than two thousand cannon shots were fired. One of the English battleships was sunk, and several of the Spanish vessels were badly damaged. Eighteen Spaniards were killed and many were wounded, and the English loss also was considerable. It was an heroic fight on the part of the English, but they were too greatly outnumbered. In spite of their utmost efforts the Spanish ships ran past them, and, turning northward, sailed up the river to within four miles of Frederica, where they cast anchor at Gascoigne's Bluff, very near where the big sawmills of the Hilton and Dodge Lumber Company now stand. The river above this point was so narrow that the Spanish commander was afraid to risk his ships under fire of Fort Frederica, until he could arrange to have his land army coöperate with him against the place; so he disembarked his soldiers on Gascoigne's Bluff.

IV. BLOODY MARSH.

The situation was now more desperate than ever. Night had come on, but for the almost exhausted soldiers of Oglethorpe there must be neither rest nor sleep. Oglethorpe knew that to prevent being cut off from his retreat to Frederica, he must move with utmost promptness and celerity. He ordered his two remaining battleships to sail at once for Charleston; for they could be of no further service here, and if they remained they would certainly be captured by the enemy.

He spiked the guns in the fort, destroyed the supplies, and blew up the magazine. Then he set fire to the eight sloops moored by the shore; and by the lurid conflagration that they made, he started a little after midnight on his retreat to Frederica, nine miles away, and reached the place just at daybreak. The fight down at Fort St. Simon's had been fierce, but well he knew that the great life-and-death struggle was yet to come!

On the morning of the 6th, the Spanish commander, finding that the English had abandoned Fort St. Simon's, marched his forces from Gascoigne's Bluff three miles across the country down to the fort, so that he might have the protection of its walls from any attack the English might make. From this point he prepared to march against Frederica.

On the morning of the 7th, the Spanish advance guard, consisting of four hundred picked men, started towards Frederica. When within two miles of the place, they came upon a company of thirty mounted rangers whom Oglethorpe had sent out as a picket, and with a single volley drove them back, killing one of their number. Oglethorpe, hearing the firing, sprang upon his horse, and at the head of the Highlanders, Indians, and three companies of British regulars, all of whom happened to be under arms at the time, dashed through the woods and drove the enemy back, with much slaughter, to an open plain, or savannah, seven miles from Frederica. He posted the forces with him in the thick wood along the edge of the savannah, and put them in charge of the Highland captains, Sutherland and Mackay, while he himself galloped back to Frederica to get the rest of the troops and bring them up.

While he was gone, the Spaniards, largely reinforced, advanced across the savannah, and with loud huzzahs charged on the forces in the edge of the woods. Two companies of British regulars, becoming panic-stricken, gave way before the charge and fled in wild confusion. The Spaniards, following hot on their heels, pursued them to within two miles of Frederica, and then turning, started back, thinking all the time that they had driven back the entire command. In the mean time, the soldiers who had remained at their post were ordered by Captains Sutherland and Mackay to conceal themselves behind the palmetto bushes in the woods, for they knew that the Spaniards would soon be coming back. So the fatal ambush was prepared. Behind every palmetto bush on both sides of the road and far back into the woods an English soldier lay concealed with his gun ready, still as death.

In a little while, sure enough, the Spaniards were seen coming down the road with martial tread and heads erect, proud of their victory, and having not the least suspicion of the death trap into which they were about to march. When near the edge of the woods they halted, stacked their guns in the road, and sat down on the ground to rest and to eat the breakfast that they carried in their haversacks. But scarcely were they seated when Captain Mackay gave to his men the signal agreed upon, by raising his Highland cap on the point of his uplifted sword; and then "bang! bang! bang!" from behind the palmetto bushes a deadly fire was poured into the poor astounded Spaniards. Quickly they sprang to their guns, but before they could form in line of battle the English charged through the rustling palmettoes right down upon them. Some of their officers bravely tried to make them take a stand, but all in vain. They broke and ran in a perfect stampede, and were charged by the English out of the woods and across the savannah as a flock of sheep are chased by a pack of wolves.

On the other side of the Savannah was an open salt marsh extending to the sea. The terror-stricken Spaniards, seeing that their way by the road was cut off by the English, tried to make their escape by rushing straight across this marsh to the shelter of the sand dunes on the other side; but they mired up in the marsh so that they could scarcely move, and were shot down there by scores, their bodies falling into the long sea grass and their life's blood staining with red the black swamp ooze. This awful place of slaughter is known to this day as "Bloody Marsh," and is pointed out to visitors as the most tragic spot on this tragic island. The forests have been mostly cleared away from this vicinity, but the open savannah, the marsh, and the white sand dunes beyond appear to-day precisely as they did when the battle was fought one hundred and sixty years ago.

Over two hundred Spaniards were killed in that day's fight, and many more were taken prisoners. Very few got back to the Spanish lines to tell the dreadful tale. In the battle no soldier on the English side behaved more heroically than did our young Indian friend, Toonahowi. He had succeeded Tomo-chi-chi as chief of the Yamacraws, and had joined Oglethorpe's army at the head of a hundred Creek warriors. In the thickest of the fray just described he was charging with uplifted tomahawk on a Spanish captain, when the captain, with a pistol ball, broke his right arm. Down dropped arm and tomahawk; but quick as a flash he drew his pistol with his left hand and shot the captain through the brain, killing him instantly. Two years later this young Indian chief was killed in a skirmish with the Spaniards down in Florida, but not until he had, by many feats of arms and deeds of valor, fulfilled the dear wish of old Tomo-chi-chi's heart, that Toona-howi should "be big warrior!"

General Monteano, commander of the Spaniards, was greatly alarmed at this terrible defeat of his advance guard, and deemed it necessary to exercise extreme caution in his further movements; he therefore postponed until the next day marching against Frederica with his main body. That night Oglethorpe, by practicing a most shrewd and cunning stratagem, which we have not space to relate here, but a full and very interesting account of which you may find in C. C. Jones's history, made the Spaniards believe that he had a large and powerful fleet at Frederica and vicinity. Brave General Monteano was anxious to go ahead and fight it out anyhow; but his soldiers were panic-stricken, and several of his generals, especially the one commanding the Cuban contingent, which composed more than half of his army, refused to act with him. So on the 8th day of July, the great Spanish host—ships, soldiers, and all—sailed away for St. Augustine; and never again did Spain attempt the invasion of Georgia. The war was continued in a feeble, half-hearted sort of way for two years longer, when it was brought to a close by a final treaty of peace between Spain and England.

Thus, with a little band of only eight hundred men and three ships, Oglethorpe had driven off a Spanish armada of thirty-six warships and an army of five thousand men and had saved Georgia and South Carolina, and perhaps the whole of English America, from Spanish conquest! There is no more brilliant event in American history. The memory of it should ever be cherished among the proudest annals of our beloved State of Georgia!

CHAPTER VIII.

"NON SIBI SED ALIIS."

On the 23d of July, 1743, James Oglethorpe left Georgia never to return. As he was tossed on the waves of the Atlantic on his way back to his old home in England, what must have been his thoughts and feelings about the work in Georgia to which he had given eleven of the best years of his life? They had been years full of trial and tribulation to him. Of some of the hardships and dangers that he had to endure, you have learned in the foregoing pages; but these were the least of his troubles. In carrying out this great enterprise he had to deal with many very mean people. He was constantly harassed (if so strong and firm a mind as his would allow itself to be harassed) by the dishonesty and treachery, the "envy, hatred, malice and all uncharitableness" of persons who should have lent him a helping hand. Yet in coming to America to undertake this hard and trying work, Oglethorpe had made many sacrifices; for he gave up a luxurious home, the delights of literature, the pleasures of refined society, and a splendid public career that was just opening to him in England, and from it all he had absolutely nothing, in a worldly sense, to gain for himself. *Non sibi sed aliis!*

Tomo-chi-chi, that grand old savage, showed a spirit as unselfish and noble as Oglethorpe's. By the practice of a little business cunning he might have obtained for himself rich rewards from the English for the great services that he rendered to them, but not one cent did he ever ask or receive. Even the presents that were made to him while he was in England, he gave away with a free hand to the poor people of his tribe on his return to America. He died at last in his humble wigwam, one of the poorest of men. In all that he did, he was governed by no other motive than to promote the best interests of his people. American history furnishes no finer illustration of pure and lofty patriotism. *Non sibi sed aliis!*

The Trustees of Georgia served without pay or reward of any kind. The work required much of their time and was full of grave responsibility. They looked after the affairs of the colony with as much care and diligence as if Georgia had been their private property and was being run as a money-making enterprise; and yet they well knew that, in a selfish sense, there was absolutely nothing in it, neither fame nor fortune, for themselves. *Non sibi sed aliis!*

Of all the American colonies, Georgia was certainly the one established on the noblest principles; and yet for a long time Georgia did not prosper. At the time of Oglethorpe's leaving, the whole enterprise seemed little better than a failure. Boundless enthusiasm, devoted self-sacrifice, strenuous work, and many hundreds of thousands of dollars had been expended on the undertaking; and yet after ten years there were less than three thousand people in the colony, and most of these were in a deplorable condition. Hundreds of people who had settled here moved away in disgust to the Carolinas and other more prosperous provinces.

The reason generally given for this discouraging state of affairs is the obstinacy of Oglethorpe and the Trustees in not allowing negro slavery and the rum trade in Georgia. And yet Oglethorpe was neither an abolitionist nor a teetotaler. He owned slaves himself on a place in South Carolina and he was fond of a glass of wine at dinner, and you have seen how liberally he dispensed rum punch to the guests at his big barbecue in South Carolina. His reason for prohibiting slavery in Georgia was (to use his own language somewhat paraphrased): "Owing to its proximity to the hostile and treacherous Spaniards, Georgia should be a sort of military colony; every citizen should also be a soldier. The people should live on small farms close together, so that, whenever need be, the men may quickly combine into an army. If slavery were introduced, rich men would buy up the lands, the State would be divided up into large plantations occupied by multitudes of negroes and only a few white men. The Spaniards would incite the negroes to rise in insurrection and murder the whites. South Carolina has already been much disturbed in this way; it would be very much worse for Georgia, lying so near Spanish Florida." His reason against rum was: "Indians are extremely fond of rum and, when they can get it, drink to great excess, bringing on madness, disease and death. For many years to come the welfare of Georgia will depend largely on the help and good behavior of the Indians, therefore rum should be kept away from them." So the prohibition of slavery and rum in Georgia was not at all a matter of morality, but purely a matter of economics or public policy. From this standpoint it was, under all the circumstances, an unwise prohibition, and worked greatly to the detriment of the colony.

Another cause of the lack of prosperity was, no doubt, in the kind of people of whom the colony was largely composed. For, if the truth must be told, many of the emigrants who came to Georgia during Oglethorpe's rule were a sorry lot of folk—debtors, paupers, beggars, and all sorts of folk who had not been able to take care of themselves at home. Oglethorpe has been much blamed for peopling Georgia with such slipshod, knock-kneed human beings; but really it redounds to his glory that he was willing to extend a helping hand to those poor creatures whom no one else would help, and to give them one more chance in the world. True, as might have been expected, these persons made poor use of the opportunity, but Oglethorpe was not to blame for that. There were, of course, many good settlers, such, for instance, as the Salzburgers, who were an earnest, sturdy, industrious folk; but they seem to have lacked spirit, enterprise, and ambition. Of all the early emigrants to Georgia, those who seem to have been made of that heroic stuff necessary to the right upbuilding of a new country were the doughty Highlanders who settled on the Altamaha River, and, alas! they were wiped out of existence in the Spanish war where they so bravely threw themselves "in the imminent and deadly breach," *non sibi sed aliis!*

But Oglethorpe's work in Georgia was far from being the failure that it seemed. He had laid deep the foundation of splendid success. He had gained the lasting good-will of the Indians. He had saved Georgia, and Carolina, too, from Spanish conquest In the face of dangers and obstacles that might have appalled the stoutest heart, he had planted a colony that was destined to grow into the great Empire State of the South!

In 1751 the Trustees of Georgia surrendered their charter to the king. For twenty years they had managed the affairs of the colony with the greatest faithfulness and zeal, though, it must be confessed, with but little wisdom. For their pains and unselfish devotion they received nothing but harsh criticism from the public and base ingratitude from those whom they had tried so hard to help. No doubt they were glad to be free from the thankless task. Georgia was at once changed into a Royal Province. Under the new *régime* the restrictions on slavery and the rum trade were removed, and a number of unwise regulations of the Trustees were abolished or changed. Many energetic, enterprising people, some of them wealthy and influential, moved into the colony, and Georgia forged rapidly forward. By the year 1766, it had ten thousand white inhabitants and eight thousand negro slaves. It had at last grown to be a prosperous and flourishing colony.

In 1744, about a year after his return to England,

Oglethorpe at the Age of Ninety-two.

Oglethorpe at length was married, aged fifty-five years. His bride was Miss Elizabeth Wright, aged thirty-five years. As he was quite an old bachelor and she was somewhat of an old maid, it is to be presumed they lived happily together. She was very wealthy, and her money came in nicely for him, since his own fortune had been much depleted from his generosity to the Georgia colony. Soon after his marriage he was made Major-General in the British army and took an active part in the famous campaign against the Pretender. Subsequently he was promoted to the higher rank of Lieutenant-General, and later still to that of full General, or Commander-in-Chief. It is often told that at the beginning of the Revolutionary War, when he was eighty-six years old, he was offered but refused the command of the army that was to fight against the Americans; but there is no truth in this absurd story.

After his retirement from the army, he was re-elected to Parliament, where he served with distinction for many years. Like his friend Tomo-chi-chi, he lived to be a very old man; and, like Tomo-chi-chi, too, to the very last his figure was erect, his step light and spry, his eye undimmed, and his faculties unimpaired. His youth had been stormy, his middle life tempestuous, but his long old age was entirely serene. He lived in great ease and luxury at his rich wife's beautiful country home, but he paid frequent visits to London, where he entered with great heartiness into the literary and social pleasures of the city. One night he would be at the Authors' Club enjoying the brilliant company of such men as Dr. Johnson, Goldsmith, Burke, Burton, and other great literary lights; and the next night he would be at a court ball, dancing with the belles of the season. Until he was ninety years old, he continued to enjoy such pastimes and gayeties with unabated zest. In his marvelous old age he was the most striking figure and the most honored man in all England, and wherever he went he was the "observed of all observers." On the 1st of July, 1785, he died at Cranham Hall, Essex, aged ninety-six years.

Georgia has a county and a town named for Oglethorpe, but, strange to say, the State has never erected a monument to his memory. The Colonial Dames and the Daughters of the American Revolution of Georgia are now trying to raise funds by popular subscription for this purpose. The movement should have the hearty sympathy and help of all Georgians and should be aided by a liberal appropriation from the State Legislature. There has never lived a man who more richly deserved such an honor at the hands of the Georgia people. To the many superb patriotic monuments that already adorn the beautiful city of Savannah, let one, more splendid than any of the others, be added to the memory of James Oglethorpe; and let there be carved on it as a suitable epitaph the noble phrase, *NON SIBI SED ALIIS!*

PART II.

REVOLUTIONARY PERIOD

CHAPTER IX.

THE STAMP ACT IN GEORGIA.

In the year 1765 the English Parliament passed the celebrated law known as the *Stamp Act.* This law required the American colonists to write all their legal documents, such as promissory notes, deeds, contracts,

English Stamps for America.*

bonds, leases, mortgages, etcetera, on "stamped paper," which they had to buy from the English Government, and which was very costly. It required them also to put expensive government stamps on all newspapers,

*From Green's "A Short History of the English People." Reproduced by permission of Harper and Brothers.

pamphlets and almanacs published in America. This was a heavy tax on the Americans, who were poor and ill able to bear it; but England declared it necessary in order to help pay the expenses of the French and Indian War, which had been fought for the benefit of the colonies. The passage of the law made the Americans very indignant, because, as they asserted, England had no right to tax them without their own consent. In Virginia the great orator, Patrick Henry, made against the Act a bold and eloquent speech that fired the hearts of the people. James Otis of Massachusetts and other able and patriotic men also spoke and wrote against it. Soon the people throughout the whole country were aroused, and they determined not to permit the outrage. All of the colonies were invited to send delegates to a convention, or congress, to be held in New York City for the purpose of protesting against the Stamp Act.

The Governor of Georgia at that time was James Wright. He was born and reared in South Carolina and belonged to a very fine family. He was appointed Governor of Georgia by George II, King of England, in 1760. He was a brave, able and honorable man, but he did not sympathize with the Americans in their stand against the Stamp Act. He believed that England had a right to tax the Americans, and that they ought to submit to it without a murmur; so he did everything in his power to keep the people of Georgia from taking part in the movement against the Act. Through his influence Georgia was prevented from sending any delegates to the congress in New York.

So Georgia was not represented in the famous First Colonial Congress, as it was called, that met in New York in October, 1765. The congress drew up a respectful petition and sent it by special messenger across the ocean to the King and Parliament of England, protesting that England had no right to tax the colonies without their own consent, and begging that the Stamp Act be repealed; but the King and Parliament were obstinate and headstrong, and were determined to enforce the Act. Ships laden with boxes containing the odious "stamped paper," and accompanied by officers appointed to sell the paper to the colonists, sailed from England for all the principal American ports. When they arrived in America, both stamps and stamp officers received rough treatment at the hands of the angry people in nearly all of the colonies, as you may learn from United States history. What we want to learn now is exactly what the people of Georgia did about it.

In spite of Governor Wright's earnest efforts to get the people of Georgia to submit quietly to the Stamp Act, they were determined to rebel against it. They had good reason to rebel; for besides the wrong principle of the Act itself, Georgia was at that time the poorest of all the colonies, and the one least able to bear this oppressive tax. In all parts of the colony the people banded

King George III.

themselves together in societies called "Sons of Liberty," and took a solemn pledge not to allow the stamps to be sold or used in Georgia. Young men formed themselves into military companies called "Liberty Boys," and vowed that they would capture and destroy the stamps as soon as they reached Savannah, and would compel the stamp officer to leave the colony or else would bind him hand and foot and throw him into the river and drown him.

The 26th of October was the anniversary of King George III's accession to the throne of England; and

Colonists Burning the Stamp Seller in Effigy.

Governor Wright, wishing to honor his royal master, called on the people to assemble in Savannah to celebrate the occasion. Big crowds came; but most of them, instead of honoring King George, spent the day in listening to speeches against him and his Parliament and their wicked Stamp Act. In the evening the crowd made images, or effigies, of Governor Wright and other prominent men who favored the Stamp Act, and putting them on high poles, paraded the streets with them, accompanied by jeers and insults, ending at last late at night by burning the effigies on the public square amid great cheering and hurrahing.

Governor Wright thought the people were very wrong to act this way and tried by talks and speeches and writings to get them to behave themselves, but they heeded him not. In all parts of the colony they continued to hold public meetings to denounce the King and Parliament and the Stamp Act.

It was expected that the ship bearing the stamps would reach Savannah about the 1st of November, but for some reason it was delayed. At last, on the 5th of December, an English vessel called *The Speedwell* was seen sailing up the river. It was laden with boxes containing the much-talked-of "stamped paper," but this fact was known only to Governor Wright and a few of his council. The Governor had the vessel stopped several miles down the river until late in the night, when it was brought up to the landing, and the boxes of "stamped paper" were secretly transferred to a strong warehouse, known as Fort Halifax, where they were locked up and put under guard. All this was done to keep the Liberty Boys from destroying the stamps, which they certainly would have done if they could have got their hands on them.

The stamp officer for Georgia, a Mr. Angus, did not come over on *The Speedwell*, but on a vessel that was to arrive later. This vessel reached Savannah on the 3d of January. Governor Wright knew that the Liberty Boys were on the lookout for the stamp officer and, if they should get their hands on him, would handle him very roughly; so he was taken off the ship away down at Tybee Island and put in a small boat and brought to the landing and then smuggled through the streets to the Governor's mansion, where he was strictly guarded.

Everything now seemed ready for the sale of the stamps to begin; but the people were determined that the stamps should not be sold or used, and this they let Governor Wright and Mr. Angus know very plainly. However, they made one exception. There were at this time sixty merchant ships at Savannah, all loaded and ready to sail; but before a ship is allowed to leave a port it must have what is called "a clearance certificate," and the Stamp Act required that all "clearance certificates" should be written on "stamped paper." It was very necessary that these ships should sail away with their merchandise, or else the commerce of Savannah and the whole colony would be utterly ruined. So the Sons of Liberty held a meeting and agreed to allow stamps to be bought and used for the clearance of these ships, but not for any other purpose; and these were the only "Stamp-Act" stamps ever used in Georgia.

The people grew more and more excited. Every night they gathered in noisy, angry crowds on the streets of Savannah. They threatened the life of the Governor and of Mr. Angus. The Governor's mansion had to be guarded day and night by forty British Rangers. For four days and nights in succession Governor Wright did not take off his clothes, not even his boots, expecting every moment to be attacked. Mr. Angus did not dare walk out on the streets or even put his head out of the door. At last he decided that it would be best for him to leave the city, so he was smuggled out to the country home of one of the Governor's friends. One day a great crowd of Liberty Boys began gathering on the streets for the purpose of taking the "stamped papers" from Fort Halifax and destroying them; but Governor Wright, hearing of it, took a company of fifty Rangers and marched to the fort, and loading the stamps on a cart drawn by two stout horses, carried them to the guard house and locked them up behind its iron doors and iron-barred windows.

Towards the end of January a body of six hundred men from nearly all parts of the colony assembled in the woods near Savannah and sent word to Governor Wright that if he did not surrender the stamps to them they would kill him and take them by force. The Governor, always energetic and prompt, instead of yielding to their threats, hurried the stamps down the river to a fort on Cockspur Island, where they were guarded by a garrison of British Rangers; but, fearing that they might not be safe even there, a few days later he had them placed on the English ship *The Speedwell*, the same vessel that had brought them over from England, and which was then at anchor just inside the harbor bar. There, at last, the precious stamps were safe from the terrible Liberty Boys!

A day or two after the removal of the stamps a body of nearly two hundred Liberty Boys from the crowd which was camped in the woods near Savannah, marched boldly into the city and took possession of the public square. The Governor quickly called the Rangers from Cockspur Island to defend the city, and a number of volunteers also joined him, so that he had nearly a hundred well-armed soldiers. It looked as if there would be a bloody battle in the very heart of the town; but the Liberty Boys, awed by the Governor's bold front, soon dispersed and returned to their camp in the woods.

You will notice that through all this trying time Governor Wright showed himself to be a firm, brave, wise man. Against great odds he protected the stamps and the stamp officer from violence, but at the same time he was very prudent in his dealings with the angry people. A single rash act on his part would have caused fighting and bloodshed. Through it all he had a number of strong friends and adherents to stand by him and help him; for there were many people in Georgia who sincerely agreed with him that the colonists ought to submit to the Stamp Act as obedient subjects of England, and that to rebel against it was treason. These persons were called Loyalists or Royalists, but afterwards they became known as Tories. Those that resisted the Act called themselves Patriots.

In the spring of 1766 all of the trouble about the Stamp Act came to a sudden and happy end. Over in England Parliament had at last repealed the hated Act. This was done, not so much on account of the pleadings of the Americans, as through the influence of certain great Englishmen who thought that the Act was wrong, and who sympathized with the Americans. The greatest of these was William Pitt, afterwards Earl of Chatham. Bent with rheumatism, swathed in flannels, suffering acute pain, he hobbled into the Parliament House on his crutches, and made on behalf of the Americans one of the greatest speeches ever delivered. All Americans should ever love the great Englishman, William Pitt, Earl of Chatham. After him, Chatham County, Georgia, is named.

The news of the repeal of the Stamp Act was hailed with mighty rejoicing by all the colonies, and by none more than by the colony of Georgia. Every colony sent earnest and grateful thanks to the King and Parliament, with assurances of loyalty to the English Government. So for a while there was again peace and love between the colonies and the mother country!

William Pitt.

James Wright was Governor of Georgia for many years, and he was one of the ablest and best Governors that Georgia has ever had. He did a great deal for the good of the colony in its early days of poverty and hard struggle. It is a pity he did not sympathize with the people in their righteous and noble struggle for independence; but he really believed they were wrong, and he acted according to his convictions. Through many hard trials he was faithful to what he thought was his duty. He was an able, brave, honest man. We should honor his memory.

CHAPTER X.

THE CAPTURE OF SAVANNAH.

I. ARRIVAL OF THE BRITISH FLEET.

The good feeling between the colonies and the mother country, that had been brought about by the repeal of the Stamp Act, did not last long. King George III and the English Parliament still insisted that they had a right to tax the colonies, and they soon passed another tax law as bad in principle as the Stamp Act. The colonies resisted it, and England tried to force them to submission. The strife between the two countries grew worse and worse, until at last it resulted in the great Revolutionary War, which began with the Battle of Lexington, fought in Massachusetts, April 19, 1775. An account of how the war broke out and of its early battles you can learn from United States history.

When the news of the Battle of Lexington reached Georgia it caused great excitement, and the patriotic people began making vigorous preparations for war. The Royal Governor, James Wright, about whom you learned in the last lesson, did his best by persuasion and by threats to keep the colony loyal to the English Government, but all in vain. At last he was forced to flee the country and take refuge in England. Many other leading Tories were driven from the colony, and those that remained were required to take a solemn oath not to do anything to aid the British. All the British officials were turned out of their positions, and the Patriots took complete possession of the government. In place of the banished Governor Wright, Archibald Bulloch,* an able and noble Patriot, was put at the head of affairs with the title of President and Commander-in-Chief.

The people of Georgia refused to carry on commerce with England or to buy anything brought over in English ships, thus voluntarily depriving themselves of many comforts and almost of many necessities of life. They sent large donations of money, clothing and provisions to the fighting American soldiers at the North. They raised a fine regiment of volunteers to defend Georgia from British invasion; and this regiment, on the 2d of March, 1776, most gallantly drove back a fleet of British warships that was trying to capture the American merchant vessels lying at the wharves of Savannah. In the fight three British marines were killed and several were taken prisoners, while the Americans had only one man wounded. This was the first bloodshed of the

---

*This Archibald Bulloch was the great-grandfather of Theodore Roosevelt, President of the United States.

Revolution in Georgia. Georgia was represented in the Continental Congresses that met in Philadelphia during the Revolution; and her three delegates, George Walton, Button Gwinnett, and Lyman Hall, signed the Declaration of Independence passed by the Congress of 1776.*

Among the men who took a leading part in the stirring incidents of the early days of the Revolution in Georgia were Archibald Bulloch, Joseph Habersham, Samuel Elbert, Lachlan McIntosh, George Houston, Jonathan Bryan, Button Gwinnett, Noble Jones, and Lyman Hall. You will observe that there is a county in Georgia named for each of these great patriots, and well do they deserve the honor.

George Walton.

During the first three years of the Revolution the war was waged almost entirely at the North, mainly in the states of Massachusetts, New York, New Jersey, and Pennsylvania; but in the latter part of 1778 the

*You will find a full account of these interesting events in the histories of Georgia by Rev. Wm. B. Stevens and by Hon. C. C. Jones—excellent books for every Georgia man and woman to read.

British commanders determined, for several reasons, to transfer the seat of war to the South. They decided to begin with the invasion of Georgia. Their plan was to swoop down on Savannah from the sea and then overrun and subjugate the whole State. The people of Georgia knew nothing of these plans. For nearly three years they had been let alone, and they hoped that the war would be fought out at the North, where it began, and that no British army would ever set foot on Georgia soil; but they were doomed to be rudely awakened from this fond dream of security.

Button Gwinnett.

Lyman Hall.

On the 6th of December, 1778, a deserter from the British

The Capture of Savannah.   135

navy, a man by the name of William Haslan, managed somehow to make his way to Savannah, and he told the people a startling story, like this: "On the 23d of November a large fleet of British warships and transports, accompanied by a big army of soldiers, sailed from the harbor of New York and is now on the high seas on its way to Savannah to capture the city. You may look for it to reach here about the 12th of the month." The story filled the people with alarm, for they were wholly unprepared to defend themselves against such an invasion. Every day after the 12th of the month they looked with fear and trembling for the appearance of the dreaded fleet, but day after day passed and not a warship hove in sight. The people began to believe that the deserter was mistaken or else had purposely told them a lie, but in this hope they were doomed to bitter disappointment. Just at sunset on the 23d of December the people on Tybee Island, about eighteen miles below Savannah, at the mouth of the

Lachlan McIntosh.

river, saw a large fleet of ships coming from the northeast with all sails spread and the English flag floating from the mastheads. On came the ships like a company of evil spirits and cast anchor off the island. The fleet consisted of five men-of-war and five transports, having on board three thousand five hundred soldiers, besides sailors and marines. The news of their arrival was quickly conveyed to the city, and you may be sure there was no "Merry Christmas" for the people of Savannah that year. Maybe the children had their Christmas trees and their stockings filled by Santa Claus, but for the grown folks there were neither feasts nor merrymakings.

Noble Jones.

Joseph Habersham.

It took the British officers several days to

The Capture of Savannah.

get their bearings before they were ready to begin the attack. The Patriots, with their utmost efforts, could get together an army of only nine hundred men to defend the city. This little army was under the command of General Robert Howe, a cousin of General Howe, of the British army. He was a true patriot and a well-meaning man, but a very stupid general, as we shall soon see. The second in command was Colonel Huger; the third in command was Colonel Elbert; the fourth in command was Colonel Walton.

General Robert Howe.

II. QUASH DOLLY AND THE FLANK MARCH.

At daybreak on the 29th of December the British army was landed on the banks of the Savannah River, in the rice fields of Mr. Girardeau's plantation, at a point just two miles in a bee-line southeast of the city. The army, which consisted of about three thousand men, was commanded by Colonel Archibald Campbell, a very able officer. As soon as the soldiers had landed, they were formed into ranks and started marching straight toward Savannah. To reach the city they had to cross a boggy marsh over a causeway, or raised road, half a mile long, and then ascend a high bluff, known at the present time as Brewton Hill. Colonel Elbert urged General Howe to marshal the American army along the edge of the bluff, so that they might pour their cannon shots and volleys of musketry into the ranks of the British as they crossed the narrow causeway; but General Howe, instead of taking good advice, drew up his men in line of battle about a mile back of the hill towards the city,* in the rice fields on Governor Wright's plantation. To the right of the American line there was a swamp, thickly covered with trees and undergrowth. Colonel Walton said to General Howe, "General, you had better have the edge of that swamp strongly guarded, lest the enemy steal a march through it and turn our flank." "Nonsense," sneered Howe, "nothing but a wildcat could get through that jungle!" and so he left the swamp unguarded—a stupid blunder, as we shall soon see.

General Howe sent Captain John Smith's company of forty men forward to Brewton Hill to watch for the

---

*This line crossed the Thunderbolt Road about where the Atlantic Coast Line Railroad freight depot now stands.

coming of the enemy and act as skirmishers. Captain Smith made his men lie flat down on their stomachs along the edge of the bluff and keep a sharp lookout in front of them. In a little while here came the British army, with drums beating and flags flying, marching over the causeway. Considerably in advance of the others marched Captain Cameron's company of one hundred Scotch Highlanders. They crossed the causeway and were just starting up the hill when Captain Smith's Americans rose suddenly to their feet and fired a volley of musketry into their ranks. Captain Cameron and three of his men fell dead and five were wounded. The company was thrown into disorder and the men started to run back, but quickly rallied when they saw the rest of the British army hurrying up to their assistance. Captain Smith's company now fell back to the main American line.

The British army marched up the hill and a considerable distance beyond, and there formed in line of battle* close behind a long rail fence. Eight hundred yards in front of them, and in plain view, was the American line of battle, drawn up behind some low earthworks that had been hastily thrown up the night before.

*This line crossed the Thunderbolt Road about where the tollgate now stands.

About midway between the two armies ran a little creek, the bridge across which had been burned by General Howe; and a short distance beyond the creek there was a ditch filled with water. The banks on both sides of the creek were miry and boggy. So to get at the Americans the British would have to labor through the bog, wade the creek, jump the ditch, and scale the earthworks. Colonel Campbell knew that to make a frontal attack on the Americans in this strong position would be a hard fight and would cost him the lives of many of his men. Looking over towards the swamp on the American right he said to a Tory standing by, "Is there any way to get through that swamp over there?" "Yes," answered the Tory; "there is a private path through it, and there is an old negro named Quash Dolly on Girardeau's plantation who can show you the way." Quickly Colonel Campbell, guided by the Tory, galloped over to the negro quarters on Girardeau's place in search of Quash Dolly. He found the old negro standing in front of his cabin calmly smoking his pipe. Quash was a native African who had been captured on the coast of Guinea in his young manhood and brought over to America and sold into slavery. He was a short, stout, chunky man, with the kinky hair, flat nose, and thick lips of his race, and as black as the ace of spades; but he was sharp and shrewd. He wore on his head a coonskin cap which he had made himself, and of which he was very proud; it was so made that the bushy and ringed tail of the coon waved from the top like a plume. Colonel Campbell asked him if he would guide him through the swamp, at the same time showing him an English sovereign, a gold coin equal to about five dollars in our money. Quash's black eyes sparkled at the sight of the gold, and he readily agreed to undertake the job. Colonel Campbell ordered two regiments of light infantry, under command of Major James Baird, to make the flank march through the swamp under the guidance of Quash Dolly, while he himself stayed with the rest of the British army in front of the Americans. So secretly was Baird's movement made that the Americans had not the slightest suspicion of what was going on. They were watching the British behind the rail fence in front of them and wondering why they did not come on to the attack. The British soldiers kept marching and counter-marching behind the fence, as if they were getting ready to charge the Americans; but not a step forward did they move. Thus hour after hour passed. "They are scared of us and will sneak back to their ships as soon as night comes. Savannah is already saved!" exclaimed General Howe; but he was badly mistaken. All this time Major Baird's two regiments of light infantry were stealing a march through the swamp so as to get to the Americans' rear. In front trudged the low, stout figure of Quash Dolly with the coon tail plume of his coonskin cap streaming proudly above his head, while behind him marched Major Baird and his thousand men, making their way as best they could through the thick bushes. By three o'clock in the afternoon they had gained the American rear. Bursting from the cover of the woods they rushed across the rice fields, and with loud yells and volleys of musketry swooped down on the Americans from behind, while at the same time Colonel Campbell's forces charged upon the patriots from the front. So the poor Americans were suddenly caught between two fires by an army that outnumbered their own nearly four to one. Brave as the American soldiers were, they could not stand against such odds. They broke and fled in wild confusion back towards the city, many of them being killed as they ran. They were pursued by the British through the very streets of Savannah, where a number of them were shot down and bayoneted almost in the presence of their wives or their mothers. On the west side of the town they were rallied somewhat by their officers near the spot where the

Central Railroad Depot now stands, and passed out in rapid retreat by the Augusta road and across Musgrove Creek. In this way many made their escape. But the British soon got possession of the road and the bridge across the creek. Colonel Elbert's regiment, finding itself thus cut off from this avenue of escape, rushed through the rice fields to the banks of the creek near where it empties into the river. The tide was up and the creek was full of water. A hundred men jumped in and tried to swim across the creek. All of them succeeded except thirty poor fellows, who were drowned in the attempt. Two hundred others, afraid to make the plunge, stood on the bank until the British came up, when they surrendered themselves as prisoners of war.

The brutal British soldiers, wild with fiendish joy at their victory, committed all sorts of outrages on the people of Savannah, such as the bursting open of doors, the robbing of houses, the insulting of women, and the maltreating of prisoners. Colonel Campbell either could not or would not restrain them.

Night came at last, and brought to a close one of the saddest and most awful days that the city of Savannah has ever known. In this fight eighty-three Americans were shot dead on the field, thirty were drowned in trying to swim Musgrove Creek, over a hundred were wounded, and many were taken prisoners, while the British lost altogether only four men killed and ten wounded. Of the nine hundred soldiers composing the American army, scarcely more than four hundred escaped. These gathered together the next day at a place eight miles above Savannah. With General Howe at their head they marched far up the river to Sister's Ferry and crossed over into South Carolina. So poor Georgia was abandoned to her fate! A few weeks later the British army had overrun and practically subjugated the whole State.

CHAPTER XI.

THREE GEORGIA TORIES.

I. THOMAS BROWN.

By the 1st of February, 1779, the British had gained almost complete possession of Georgia. Their commander, Colonel Campbell, issued a proclamation calling on the people to take the oath of allegiance to the King and the Government of England. He promised that those who would take the oath should not be molested, but declared that those who refused would be driven from the colony and would have all their property confiscated. Frightened by this threat a great many people took the oath and became British subjects; these people were called *Tories*. But many refused to take the oath because they would rather suffer banishment and the loss of their property, or even death, than give up their heroic struggle for American independence; these were called *Patriots*. So the people of Georgia were divided into these two parties, Tories and Patriots, which hated each other with a bitter hatred.

In proportion to the population there were more Tories in Georgia than in any other state. Some of them were no doubt good, honest people who really believed that the Americans were wrong in rebelling against the English Government; but many of them were mean, selfish men who only wished to be on the strong or winning side.

By the British subjugation of Georgia nearly all of the Patriots of fighting age were driven out of the State, leaving their property and their helpless families behind, while the Tories remained unmolested in their homes. James Wright, the royal Governor, came back from England and was once more placed at the head of the Georgia Government.

So the British and the Tories now held full sway in Georgia, and most cruelly did they use their power. The Tories were far worse than the British. They formed themselves into military companies that were nothing more than bands of ruffians. They roved over the country on horseback and on foot committing all sorts of outrages, robbing the people, burning houses, throwing old men into prison, insulting women, hanging every Patriot soldier that they could lay their hands on, sometimes even murdering children, and showing no mercy to any one who favored the American cause. In no other state were the Tories so wicked and cruel as in Georgia. They were even worse than the savage Indians, whom they employed to help them.

The worst of these Georgia Tories was a man by the name of Thomas Brown. He had always been a Tory; and in the early days of the Revolution he had made himself so obnoxious to the patriotic people of Augusta, where he lived, that one day a crowd of men dragged him out of his office, and, stripping him to the waist, poured over his naked body a pot of soft tar and over that emptied a pillow case full of feathers, which stuck to the tar and made poor Brown look like a big, ugly frizzled chicken. Thus "tarred and feathered," they seated him in an open wagon drawn by three mules and hauled him about the streets of Augusta, while a great crowd followed with hoots and jeers. After parading him for an hour or two they turned him loose with the warning that if he did not leave town within twenty-four hours they would kill him. For several hours Brown kept his negro servant busy washing the tar and feathers from his body; then he put on his clothes, and, raising his right hand towards heaven, he took a solemn oath that he would be avenged for this great shame and outrage that had been done him. He left the city and the State, but many months afterwards he came back, and how well he kept his oath is a story that has been written in blood!

It was when Georgia fell into the hands of the British that Brown came back, and soon he became the chief leader of the Tories in the State. He was a well educated, intelligent man, and had fine military ability, so that he was made a colonel in the English army and was placed in command of Augusta, his old home. His army was composed about half and half of Tories and Indians. His opportunity had now come, and he kept his oath. All of the Patriots of fighting age had left Augusta and were in the American army. Brown confiscated their property, threw their old gray-haired fathers and grandfathers into prison, expelled their helpless wives and children from their homes, and drove them two hundred miles away into North Carolina. Their sufferings on the journey were awful. A number of them died from exposure and exhaustion, and many others had their health ruined for life by the hardships they endured on that dreadful march.

From an old print.
Residence of George Walton at Augusta.

In September, 1780, General Elijah Clarke, with a

small army of Patriots, undertook to recapture Augusta. He succeeded in driving Brown's army out of the city, and they took refuge in a large building just outside of the town known as the "White House." Brown had the doors and windows barricaded and bored holes through the walls, through which his marksmen, with their long-range rifles, held the Americans at bay. The building was completely surrounded by the Americans, and it seemed impossible for Brown and his men to escape. General Clarke had no cannon with which he could batter down the house, so he had to depend on starving out the Tories. For four days and nights he held them besieged. Their provisions were nearly exhausted, and every drop of water was gone. In one of the large upper rooms of the house lay forty poor wounded Tory soldiers with no medicines and no bandages or salves for their wounds, and not a drop of water to slake their feverish thirst. Their shrieks of agony and their wild cries for "water! water!" could be plainly heard in the American camp. Brown himself was severely wounded, shot through both thighs, and was suffering dreadfully; but he never gave up. He had himself carried around in a big arm-chair from room to room to direct and encourage his men, who were nearly crazed with famine and thirst. General

Clarke sent a flag of truce to him and begged him in the name of humanity to surrender, but he positively refused. He was as brave and heroic as he was bad and cruel.

At last, on the morning of the fifth day, the relief for which Brown had been looking came. Colonel Cruger, with a large regiment of British regulars, suddenly appeared on the other side of the river. Brown had sent a secret messenger for them on the day he had been driven from Augusta, and at last they had arrived. General Clarke, knowing that he could not contend against this large force, withdrew his army from the vicinity of Augusta and quickly retreated. He left behind thirty wounded Americans who were unable to march. He supposed, of course, they would be treated as prisoners of war. He knew not then the cruel heart of Thomas Brown, though he afterwards learned to know it well.

Brown selected thirteen of the wounded Americans and had them hanged from the high balustrade of the staircase in the "White House," so that he might witness their dying agonies as he lay on his couch in the hall below. As each victim was pushed from the balustrade and fell with a dull thud at the end of the rope, Brown would utter a grunt of satisfaction. He turned the rest of the prisoners over to the tender mercies of his Indian allies, who, forming a circle around them in the front yard of the "White House," put them to death by slow and horrible tortures. A long chapter might be filled with the inhuman cruelties of Brown, but it would be too horrible a story for you to read.

When in 1781 Augusta was at last captured by the Americans, Brown was taken prisoner. Knowing that if the soldiers could get their hands on him, they would tear him limb from limb, the American commander had him carried down the river in a boat under a strong guard. It is strange that he was not court-martialed and hanged, a fate that he richly deserved. The Americans were only too merciful to him. He was soon afterwards exchanged and rejoined the British army, and till the end of the war he continued his fierce fighting and cruel deeds. After the war was over, knowing that he could not live in America, he took refuge in England. There, in the year 1812, he was convicted of forgery and thrown into prison, where he ended his infamous life in disgrace and ignominy.

II. DANIEL McGIRTH.

Daniel McGirth was another notorious Tory of Georgia. Unlike Brown, he was an ignorant, uneducated man; and unlike Brown, too, he started out as an ardent Patriot. He was born and reared in South Carolina when that was a new, wild country. He was a good woodsman and as active and lithe as a panther. He was a fine horseman and a splendid shot. He was among the first to take up arms in the American cause. Somehow he drifted down to South Georgia, where he belonged to the little band of Patriots that so bravely resisted the invasion of the British from Florida. He acted as a scout and spy for the Americans, and he rendered them extremely valuable service.

He brought with him from South Carolina a thoroughbred horse, of which he was very proud. She was an iron-gray mare with a snow-white blaze in her forehead, and he called her Gray Goose. She was considered the finest horse in the American army, beautiful, intelligent, and swift as the wind. A captain in the American army took a great fancy to the animal and tried to buy her from McGirth, offering him a large price; but McGirth refused to part with her. This angered the captain who, out of spite, mistreated McGirth in many mean, petty ways, as an officer can mistreat a subordinate, if he chooses. McGirth was a high-spirited fellow. Irritated beyond endurance, he one day insulted the officer and raised his arm to strike him; but some one intervened and stopped the blow.

Now, to strike a superior officer is a grave crime in the army, so McGirth was tried by court-martial and sentenced to receive ten lashes with a cowhide on his bare back three days in succession. The first whipping was administered and he was put in the guard house to await his second humiliation. You can imagine the feelings of this high-spirited man, as he paced up and down in his cell brooding over the bitter shame to which he was being subjected! About twilight, as he was gazing through his prison bars, he spied Gray Goose hitched to a tree not far away. He gave a low, peculiar whistle, and Gray Goose, recognizing the signal, raised her beautiful head and uttered an affectionate whinny in response. This was more than he could stand. With a broken trowel that he found in his cell and with his bare hands, he tore the masonry from around the prison bars; then, with almost superhuman strength, he pulled out one of the bars and through the narrow crack thus made squeezed his long, lithe body and rushing out, sprang on Gray Goose and dashed away! The guards called to him to halt, but he only shook his fist at them and yelled a dreadful curse, and dashed away in the darkness on his fleet-footed steed, heedless of the musket balls that whistled about his head!

His whole nature seemed perverted by the bad treatment which he had received. He deserted to the enemy and joined the British army, and from then to the end of the war fought ferociously against the Americans. Of course, the bad treatment he had received from the American officer was no excuse for this, but McGirth was as unprincipled as he was brave and fierce.

He was made a colonel in the British army and was put at the head of a powerful Tory band, which for many months was the scourge of the State. He was a perfect ruffian in his manner of warfare. From the Florida line to Elbert County and over into South Carolina his name was a terror to the people. Many were the fearful stories told of "McGirth and his blazed-faced horse!" A whole book might be written about his daring deeds and his inhuman cruelties. He was twice wounded, but was never taken prisoner. A big reward was offered for his capture, and a thousand people were trying to catch him and often had him in a tight place; but in every emergency he was saved by the fleet foot of his best friend, Gray Goose!

After the war was over, he went to Florida, which was then owned by the Spaniards. For some offense or crime there he was arrested and thrown into prison in the old fort of St. Augustine. After five years' imprisonment he was released, so weak and broken in health that he could barely drag himself back to his wife in their rude country home in Sumter District. South Carolina. There he soon died in peace, and there he now lies buried!

III. COLONEL GRIERSON.

Colonel Grierson was another bad Tory. He was Brown's right-hand man. They were two of a kind. They were companions in arms and companions in many acts of cruelty. Never was there joined together in the commission of wicked deeds two men worse than Brown and Grierson, the Georgia Tories.

Grierson, like Brown, was a colonel in the British army. Fort Grierson, at Augusta, was named for him. It was one of the strongest forts in Georgia, and around it at the siege of Augusta was fought one of the bloodiest battles of the Revolution in the State. When Augusta was captured by the Americans, Grierson, like Brown, was taken prisoner. To save him from being mobbed by the soldiers, the American commander had him hid away in a little house some distance from town and placed a strong guard around him; but suddenly about twilight a soldier on horseback galloped up and, before the guards knew what he was about, threw his gun to his shoulder, shot Grierson through the window, and then, wheeling, galloped away. That night Grierson died of the wound, in dreadful agony. The man that shot him was supposed to be Samuel Alexander, the son of John Alexander, an old man seventy-eight years old, whom this Grierson had treated with horrible cruelty when he and Brown held sway in Augusta. Young Alexander was never arrested or tried for the deed. "Vengeance is mine, I will repay!" says the Bible, but perhaps a merciful God will pardon a man for taking vengeance in his own hands in a case like this.

CHAPTER XII.

THREE GEORGIA PATRIOTS.

I. ELIJAH CLARKE.

Nearly all the Patriots of fighting age had left the State to join the American army elsewhere, so there was nothing to restrain the demon Tories. The people became cowed and hopeless. Many who had been Patriots gave up the struggle and took the oath of allegiance. The State seemed to be abandoned to her unhappy fate. But by the blessing of Almighty God there arose in this dark day a few great, heroic souls to redeem Georgia and avenge her wrongs!

The greatest of these heroes was Colonel Elijah Clarke. Just a year before the war broke out he moved with his wife and children from North Carolina to Wilkes County, Georgia, where he settled as a farmer. In the early part of the war he joined the Patriot army, and in a fight with the British in Florida he was desperately wounded and for a long time disabled. He was at his home in Wilkes County recovering from this wound when the British, under Colonel Campbell, captured Savannah and began overrunning the State. As soon as Colonel Clarke heard the news, he buckled on his good sword, mounted his horse, and, leaving his wife and children on the farm, rode day and night over the country, getting together a band of Patriots to fight the British if they should come into that section of the State. He mustered one hundred dragoons, all Georgians, and as good fighters as ever mounted a horse or shouldered a gun.

Colonel Boyd, a British officer, with a band of a thousand Tories, while marching through north Georgia on his way to Augusta to join Colonel Campbell, camped one night in an open field on Kettle Creek, in Wilkes County. The following day Colonels Pickens, Dooly, and Clarke, with a band of five hundred Carolina and Georgia Patriots, bursting through the thick cane brakes, made a surprise attack on them and a desperate battle took place. The Tories greatly outnumbered the Patriots and were getting the best of them, when Colonel Clarke, with his hundred Georgians, made a bold flank movement, and, gaining a hill on the other side of the creek, poured a deadly fire into the enemy's rear, and "snatched victory from the very jaws of defeat." The

Colonel Andrew Pickens.

Tories were completely routed. Seventy-two of them were killed, more than a hundred were wounded, many were taken prisoners, and the rest were scattered to the four winds. Colonel Boyd himself fell mortally wounded, and died the next day. This battle of Kettle Creek, fought February 12th, 1779, was the most brilliant American victory in Georgia, and Colonel Elijah Clarke was the hero of the day.

For months Colonel Clarke, at the head of his little band of Patriots, carried on a guerrilla warfare with the British and Tories throughout what was then north Georgia, including especially Elbert and Wilkes counties. Constantly in the saddle, moving rapidly from place to place, suffering from hunger, thirst, fatigue, and all kinds of hardships, rarely ever sleeping under a roof, living in swamps and jungles, striking the enemy a blow whenever a chance offered, he was the only protection the people had from the outrages of the brutal Tories. Through it all, by his side rode and fought his son, John Clarke, a youth of seventeen years, who afterwards became a famous man in Georgia.

Worn out with the hard life that they had to endure, many of Colonel Clarke's men left him and returned to their homes or crossed over to South Carolina and joined the regular American army, and some of them even took the oath of allegiance to the British Government. At one time his command had dwindled down to less than twenty men; but the heroic spirit of Elijah Clarke would not be discouraged. He rode day and night among the mountains of north Georgia and over into South Carolina stirring up the people and calling them to arms. By this means he increased his force to three hundred men. With these he marched against Augusta and made an unsuccessful attempt to capture the city from the Tory, Brown. After this failure he saw that for the present he could do nothing more in Georgia; so, accompanied by his devoted followers, he crossed over into South Carolina and joined the American army in that State, where he fought with great gallantry in many fierce battles.

In the spring of 1781 he returned to Georgia for the purpose of making another attempt to capture Augusta. Together with the commands of Pickens, Jackson and McCall, he succeeded in surrounding the city. About the 1st of June the investing army was reinforced by the famous Legion of "Light Horse Harry" Lee, and that officer assumed principal command. The main defense of Augusta was a powerful fort which stood on a bluff of the river and in the yard of St. Paul's Episcopal Church. This fort was built by Ogle-

pe in 1736, and had always been known as Fort
gusta. Colonel Brown, the Tory, had enlarged and
ngthened the structure and had changed its name to

"Light Horse Harry" Lee.

t Cornwallis. Towards the close of the siege the
ish army, driven back from the outposts, took
ge in this fort, which seemed absolutely impreg-
le.

For several days the Americans were greatly puz-
what to do. At length they resorted to the strata-
of the "Mayham tower," so called because the de-

vice was invented by Major Mayham of the American army. It consisted of a square tower built of huge unhewn logs and rising forty feet high. As the tower rose, the inside of it was filled with dirt packed down hard. Near the top an embrasure, or opening, was made through the logs; and through this opening a single little six-pound cannon, the largest piece of artillery the Americans had, looked down into Fort Cornwallis, which was within easy range of its plunging fire. For days this terrible little war dog poured a tempest of well-aimed shot and shell down into the fort, destroying its barracks, demolishing its walls, and killing and wounding its garrison by scores. The poor, pent-up soldiers, driven to desperation, dug holes in the ground, into which they crept for protection from the pitiless iron hail.

At length, on the 5th of July, Colonel Brown, seeing that further defense was worse than useless, surrendered himself, the entire garrison, the fort, and the city (or village as it then was) to the Americans.

This device of the Mayham tower was one of the most brilliant stratagems of the Revolutionary War. The fort, which had been practically destroyed by the plunging fire of the little six-pounder, was never rebuilt. The spot on which it stood has been marked by a stately and beautiful monument, erected by the Colonial Dames of Georgia. It is made of granite from the quarries in Oglethorpe County. This noble memorial of both Colonial and Revolutionary history was unveiled with impressive ceremonies on November 23, 1901. The Mayham tower was located near where the Cotton Exchange of Augusta now stands.

Till the close of the war Colonel Clarke (or General Clarke as he had now come to be) continued to do glorious service for Georgia. His martial tramp was heard from one end of the State to the other, and his strong right arm dealt blow on blow upon the doomed heads of British and Tories. He was four times wounded, twice nigh unto death. In camp he contracted a severe case of smallpox, from which he lay prostrate for six weeks; but in each instance, as soon as he was able to mount a horse, he was up and about again, encouraging the faint-hearted and leading the brave to battle.

Elijah Clarke was an uneducated man and was rough and uncouth in his manners. He had his faults of character, too, but with it all he was a truly great man. He dealt severely with the Tories that fell into his power; hanged a number of them, burned their homes, confiscated their lands, and destroyed their property. Some people have blamed him for this, but he believed he was justified in it. These horrid Tories had driven his own wife and children from home and burned his house. They had treated old men, women and children with inhuman cruelty, had murdered scores of Patriots in cold blood, and had spread ruin and desolation throughout the land. He believed it was but a mild retaliation to hang a score or two of them; and who will say that he was wrong? Among the many heroes that Georgia produced during the Revolutionary War, Elijah Clarke stands out in bold relief as the most heroic figure of them all.

II. JAMES JACKSON.

Another great Patriot of the times was James Jackson. He was born and partly reared in England. His father was a worthy, well-to-do, intelligent man, who sympathized keenly with the Americans in their struggle against English tyranny and often talked to his son about it; so James was in spirit an American Patriot before ever he saw America. In 1772, when he was fifteen years old, his father sent him over to America to become an inmate of the household of John Wereat of Savannah, an old and intimate friend of the family, who was anxious to have the boy. His father was glad to give him this opportunity of growing to manhood in the new and promising country. He went to the best schools then in Savannah and at the same time studied law.

When the Revolutionary War broke out, young Jackson, though only eighteen years old, was among the

General James Jackson.

first to shoulder a musket in the American cause. In the fight at Savannah with the British troops in March, 1776, he behaved so bravely that President Bulloch wrote him a letter of thanks and commissioned him a captain. When in January, 1779, the British, under Colonel Campbell, captured Savannah and destroyed the little American army defending the place, Jackson managed to make his escape into South Carolina. His command was now gone, but he was determined to enter the army again as a private. Friendless, penniless, ragged and barefooted, he and young John Milledge were making their way through the country to join Colonel Moultrie's regiment in the northern part of the State, when a party of American soldiers took them for spies. In vain did they protest their innocence. They were condemned to be hanged the next day, and the gallows was already prepared for them, when Major Devaux, happening to come along, recognized them and had them set free. Thus the two noble youths had a narrow escape from an awful and ignominious death.

Jackson joined Colonel Moultrie's Carolina regiment as a private, but on account of his fine ability and great courage he was rapidly promoted until he got to be a major. He distinguished himself at the famous battles of Cowpens and Blackstocks in South Carolina. Afterwards he came back to Georgia and was put in command of a legion of militia.

In the spring of 1781 the Americans besieged Augusta. The town was surrounded by an army of militiamen who were ordered to guard the place until General Lincoln and "Light Horse Harry" Lee could come down from South Carolina with an army of Continentals* and take the place by storm. The wait was a long and trying one. It looked as if Lincoln and Lee would never come. The militiamen, whose time of enlistment was out, became discontented and insubordinate. They threatened to disband and go home. The great colonel, Elijah Clarke, was sick with smallpox; and Colonel Hammond, who was then commanding in his stead, could do nothing with the men. Hammond called on Major Jackson for help. Jackson said, "Get the men together and let me talk to them."

General Benjamin Lincoln.

So the soldiers were assembled in a great crowd in an open space in the middle of the camps. When Jackson rode up in front of them, they scowled at him with morose and surly faces, and some of them even started to hoot and jeer him. He began to speak to

*Continental troops were those in the service of the Congress of the United States, and not under the control of any one state, as were the militiamen.

them. He was a born orator as well as a born soldier, and he spoke with burning eloquence. He did not scold or chide or threaten them; he appealed to their manhood; he spoke straight to their hearts; he stirred the nobler spirit in them, and soon the scowls vanished from their faces and they were cheering wildly. They were carried away by his eloquence. When he had finished he called on all who were willing to stand by the post of duty to hold up their right hands, and the hand of every man went up. They kept their promise and stood guard faithfully around Augusta until a month later, when Lincoln and Lee, with the Continental troops, came from South Carolina and joined in the capture of the city.

Many other times Jackson used his eloquence to good purpose in reviving the sinking spirits of the people and the waning heroism of the soldiers. But on one occasion he had to use sterner means than this to teach his men their duty. The legion was made up about half and half of dragoons and infantrymen. The dragoons were picked men and were faithful to him; but the infantrymen, exasperated by the hardships of war, formed a conspiracy by which they were to assassinate Jackson and then disband and go to their homes. A faithful servant told him of the plot two days before

Lee's Cavalry Skirmishing.

it was to be executed. Without appearing to know anything about it, he ordered the infantrymen to assemble without arms on the parade ground at sunset to hear a very important proclamation that he had to read to them. Suspecting nothing, and curious to know what the proclamation could be about, the men gathered on the parade ground promptly at the appointed hour. Jackson rode slowly in front of them as if about to read the proclamation, but instead of doing so he made a signal by waving his handkerchief over his head, whereupon the dragoons, fully armed, came galloping up and surrounded the astounded infantrymen and held them prisoners. All night they were guarded like criminals. The next day Jackson picked out the six ringleaders of the conspiracy and had them hanged in the presence of the whole legion. Then he made a speech to the men, in which he told them he knew they had been led into this foul plot by the few bad men who had been hanged, and from whose fate they must take warning; he would pardon them for what they had done. Then he appealed to them to return to their duty like true soldiers. The lesson sank deep into their hearts, and they gave him no further trouble. Jackson was a kind-hearted man, but he could be severe when duty required it.

Towards the close of the Revolutionary War, Jackson and his men had harder service to perform than any other soldiers in Georgia. At last, when the war was brought to a close by the British surrendering Savannah, General Anthony Wayne, Commander-in-Chief of the American army in Georgia, said: "The keys of the captured city must be handed not to myself, but to my young brother officer, Colonel James Jackson; for to him more than to any other man is due the triumphant issue of this trying campaign!" Thereupon the keys were formally handed to Jackson, and he was the first American soldier to tread the streets of recaptured Savannah, from which he had been driven by the bayonets of the British four years before. He was still only twenty-three years old.

General Anthony Wayne.

James Jackson, unlike Elijah Clarke, was an educated, cultured gentleman. He had a splendid intellect, and afterwards became a great lawyer and statesman. He was a man of medium height and slender figure, but was perfectly formed. He had light hair, clear penetrating blue eyes, and commanding features.

He was noble natured and warm hearted, but very high tempered. He was a brilliant soldier of the Revolution, but the most glorious part of his career came after the war was over.

III. JOHN TWIGGS.

Another great Georgia soldier of the Revolution was General John Twiggs. Not long before the war started, he came to Georgia from Maryland as a young mechanic. He entered the army as captain and rose rapidly to the rank of brigadier-general. Brave, active, talented, and influential, he was a tower of strength to the Patriots. No partisan leader in Georgia was engaged in more fights and battles with the enemy, and never once did he suffer defeat. He lived for twenty-five years after the war was over, and filled many positions of honor and trust in Georgia. He was a member of the State Legislature for a number of years, and was a trustee both of Richmond Academy, Augusta, and of the University of Georgia. He died in Richmond County in April, 1816.

Each one of this great trio of Revolutionary heroes, Clarke, Jackson, and Twiggs, became the founder of families that have given to Georgia a number of able and distinguished men.

CHAPTER XIII.

SIEGE OF SAVANNAH.

I. D'ESTAING OUTWITTED.

You remember that Savannah was captured by the British on the 29th day of December, 1778. For eight months they kept undisturbed possession of it, but in the early fall of 1779 the Americans laid a careful plan to recapture the city. Already, France had espoused the cause of America, and had sent a large fleet of warships and an army of men to help in the struggle for independence. This fleet and army, which was under the command of Count d'Estaing, a noted French general, was ordered to proceed to Georgia and aid the Americans in the recapture of Savannah.

Count d'Estaing.

The plan was for the American and the French forces to get to Savannah about the same time, to surround the city and demand its surrender. It happened, however, that the French fleet under d'Estaing reached the mouth of the Savannah River before Lincoln's American forces had arrived from South Carolina. Instead of waiting for Lincoln's arrival, as he should have done, d'Estaing landed his army at once, and, advancing within two miles of Savannah, called on the British general, Prevost, to surrender. General Prevost seemed much alarmed, and talked as if he might comply with the demand, but asked for twenty-four hours to consider the matter. He also insisted that during this time d'Estaing should withdraw his forces four miles from the city and remain there until the twenty-four hours had expired. D'Estaing very unwisely agreed to this truce and withdrew his troops to a distance Shrewd General Prevost spent the twenty-four hours in vigorous preparation for defense. He kept fifteen hundred men, soldiers and negroes, working in relays night and day, constructing fortifications, or redoubts, around the city. He took many large cannon from the warships lying in the river and placed them in the redoubts. He sent a secret messenger to Colonel Maitland over in South Carolina to hurry to his assistance. That officer managed, in a wonderful way, to slip past the French fleet in the mouth of the river and to land safely at

Siege of Savannah. 175

Savannah with his regiment of five hundred men. The pent-up garrison was overjoyed at the arrival of this strong reinforcement. During this time Prevost was keeping up a cunning correspondence with d'Estaing, leading him to believe that he would surrender at the end of the twenty-four hours if satisfactory terms could be agreed upon.

In the meantime, General Lincoln arrived from South Carolina with the American forces. In

Count Pulaski.

Lincoln's command was the famous Pulaski Legion, led by the valiant Count Pulaski, a Polish nobleman and soldier, who, having been driven from his own country by Russian despotism, had come over to the United States and joined the American army. He had been put in command of a legion of cavalry, and had rapidly gained great distinction as a daring and successful leader. At this time he was about thirty-five years old, the very *beau ideal* of a soldier—tall, stalwart, handsome, with a fine military bearing.

As soon as Lincoln arrived, d'Estaing said to him,

with great elation: "I have Savannah already surrounded, and it is completely in our power. Negotiations are now going on for its surrender, and the city will be ours before sunset without the firing of a gun!" But in this, poor d'Estaing was wofully mistaken. He had "reckoned without his host." When the twenty-four hours' truce had expired, General Prevost sent word to the Americans that he had no idea of surrendering, but would defend Savannah to the bitter end. D'Estaing and Lincoln were greatly surprised and disappointed at this reply, and all the more so when they approached the city and found it too strongly protected to be taken by storm. D'Estaing had been completely outwitted by Prevost.

II. THE BOMBARDMENT.

Deciding that Savannah could not be taken by storm, Lincoln and d'Estaing determined to try to take it by siege and bombardment. The bombardment was begun on the 26th of September; and from then until the 8th of October the Americans and the French boomed and boomed away at the British, and the British, in reply, boomed and boomed at them; but with all the cannonading not much damage was done on either side. The American cannon balls passed mostly over the heads of the British in the redoubts and fell in the city. Many houses were struck, several were demolished, and two were set on fire and burned. Nearly all the women and children were taken over to Hutcherson Island, where they lived during the siege in the great rice barns there. Those that remained moved into the basements and cellars of their houses, where they would be in less danger. In the cellar in which General Prevost's wife and children stayed, the walls were lined with mattresses and feather beds, so as to make them bomb-proof. A bomb shell penetrated a cellar in which a family was living and, bursting, killed two of the negro servants. Another shell crashed into a room and killed a young mother and her three-weeks-old infant. Several negroes were killed on the streets by exploding shells. Savannah at that time was one great sand bed, and the shells falling in the streets or in the squares would generally bury themselves in the sand and have their fuses extinguished, for a bomb shell is burst by a fuse just as fire-crackers are. The negro children got so accustomed to the shells that when they saw one fall they would run up and extinguish the sputtering fuse by stamping it with their feet or by throwing sand on it, and would take the unexploded shell and sell it to the artillerymen for sixpence. A dangerous business surely for such small pay!

For two weeks the bombardment was continued without making any progress towards forcing the British to surrender. The French fleet in the mouth of the Savannah River was now in constant danger of being attacked by a more powerful British fleet that might at any time be sent against them from England. Count d'Estaing was therefore naturally restless and anxious to get away. So he and Lincoln determined to try to take Savannah by one brave, desperate assault.

III. THE ASSAULT AND PULASKI'S DEATH.

The American and French generals planned very carefully for the grand assault. It was to take place at daybreak on October 9th.

On the east side the approach to Savannah was mostly over dry, firm, level ground, by good roads, and through concealing forests; so for defensive purposes that was the weak side. Hence the British had placed their strongest fortifications there. On the west side the approach was more difficult; for over there were Musgrove Creek and swamp, and marshy rice fields lying below the level of the city. The French and the Americans determined to make the attack on that strong west side for the very reason that the British would not be expecting it at that point. To mislead them still further, they ordered General Huger's regiment to make a vigorous

Siege of Savannah.

pretended, or feigned, attack on the east side just before daybreak, so as to cause the enemy to concentrate his forces at that point, while the real assault was being made on the west side. The plan was a splendid one, and might have succeeded if treachery had not taken a hand in this exciting game of war. On the night of the 8th of October, James Curry, of Charleston, sergeant-major of a regiment of South Carolina volunteers, deserted and made his way into Savannah and revealed the whole plan to the British.*

At three o'clock on the morning of October 9th, in the darkness before dawn, the French and American forces concentrated in the woods of Musgrove swamp to the west of Savannah, and were there marshalled into battle array for the grand assault. Three hundred yards in front of them was the line of British redoubts manned with cannon, and in front of the redoubts were trenches for the infantry. The assault was to be directed mainly against Spring Hill redoubt, which stood very near where the "round house" of the Central Railroad shops now stands. The assaulting column consisted of about four thousand men, three thousand French and one thousand Americans. About eleven

---

* It is gratifying to know that a year later the Americans captured this traitor at Hobkirk Hill (N. C.), and hanged him.

hundred men were held in reserve to strike in at the critical time whenever their services might be most needed. Pulaski's Legion was among these reserves and occupied a position to the left and back of the assaulting column, where, from an elevated piece of ground, Pulaski could clearly see the whole battlefield.

A little before sunrise, in the gray light of the breaking day, the assaulting column emerged from the woods and started at quick-step across the open space toward the enemy's works. As they approached the redoubts they were disappointed to find that the British were not surprised, but on account of the information brought by the traitor Curry, were ready to give them a warm reception. Fifty cannon poured an iron storm of grape, canister and chain shot into their ranks. They fell like grass before the mower. Their line was torn into fragments and went reeling back, but under the rallying cry of their brave officers they gathered themselves together and charged forward again. As they drew still nearer to the enemy's works, a leaden hail from the muskets in the trenches was added to the iron storm from the cannon in the redoubts. Still they pressed on, until some of the trenches were captured and the American flag was planted on one of the redoubts. The opposing columns stood within a few feet

Siege of Savannah.

of each other, and fired point blank into each other's faces.

At this critical moment Count Pulaski said to General Lincoln: "Let me take my horsemen, dash in between those two redoubts on our left and gain the enemy's rear. We will spread havoc among them from behind, while the infantry press them in front, and the victory will soon be ours!" General Lincoln readily agreed to this bold stroke. The bugler blew the rally, the two hundred cavalrymen formed in column for the charge. Pulaski, galloping to the front on his superb black charger, raised his sword aloft and cried "Forward!" The men put spurs to their horses and away they dashed, swift as the wind, straight towards the open space between Spring Hill redoubt and the one next to the right of it. A more splendid cavalry charge was rarely ever seen on earth. But as they came sweeping like a cyclone up to the enemy's works, Pulaski saw that the infantry whom he had come to support, driven back by the terrible fire, had abandoned the assault and were streaming to the rear in a wild stampede. Still on dashed Pulaski and his horsemen. The concentrated fire of both redoubts was now turned upon them. Pulaski, on his black charger, leaped the entrenchments and dashed into the gap between the two redoubts.

Only a few of his horsemen and some infantry whom he had rallied were with him now. All the rest had been shot down or driven back. At this moment a small cannon ball, called grape shot, fired from the Spring Hill redoubt, struck the gallant Polander in the right groin. Still retaining his sword in his right hand, he threw his left hand over to the wounded side. His horse, feeling the reins slacken, made a great lunge. Pulaski reeled in his saddle and fell heavily to the ground. His brother Polander, Major Rogowski, sprang from his horse and knelt by his side. "Jesus! Mary!" faintly groaned Pulaski, for he was a devout Roman Catholic. A glancing musket ball struck Rogowski on the forehead, making only a slight wound but filling his eyes with blood and knocking him senseless by Pulaski's side. Several of Pulaski's brave soldiers rushed up at the imminent risk of their own lives, bore their chieftain through the sulphurous smoke and death-dealing missiles to the rear of the battlefield, where Dr. James Lynah of Charleston extracted the ball—an operation which, though exceedingly painful, was borne by Pulaski with inconceivable fortitude. The grape shot is still in possession of Mr. J. H. Lynah of Savannah, a great-grandson of Dr. Lynah.

This was one of the fiercest and bloodiest battles of

the Revolutionary War, and in it the Americans with their French allies suffered a complete and crushing defeat. Men never fought more bravely than they did, but nothing human could stand before the terrible cannonade from the enemy's lines. Out of the 5,000 soldiers actually engaged on the American side 1,133 were killed or wounded, 821 French and 312 Americans. Nearly all of the officers were either killed or wounded. Count d'Estaing, who most bravely led the assault, was wounded in the early part of the battle, but refused to leave the field until he was prostrated by a second shot and had to be borne away by his men. He finally recovered from his wounds, and afterwards had a very distinguished career in France. The British lost only one hundred men all told. The battle started at sunrise and by nine o'clock it was all over; the last sound of the strife had died away, and amid the drifting smoke the black-robed Angel of Death brooded in silence over that bloody plain.

All hopes of taking Savannah were now abandoned. Immediately after the battle General Lincoln retreated to Ebenezer, and a little later crossed over the river into South Carolina. In a few days d'Estaing with the whole French fleet and army sailed away for France.

On the day after the battle, as soon as Dr. Lynah

had attended to his wound, Pulaski was put on board a ship to be carried to Charleston for safety and proper attention. But he had received a mortal hurt, and, in spite of the best surgical attention, he died on shipboard the next day. He was buried in the sea, somewhere between Savannah and Charleston.

In 1853 the city of Savannah erected a magnificent marble monument to this heroic foreigner who had sealed with his life's blood his devotion to the cause of American liberty. The monument stands in Monterey Square, in the heart of the city. It was made in Italy, at a cost of eighteen thousand dollars, and is probably the finest piece of tombstone work in Georgia. The figure of Pulaski falling from his horse as he receives his death wound, carved in high relief on one side of the monument, is especially beautiful, and is regarded by art critics as a masterpiece of sculpture.

Monument to Pulaski.

Georgia has honored Pulaski also by naming one of her counties for him.

IV. DEATH OF SERGEANT JASPER.

In the assault on Savannah an American soldier of immortal fame received his death wound within a hundred yards of where Pulaski fell, and at almost the same moment. His name was William Jasper, a young volunteer from South Carolina. He was a man of humble origin. His parents were poor, honest Irish, who emigrated to America and settled in South Carolina, where they earned a livelihood by the toil of their hands. Their famous son was brought up not only in poverty, but in ignorance, for in those days the children of the poor had little or no chance for getting an education. William Jasper never went to school a day in his life, and he grew to manhood without being able to read or write.

At the outbreak of the war he joined the Second South Carolina Regiment, one of the finest regiments in the American army. He proved a model soldier and won the admiration of his officers. He was a splendid specimen of physical manhood. There was not a loose stitch in his body nor in his character. Although entirely uneducated, he was endowed with an abundance of mother wit and the gift of ready and eloquent speech.

In the Battle of Fort Moultrie, at Charleston, S. C.,

in the early part of the war, he distinguished himself by a deed of great daring. In the midst of the fight a cannon ball fired by the British struck the flag staff on the fort, and the American flag fell to the ground. Jasper picked it up, and, amid shot and shell, clam-

From the painting by Oertel.
Sergeant Jasper at Fort Moultrie.

bering to the top of the fort, replaced the flag in its former position, shouting, "God save liberty and my country forever!" In recognition of his bravery, Governor Rutledge, in the presence of the whole regiment, offered him the commission of lieutenant; but Jasper replied in these words: "Governor, I thank you most heartily for this honor, which is more than I deserve, but I can't accept it. I am a poor, ignorant body; I can't write my own name or even read a line. As sergeant I may do pretty well, but as lieutenant I would only get myself laughed at and lose the respect of my fellow soldiers." The Governor replied: "Good sergeant, that was nobly spoken! I see that you are as modest as you are brave. Since you will not accept the commission, I beg that you will accept this sword as a personal gift from me." At the same time, he unbuckled his own weapon from his side and handed it to Jasper, who received it, saying, with tears in his eyes: "Governor, I pray that I may never do anything to dishonor this sword!"

In the years after the Battle of Fort Moultrie, Jasper was frequently detailed to act as scout and spy for General Lincoln. This is the most dangerous service that a soldier can perform, and requires not only courage, but great shrewdness and intelligence. Many were the daring deeds done by Jasper in discharge of the duties of this position. In a number of his expeditions he was accompanied by another famous scout and spy, Sergeant Newton.

On one occasion, in the darkest days of the Revolution in Georgia, six American soldiers were being conducted under a strong guard from Ebenezer to Savannah, where they were to be tried for their lives for entering the American army after having taken the oath of allegiance to the British Government. They were accompanied by a Mrs. Brown, whose husband was one of the prisoners, and her little seven-year-old boy. She was going to Savannah to plead with the authorities for the life of her husband. Jasper and Newton, while spying through the British camp at Ebenezer, found out all about this intended expedition, and they determined to try to rescue the prisoners. On the road that the prisoners and their guard would have to travel, and only a few miles from Savannah, there was a famous spring known as The Spa. Jasper knew that the party would probably stop at this spring to rest before proceeding to the city. So he and Newton went ahead through the woods, and concealed themselves behind the thick bushes near the spring, and awaited the coming of the party. After a short while the party arrived and halted. The soldiers, leaving two of their number to guard the prisoners, stacked their muskets; and, after quenching their thirst at the spring, the whole party sat down on the ground to rest. Quick as a flash Jasper and Newton sprang from their covert, snatched two muskets from the stack, shot the two armed guards dead, and then, seizing two other muskets, held at bay the other guards, who were required to remove the manacles from the wrists of the Americans. Then the Americans transferred the manacles to the wrists of the British, and so the tables were completely turned! The British prisoners, eight in number, were marched to an American camp ten miles away. This was one of the most daring and wonderful exploits of the Revolutionary War. The spring at which it occurred became a noted historic spot, and has ever since been known as Jasper Spring. In the year 1902 the Lachlan McIntosh Chapter of the Daughters of the American Revolution erected at the place a memorial in the form of a beautiful fountain made of white Georgia marble. All travelers who pass that way stop to drink at the spring and to ponder on its tragic story.

The assault on the British works in the siege of Savannah, already described, was led by the Second South Carolina Regiment, to which Jasper belonged. They carried the first line of works and planted their flag on one of the fortifications. This flag had been presented to the regiment several years before by Mrs. Elliott, of Charleston, one of the leading ladies of South Carolina. In a few moments British reinforcements came up and drove the Americans back from the position which they had gained. As they were retreating,

Jasper remembered that the flag floating from the breastwork had been left behind, and was about to fall into the enemy's hands. Determined to rescue it at the hazard of his life, he turned, rushed back, and mounted the fortification; but just as he seized the flag, a cruel musket ball from the enemy tore through one of his lungs. Holding one hand to his wounded side, he painfully made his way to the rear with the rescued flag.

Monument to Sergeant Jasper.

The next day he died of his wound, surrounded by devoted comrades. To Major Horry, who was holding his hand, he said: "Major, I am not afraid to die. When I was a little child my good mother used to take me on her knee and tell me about the Great Hereafter, and I believe it. There has hardly been a day, even during all this bloody war, that I have not said my prayers night and morning. I believe I am prepared for the Great Hereafter. Tell my old father that his son died in hope of a better life. Tell Governor Rutledge that I never dishonored the sword which he gave me; and if you should ever see that grand gentlewoman (Mrs. Elliott), tell her I lost my life saving the flag which she presented to our regiment." With these words he expired.

Georgia has honored this gallant Irish-American patriot by naming a county for him, and another county she has named for his brave comrade, Sergeant Newton.

In one of the public squares of Savannah a superb monument has been erected to Jasper's memory. It is surmounted by a bronze figure of heroic size, representing Jasper in a noble attitude, holding aloft in one hand the flag that he had rescued from the enemy at the Battle of Savannah, and in the other the drawn sword presented to him by Governor Rutledge.

CHAPTER XIV.

NANCY HART.

Nancy Hart was a famous woman who lived in Georgia during the Revolutionary War. She lived with her husband, Benjamin Hart, and their eight children in a log house on their little farm away out in the country, in what is now Elbert County, about ten miles from the present pretty town of Elberton.

Nancy was six feet tall, spare, big boned, and very strong. She could ride a horse, shoot a gun, and handle an axe as well as any man. She had brilliant red hair and a fiery temper; she had penetrating blue eyes and a keen wit. She was a high-spirited, energetic, and brave woman. She had a strong will, and "bossed" everything and everybody about her. Her education was limited, but this deficiency was overcome by her natural shrewdness. Notwithstanding her fiery temper and overbearing will, she was really a kind-hearted woman. People feared and loved her at the same time, and far and wide she was known by the fond pet name of "Aunt Nancy."

Nancy was a great patriot, and was devoted to the American cause. Her love for the Liberty Boys was sincere, while her hatred of the British and the Tories was bitter. During the latter days of the Revolution, when the war was raging in Georgia, she took an active part against the enemy, and many are the wonderful stories told of her daring deeds. She was of great assistance to General Elijah Clarke in his campaigns against the British. On one occasion General Clarke was very anxious to know the strength and position of the British army in Augusta, and Nancy offered to find out for him. She disguised herself as a man, which, on account of her tall and stalwart figure, she could easily do. She pretended to be a poor, half-witted countryman; and, taking a basket of eggs on her arm, she walked boldly into the enemy's camp. After selling the eggs, she spent the entire day in the camp, entertaining the officers and soldiers mightily with her crazy antics and songs and dances. No one suspected she was anything but a poor, half-witted, harmless countryman, so she was permitted to rove through the camps at will; but while she was cutting up foolish capers, her keen eye and shrewd mind were busy making observations and taking notes. Late in the afternoon she walked out of the camp without hindrance and carried to General Clarke information that enabled him a few days later to capture the city of Augusta.

One day a young Patriot soldier, or Liberty Boy, came riding furiously up to Nancy's door, scared out of his wits, and crying at the top of his voice, "Aunt Nancy, the Tories are after me, the Tories are after me!" "Ride straight through the house and make for the swamp!" commanded Nancy, as she flung the front door wide open. The frightened youth lashed his horse and made him dash up the steps, through the hall, out of the back door, across the fields, and away to the swamp in the rear. Quickly Aunt Nancy shut the doors and was as still as a mouse. In a few seconds a band of armed Tories came galloping up and began knocking on the door with the butts of their guns. Aunt Nancy, grunting and groaning as if in great pain, hobbled to the door and opening it slightly peered out, and in a whining voice asked what was the matter. "We are looking for a rebel on a gray horse that came this way just now. Which way did he go?" demanded the Tories. "I haven't seen nor heard no rebel nor no horse; they haven't been this way. Ain't you men ashamed to come here skeering a poor, lone, sick woman to death!" whined Nancy. She acted the part so well that they believed every word she said, and turned and rode back the way they had come. Thus Aunt Nancy saved the life of the young Patriot soldier, for if the

Tories had caught him they would certainly have killed him.

Nancy soon became famous all through Georgia and the Carolinas. She was loved and admired by the Americans, but mortally feared by the British and the Tories. It is a great wonder that they did not kill her, unprotected as she was in her country home; but somehow they stood too much in awe of her to attempt any violence. However, they kept spies prowling about her home to see what she might undertake to do, for they knew that she was herself a most valuable spy for the Americans. One night as Nancy was boiling a pot of "lye soap" in the big fireplace in her log cabin, stirring the soap with a long ladle, and chatting and laughing with some neighbor women who had called—for she was full of joke and humor—suddenly she noticed a pair of eyes in a bearded face peering at her from outside through a crack between the logs of the cabin. Pretending not to notice it, she went on stirring the soap and chatting and laughing. Then suddenly with a quick, deft motion, she lifted a ladleful of the boiling fluid and threw it full in the face of the eavesdropper. He fell upon the ground roaring with pain. Nancy snatched up a rope and rushed out; and, although he was a big, powerful man, she soon had him securely tied. She took him into the house and dressed his burns, and made him as comfortable as possible, for she was really a kind-hearted woman. Early the next morning she shouldered a gun, and making her big prisoner with his hands tied behind him walk before her, marched him to the American camp, four miles away. On the way they had to cross the broad river at a ford. The water was not very deep, and Nancy, holding her gun in one hand and her petticoats lifted above her knees in the other, waded right through, still driving her prisoner before her. She took him to the American camp and delivered him up to General Clarke.

During the spring and summer of 1780 the condition of affairs in Georgia was dreadful. The little American army in the State, though brave and heroic, was too small and weak to cope with the powerful enemy. Armed bands of cruel, bloodthirsty Tories roved over the country at will, committing murders, robberies, and all sorts of outrages on the defenseless people. General Elijah Clarke, the American Commander in Georgia, ordered all the women and children to move away from the region to a place of safety that he had provided for them in Tennessee, and most of them went, but Nancy positively refused to go. "I shan't budge a peg, not if me and my children die for it!" she said. She and her children remained in their lonely country home, her life in constant danger. Her husband, Benjamin Hart, was captain of a small company of American soldiers, known as "Partisans," placed on duty in the neighborhood to protect the people as best they could. The men composing the company had to lie concealed in the swamps most of the time, sallying forth only when they saw a chance of striking the enemy an effective blow. Nancy acted as a spy and kept her husband informed of the movements of the British and the Tories. Her house was a meeting-place for his company. Down by the spring near the house she kept a large conch shell, on which she and her children could blow with great skill, making a bugle-like sound that could be heard for miles around. On this conch shell they would blow signals for Captain Hart's company. The principal signals were these: One blast, "Big force of the enemy near; lie low!" Two blasts, "The enemy gone!" Three blasts, "Come to the house quick!"

One night a band of ruffian Tories went to the house of John Dooly, an old gray-haired gentleman, and one of the foremost and most beloved men in Georgia, and murdered him in cold blood in the presence of his family. John Dooly was a warm personal friend of Nancy's, and, when she heard of his murder, her fiery blood boiled like a volcano in her veins. A few days after this terrible event a band of five armed Tories rode to Nancy's house, and, hitching their horses in the grove outside, walked into the house and ordered her to get dinner for them. As you may well know, this service was not to Nancy's liking, but she could not help herself and had to obey. With eyes snapping fire and with anger in every motion of her long, lithe body, she went about the hateful task. The Tories withdrew to a corner of the room and began conversing in a low tone. Nancy pricked up her ears and listened keenly. She soon caught from their talk that these were the very men who had murdered John Dooly a few nights before. Nancy's brave heart beat fast and furious, as she thought to herself, "Oh! you bloody villains; now I'll avenge John Dooly's death!" Her manner towards the Tories quickly changed. She became pleasant and suave. Soon she was chatting and laughing at a great rate with the men, for Nancy was full of joke and humor. She went to the cupboard and got out a jug of whisky and they all took a big dram, Nancy pretending to drink with them, barely moistening her lips with the liquor. Nancy was a splendid cook, and soon had a fine dinner ready for them. The Tories leaned their guns against the walls of the cabin and took their seats at the table. Nancy called to her thirteen-year-old daughter, "Laura, go to the spring and fetch a pail of water"; and at the same time she made a secret signal to the girl by raising three fingers, which, as Laura well knew, meant "Blow three blasts on the shell!" The dram of whisky had made the men merry, and they joked and laughed mightily with Nancy as they ate her good dinner with a keen appetite. In a little while there came from down by the spring three clear blasts from the conch shell, but the Tories did not notice it. As Nancy served them she passed back and forth between them and the wall; and as she did so she would, ever and anon, take a gun and slip it outside through a crack between the logs of the cabin, the same crack through which the hapless spy had peered. She had slipped two guns through without being detected, and had the third in her hand when she was noticed by one of the Tories. "Look at that woman," he shouted. All of the men jumped from the table and started to rush at Nancy. Quick as a flash she had the gun at her shoulder, pointed straight at them, her finger on the trigger, while determination and defiance gleamed from her brave blue eyes. To take a step towards her seemed certain death. Nevertheless, one of the men made a bold spring at her. "Bang!" went the gun, and down rolled the venturesome Tory dead at her feet. The others fell back in dismay. Nancy snatched another gun, and in a jiffy had that at her shoulder, pointed straight at them, her finger on the trigger. The men huddled together in a corner of the room and began to consult what to do. About this time Laura returned from the spring. "Set down that pail o' water, take that gun from agin' the wall, cock it, stand behind me, and hand it to me quick when I want it," ordered Nancy, without moving a muscle or taking her eye off the Tories. The girl obeyed, and the sharp metallic "click, click" of the cocking guns was the only sound to break the death-like silence. The four Tories were now completely cowed. They began trying to make terms with Nancy. They offered her all the money they had and their five horses hitched in the grove, and promised to leave the country for good if she would let them go; but Nancy answered not a word. You can imagine the picture—the four men cowering in the corner, afraid to move; Nancy, tall, stalwart, determined, standing motionless with her gun pointed at them, the dead Tory lying at her feet, and her daughter with a cocked gun standing behind her! Thus for some time they stood in death-like silence, the wretched Tories wondering what would happen next, for they knew nothing of the conch-shell signal or what it meant. After a while the tramping of feet was heard outside, and there was a loud knock at the door. "Come in!" shouted Nancy, and in rushed Captain Benjamin Hart and a squad of eight "Partisan" soldiers. "These are the villains that murdered John Dooly in cold blood, and they must hang for it!" cried Nancy, pointing at the Tories. When the poor wretches heard this they turned pale as ashes, for they saw their doom. They began to deny bitterly that they had anything to do with the killing of John Dooly. "You are liars as well as villains," cried Nancy. "You done it; I heard you say yourselves you done it! You murdered John Dooly in cold blood, and you shall hang for it!" They were bound and held as prisoners. The next day they were tried by court-martial, and it was proved that they were the men that had murdered John Dooly; therefore, they were condemned to be shot. "No, not shot! Hanged! They murdered John Dooly in cold blood, and they must hang like dogs for it!" ordered the imperious Nancy, and as usual she had her way. The miserable wretches were taken out and hanged to the limbs of a big oak tree that stood near the spring by which the conch shell lay. Aunt Nancy herself witnessed the execution with great satisfaction, and she always regarded tne capture of the Tories that had murdered John Dooly as the most glorious of all her deeds.

Soon after the close of the Revolutionary War, Captain Benjamin Hart died. Nancy mourned his loss for a year or two and then married an industrious, thrifty farmer, younger than herself. They moved out to the Mississippi Valley and were doing well when a great freshet came and ruined their fortune. Her second husband died, and poor Nancy was again a widow. She wandered back to Georgia, where she lived for some time with one of her married daughters near Brunswick. Finally she moved out to Kentucky, where she had relatives living; there she spent the rest of her days, and there she lies buried. Nancy had never been a pious woman; but towards the end, when old age had turned her red hair gray and had plowed wrinkles in her strong, brave face, she "got religion" at a big Methodist revival, and, as a famous writer* has wittily said of her, "She spent the rest of her days fighting Satan and sin with as much vigor as in her prime she had fought the British and the Tories."

Georgia has honored this brave, heroic woman by naming one of its counties for her, the only county in the State named for a woman.

*Joel Chandler Harris in his "Stories of Georgia."

In Elbert County, Georgia, there is a bold, romantic stream known as "War Woman's Creek." This was named by the Indians in honor of Nancy Hart, for the savages greatly feared and admired her. One of the most flourishing chapters of the Daughters of the American Revolution in Georgia is the "Nancy Hart Chapter," at Milledgeville, Baldwin County.

A part of the log house in which Nancy lived is still standing on the old Hart farm in Elbert County, and in the canebrake near by still flow the cool crystal waters of the famous spring by which the conch shell lay. A hundred yards from the spring there is pointed out to travelers a big oak tree from the limbs of which it is said dangled the bodies of those villainous Tories who "murdered John Dooly in cold blood!"

Recently the Daughters of the American Revolution (the Stephen Heard Chapter, of Elbert County, and the Nancy Hart Chapter, of Baldwin County) have arranged to buy this old Nancy Hart homestead, and to properly mark and preserve it as a perpetual memorial to one of Georgia's truest and most heroic patriots.

PART III.

DEVELOPMENT PERIOD

CHAPTER XV.

ALEXANDER McGILLIVRAY.

I. McGILLIVRAY'S PEDIGREE AND EARLY CAREER.

By all odds the most striking and interesting figure in Georgia history during the first ten years after the Revolutionary War was Alexander McGillivray, a half-breed Indian Chief.

In the year 1735 there came to Charleston, South Carolina, on a ship from Liverpool, a Scotch youth, seventeen years old, by the name of Lachlan McGillivray. His father was a Scotch nobleman of wealth and distinction; but the boy, in a wild spirit of adventure, ran away from home and came to the New World to try his fortunes.

He had in his pocket a neat sum of money; so taking up his quarters at the best tavern in Charleston, he spent several days in viewing the city and the surrounding country. One day while wandering out in the suburbs, he came across the camp of a party of Indian traders—white men whose business was to carry merchandise on pack horses to the various Indian tribes away off in the back woods. One of the traders persuaded young McGillivray to go with him as his assistant. From this beginning he became much attached to the business and followed it for many years. By his intelligence, industry and business shrewdness he became, in course of time, one of the best-known and most successful Indian traders in America. He was of a daring disposition, and ventured farther with his train of pack horses than any other trader in the South. He used to go up into the French possessions in the neighborhood of Fort Toulouse, where the town of Wetumpka, Alabama, now stands. There he met and fell in love with, and subsequently married, a beautiful half-breed Indian girl, bearing the beautiful name of Sehoy. Her mother was a full-blooded Indian princess, daughter of a noted chief and descended from a long line of chiefs of the Tribe of the Wind of the Great Creek Nation. Her father was Captain Marchand, commander of the French garrison at Fort Toulouse, and a gentleman of distinguished family, culture and refinement. So pretty Sehoy of the Tribe of the Wind was a high-bred lady. One who knew her well at the time of her marriage describes her thus: "A maiden of sixteen, beautiful in countenance, cheerful in looks, bewitching in manners and graceful in form." There can be no doubt that the marriage of this dusky Indian girl of the lustrous eye and coal-black hair to the fair-complexioned, blue-eyed, red-headed young Scotchman was a true love match.

McGillivray had acquired considerable wealth as an Indian trader. He owned a plantation on the Coosa River in Alabama. There shortly after his marriage he settled, and there were born to him and beautiful Sehoy of the Tribe of the Wind three children, a son and two daughters. To the son was given the name of Alexander. Lachlan McGillivray subsequently bought a plantation on the Savannah River in Georgia, whither he moved with his young family.

Pretty Sehoy of the Tribe of the Wind had now become a dignified Georgia matron with her children about her knees. There was no school to which she could send the children, so, being a woman of some education, she taught them how to read and write. When Alexander was ten years old his father sent him to New York, where for four years he attended the best schools in that city. He afterwards went to school in Savannah, and later still was sent to Charleston to study Latin and Greek under a learned clergyman and famous teacher of that day. Young McGillivray was an apt student and had a great love for books, and he was specially fond of the noble Latin and Greek classics— a sure sign of a fine and lofty intellect.

After he had finished his school education he was placed in a large mercantile firm in Savannah in which his father was a partner, but he had no taste for this hum-drum, prosy business. At his earnest entreaty his father allowed him to go on a year's visit to his mother's people, the Tribe of the Wind, in north Alabama. He was received with honor and hailed with joy by the Indians, for he was their own. Proud of him were they, and they had reason to be. He was six feet tall and straight as an arrow. He had his mother's large, dark, lustrous eyes and a dash of her dusky complexion; he had his father's strong, intellectual head, and his French grandfather's long, tapering, fingers, high instep, and mien and bearing of a gentleman. He was made chief of the Tribe of the Winds, and never more did he return to the hum-drum life of a grocery merchant.

Here we lose sight of him for a few years, but during this time there is no doubt that his masterful ability was asserting itself among the Creek Indians.

II. McGILLIVRAY IN THE REVOLUTION.

About the beginning of the Revolutionary War, Mc-

Gillivray came again into the field of vision, this time standing out in bold relief as an historical character. A great council of all the chiefs of the great Creek Nation was being held at Coweta Town, right where the little village of Fort Mitchell, Ala., now stands, the same place that Oglethorpe had visited some thirty-five years before. There were three thousand chiefs and head men present at the meeting. The principal business before the council was the determination of the position which the Creek Indians should take in the Revolutionary War, then opening. McGillivray, by sheer force of native ability, got complete control of the assembly and persuaded them to espouse the cause of the British. From that moment he became supreme chief of the Creeks, and from then till near the end of his life he held them absolutely obedient to his will. The Creeks were by far the most numerous and powerful of the Indian nations in the South. Its numerous tribes occupied nearly all of Georgia, the whole of Alabama, and a part of Mississippi. They could furnish many thousands of the bravest and fiercest warriors. For his great service in winning the Creeks to the English side, McGillivray was given the rank of colonel in the British army, with a colonel's full pay.

McGillivray had really wished his people to be entirely neutral in the war, but this they were not permitted to be. Their situation was such that they were compelled to join one side or the other. He knew that the British were far stronger than the Americans; and believing that they would triumph in the war, he naturally wished to be on the winning side. But, on the other hand, he was afraid to antagonize the Americans too strongly; for if they *should* triumph in the war,—an issue entirely possible,—he knew it would be in their power to visit a terrible vengeance on his people. So he proved a rather luke-warm, half-hearted ally to the British. Throughout the war he helped them some; but had he chosen so to do, he could have helped them a great deal more. When Georgia was invaded he took an active though not very vigorous part with the British and the Tories against the Patriots. He was no fighter himself, for he had not inherited the fighting instinct with his Indian blood, and he was never in a battle; but he furnished Brown and McGirth and other Tory leaders with their Indian allies, in rather sparse numbers.

Lachlan McGillivray, the father, was a much stancher Tory than his son Alexander, and with his great wealth he did much to help the British cause. When the war was over nearly all of his property was confiscated by the Americans, and his family was reduced to poverty.

III. THE OCONEE WAR.

During the Revolutionary War, nearly all of the Indian tribes of Georgia had sided with the British and had engaged in open hostilities against the Patriots. Now that the war was over, they had, of course, to share the fate of the conquered and submit to any terms that Georgia might exact.

In the northwest corner of the State dwelt the Cherokee Indians, a small nation very little related to the Creeks. In May, 1783, the chiefs of the Cherokees met at Augusta commissioners appointed by the Legislature of Georgia for the purpose of making a treaty. The commissioners demanded a large cession of Cherokee lands, which was granted, thus adding considerably to the territory of Georgia towards the northwest. For a long time afterwards, Georgia had no further trouble with the Cherokees. They kept the treaty because they couldn't help themselves, for they were a feeble people and had no strong McGillivray back of them.

In November, 1783, Governor Lyman Hall called the chiefs of all the Creek tribes to meet at Augusta for the purpose of making a treaty with commissioners appointed by the Legislature. When the day for the meeting came, only a few of the chiefs were present; and McGillivray, the supreme chief, was conspicuous by his absence. Nevertheless, the Georgia commissioners went ahead and made a treaty with the few chiefs that were present. These chiefs assumed to act for the whole Creek Nation, and ceded to Georgia all of the lands lying between the Ogeechee and Oconee rivers and extending up to the mountains in the Cherokee country.

By this cession Georgia had added to her territory a vast, beautiful and fertile region of country. She at once divided it into two large counties, Washington County to the south and Franklin County to the north.* Parties of government surveyors were sent into the region to lay it off into townships and lots. A large portion of it was set apart to be distributed as bounties and rewards to the Georgia heroes of the Revolutionary War. The rest was to be thrown open to any settlers who might choose to come and pay the small purchase price of the lands. Every encouragement was given for the rapid peopling and development of this choice region, and a good many settlers actually moved into it. Though only a few of the Indian tribes had been party to the treaty, *all* seemed to acquiesce in it. They

* These two counties were subsequently cut up into twelve counties of the present day.

uttered no protest; they did not interfere with the surveyors or the incoming settlers and moved rapidly away from the east to the west side of the Oconee. Everything seemed peaceful and serene, but these appearances were deceptive.

Alexander McGillivray was strongly opposed to the Treaty of Augusta, for he believed that it had been unfairly obtained and that it greatly wronged his people. He determined that it should not be carried out; but with Indian cunning he concealed his feelings and designs, while he went quietly to work to accomplish his purpose.

As soon as he heard of the treaty he hastened to Pensacola, Florida, where, acting for the whole Creek Nation, he made a secret treaty with the Spanish Government by which he made the Creeks the allies of Spain. This was a master stroke of diplomacy. Spain at that time claimed the country between the Chattahoochee and the Mississippi rivers, including the southern part of the present States of Alabama and Mississippi. Georgia claimed the same region under the original grant from England. The country in dispute was inhabited mainly by Creek Indians, and by McGillivray's treaty the Creeks pledged themselves to support the claims of Spain as against Georgia. In return for this support

Alexander McGillivray. 213

Spain was to protect the Creeks, as far as she could do so, from the Georgians and from all other enemies.

Having accomplished this, McGillivray hastened back to Georgia, where he moved quietly from tribe to tribe of the Creeks firing their hearts and stirring them

Indians Plundering Cattle on a Frontier Plantation.

to revolt against the Treaty of Augusta. The blow fell, as Indian outbreaks usually do, when least expected. In May, 1785, a party of painted savages crossed the Oconee and went on the warpath into the lately ceded region, killing the settlers, burning the houses, stealing the cattle and whatever else they could carry off. General Elijah Clarke, of Revolutionary fame, quickly got up a party of white men and drove the marauders back across the river. This was the beginning of what is known in Georgia history as "The Oconee War." It lasted in a fitful, irregular sort of way for ten years, being repeatedly interrupted by "treaties of peace," which the Indians always violated at the first opportunity. The prime mover and instigator of it all was Alexander McGillivray.

The first attempt to put an end to this so-called Oconee War was in the fall of 1785. In November, the chiefs of the Creek tribes were summoned to meet the Georgia commissioners at Galphinton, on the Ogeechee River (a few miles below the present town of Louisville) for the purpose of making another treaty. McGillivray used his powerful influence to keep the chiefs from attending, consequently only a few of them were present. It was the story of the Treaty of Augusta over again. The few chiefs present, assuming to act for the whole Creek Nation, signed a treaty by which they not only confirmed all the concessions that had been made at the Treaty of Augusta, but in addition gave up to the whites a large and choice region in southeast Georgia, known then as the "Tallassee Country," including a vast tract between the Altamaha and St. Mary's rivers, and extending considerably to the west.

Of course, McGillivray repudiated this treaty, and under his instigation it was soon broken by the Indians, and the "Oconee War" was resumed. It consisted, as before, of occasional Indian raids into the ceded territory on the east side of the Oconee River, with murder of settlers, burning of houses and stealing of cattle. The Indians were usually quickly driven away with severe punishment.

In October, 1786, another council was held on Shoulder Bone Creek, in Hancock County. It was the same old story that had already been enacted at Augusta and Galphinton. Only a few chiefs were present. A new "treaty" was made confirming the Treaty of Galphinton and adding some new provisions. In a few months the treaty, under the instigation of McGillivray, was again broken by the Indians, and the Oconee War went on as before. In this Oconee War (so called), during its continuance of ten years, hundreds of white settlers were murdered, many homes were burned, and tens of thousands of dollars' worth of property was destroyed. A volume of blood-curdling stories might be written about the times.*

The authorities of Georgia had long known that Alexander McGillivray was the instigator of all these

---

*Some tragic incidents connected with this war are graphically related in Joel Chandler Harris's little book, "Stories of Georgia."

troubles, and they had used their utmost efforts to have a meeting with him and come to some understanding, but he evaded them every time. He had led them to believe that he would attend the meeting at Augusta, but he was not there. He had positively promised to be at Galphinton; but he had not the least idea of going, and not only absented himself, but kept the other chiefs away. He was full of deceit and double dealing. In his letters to the Georgia authorities (he was a strong and forceful writer) he was never defiant, but always courteous, reasonable, and apparently anxious for peace; but he never, or rarely ever, meant what he said. His aim was to drag out the fitful, desultory "Oconee War" as long as possible, until he could unite all of the Indian nations east of the Mississippi into one mighty combination and bring affairs to a state where the interests of Spain would be involved, so that he might reasonably call on that great power for aid.

At last the United States took a hand in the game and united with Georgia in trying to bring the crafty Indian to terms; but with his fine address McGillivray baffled them at every point, and the "Oconee War" still went on. Finally the United States commissioners succeeded in making an engagement with him for a meeting that he could not evade. It took place on the

20th of September, 1789, at Rock Landing, on the banks of the Oconee River, not far from the present town of Milledgeville. On the east side of the river appeared the commissioners, accompanied by a battery of light artillery; on the other side of the river was McGillivray, with two thousand warriors armed *cap-à-pie!* He had brought this army to overawe the commissioners. McGillivray, with some of the leading chiefs, rowed across the river in canoes, and the conference with the commissioners began. It lasted several days. McGillivray was, as always, dignified, courteous and self-contained, appearing anxious for peace and well pleased with the terms offered by the commissioners. The treaty was drawn up in writing, and was to be submitted to a grand council of all the chiefs the next day. McGillivray and his companions rowed back across the river to notify the chiefs. Late that night the commissioners heard a mighty commotion in the Indian camp across the river. When they arose the next morning they saw that McGillivray and his host of two thousand warriors had vanished! Soon two negroes came rowing across the river in a canoe bearing a letter from McGillivray to the commissioners, which said: "The terms you offer are not satisfactory. We are compelled to move away from here to find forage for our horses. Further negotiations will have to be deferred until next spring." The commissioners were astounded and bitterly disappointed, for the wily fox had given them the slip. These august officers had come from New York City to middle Georgia—a toilsome journey of more than a month in those days—and their mission had failed to accomplish anything. Yet, from the Indian standpoint, McGillivray is not to be blamed; for the terms of the treaty offered by the commissioners demanded of the Indians the surrender of vast tracts of their choicest lands (the same as the Treaty of Galphinton) without the least compensation. No wonder the supreme chief found it "unsatisfactory."

From the painting by Gilbert Stuart.
George Washington.

IV. THE TREATY OF NEW YORK.

In the year 1790 the United States was organized under the new Constitution which gave to the Federal Government much greater powers than it had ever had before—among others, entire control of Indian affairs.

The Georgians appealed to President George Washington to exercise this new power by sending a Federal army down to Georgia to conquer the Creek Indians and force them to stand by the treaties which they had made with the whites. But Washington decided not to do this until he had first tried his own hand at treaty making with the Indians. He went about it wisely and cautiously. He sent to Georgia Colonel Marius Willett, of New York, as a secret and confidential agent to negotiate with the Creek Nation; that is, with Alexander McGillivray.

Colonel Willett reached Georgia and proceeded directly to McGillivray's country home, "Little Tallassee," on the Coosa River, where he had a long confidential conference with the great chief. McGillivray was a sensible man, and he knew that the time had now come when he *must* make and keep a treaty with the whites. He preferred to make it with the United States rather than with Georgia, becaused he believed that the United States would be more liberal with him. He agreed to go to New York (which was then the capital of the United States), accompanied by the principal Indian chiefs, to meet the great George Washington face to face, and to settle with him all difficulties between the Creek Nation and Georgia.

It took some time to get the delegation for New York together. At length, however, it was accomplished. The party consisted of McGillivray, twenty-three Indian chiefs, six attendants, three servants, one interpreter, and Colonel Willett—thirty-five persons all told. On the 9th day of June, 1790, they assembled at

From an engraving of 1841.
Stone or Rock Mountain.

Stone Mountain, in DeKalb County, and started immediately on their long overland journey to New York. They traveled in wagons and on horseback. McGillivray was on horseback and Colonel Willett rode in a single-seated buggy, called a sulky. As they traveled through South Carolina, North Carolina, Virginia, Pennsylvania and New Jersey, they excited everywhere the greatest interest and curiosity. In the larger towns they were received with much honor and were hospitably entertained.

At Guilford Court House, North Carolina, a pathetic incident occurred. McGillivray was standing in the court house surrounded by a throng of ladies and gentlemen who had called to pay their respects. Suddenly a woman came rushing through the assembly, and, grasping McGillivray by both hands, burst into a flood of tears and poured forth a profuse and eloquent speech of gratitude and thanks, ending by exclaiming with great feeling, *"God bless you! God bless you, forever!"* The woman was a Mrs. Brown, whose husband, several years before, had been murdered by the Creek Indians in Georgia, after which she and her children had been captured and made slaves. McGillivray, hearing of their sad condition, had paid their ransom from his own pocket and thus redeemed them from slavery. For a year he had maintained them at his own home, and then sent them to their friends in North Carolina. Since her liberation this was the first time Mrs. Brown had seen McGillivray, and for this meeting she had traveled many miles through the country. The kindness which McGillivray had shown to Mrs. Brown was only one of the many instances in which he had paid heavy ransoms to the Indians for the sake of captive women and children.

McGillivray's party reached New York City at noon on Tuesday, July 20th, 1790, and were received with great splendor by the Tammany Society (which has since become so famous) in the full regalia of their order, and were conducted with much pomp and parade to the President's house, where they were introduced to George Washington and the members of his Cabinet. They then repaired to the City Tavern, where an elegant entertainment closed the day. Practically all the people of New York came out from their houses to see McGillivray and the Creek chiefs, for they were the most imposing Indian delegation that had ever visited the national capital.

The treaty making proved to be a slow process. Washington had several long conferences with McGillivray, whom he found to be a man of great ability and force of character. McGillivray agreed to surrender to Georgia absolutely and without pay the long and rich strip of country lying between the Oconee and the Ogeechee rivers and extending clear up to the mountains; but he firmly refused to give up the "Tallassee country," between the Altamaha and the St. Mary's, which the whites claimed on account of the so-called Treaty of Galphinton. He agreed to pledge the firm allegiance of the whole Creek Nation to the United States, and in return required that the United States should protect the Creeks in the peaceful possession of all their lands lying west of the Oconee River. He also had himself made an American brigadier-general with full pay. On these terms the treaty was made. It was drawn up in writing, and on the 6th of August, 1790, was formally signed by General Knox, Secretary of War, acting as commissioner for the United States, and by Alexander McGillivray and the twenty-three chiefs acting for the whole Creek Nation. The next day it was duly confirmed by Congress, and the deed was done!

In making this treaty McGillivray had deliberately violated his solemn treaty with Spain, by which, in all good faith, he was still bound. At this very time he was holding the commission and drawing the pay of a colonel in the Spanish army. He knew that, as things had turned out, it would be to the interests of the Creeks to put themselves under the protection of the United States rather than Spain; so without a scruple he broke faith with Spain and transferred his allegiance to the United States.

The Treaty Delegation returned to Georgia by water, sailing from New York in a specially chartered ship and landing in Georgia at the mouth of the St. Mary's River, in the beautiful "Tallassee country," which had been saved to the Indians by the masterful diplomacy of their supreme chief, Alexander McGillivray.

Undoubtedly this famous Treaty of New York was good, wise and fair to both parties, but it pleased neither the Creeks nor the Georgians. The Creeks complained of it bitterly because it forced them to surrender the extensive and rich region between the Ogeechee and the Oconee, for which they had been so long contending. The Georgians protested against it violently because it compelled them to give back to the Indians the "Tallassee country," which had been yielded to the whites at the Treaty of Galphinton.

In making this Treaty of New York the United States had deliberately annulled the Treaty of Galphinton made by Georgia. Georgia contended that the United States had no right so to do. Thus arose the first assertion under the new Constitution of the "State Sovereignty," or "States' Rights," for which the South always contended. For a while Georgia and the United States Government quarreled bitterly over the matter. Furthermore, by this Treaty of New York both the Creek Nation and the United States were placed in awkward and unpleasant relations with Spain; and, on the whole, it looked as if the two great chiefs, Alexander McGillivray and George Washington, instead of removing troubles, had only added to them, for their agreement gave rise to several years of wrangling and one or two "Indian Wars." However, through the wise, cautious policy of George Washington, the troubles were gradually adjusted, and in the year 1796, several years after McGillivray was dead, commissioners representing Georgia, the United States and the Creek Indians met in South Georgia at a little place called Coleraine (now vanished), and made a treaty confirming in every particular the Treaty of New York. This Treaty of Coleraine put an end to the Indian troubles, and for a long time thereafter there was peace between the white man and the red man in our beloved State. In the mean time poor Spain had become so involved in European disturbances that she required all of her strength and resources at home. She was finally compelled to lose sight of her claims to any part of North America, and eventually sold Florida (1819).

V. WILLIAM AUGUSTUS BOWLES.

After the Treaty of New York, McGillivray rapidly lost favor with the Indians. There was in Georgia at that time a notorious adventurer by the name of William Augustus Bowles, who proved to be McGillivray's evil genius. Bowles was a prince of scoundrels. He was born in Maryland in 1763. His family were Loyalists, or Tories; and during the Revolutionary War, William Augustus joined the British army at the early age of sixteen years. Though but a boy, he was

William Augustus Bowles.

given the commission of ensign. In less than a year, while his regiment was stationed in Pensacola, Florida, he was expelled from the army for some disgraceful conduct. He bundled up his uniform with bitter curses and threw it into the sea. He then joined a party of

Creek Indians who happened to be in Pensacola at the time, and returned with them to Georgia. There he lived for some time among the savages, learned to speak their language fluently, and married the daughter of a chief. Later he rejoined the British army and so distinguished himself that his old commission of ensign was given back to him, and the "stain on his escutcheon" was supposed to be wiped out.

After the war was over he joined a theatrical company and went to the Bahama Islands, where he made quite a reputation as a comic actor and portrait painter, for he possessed marvelous versatility of talent. In the year 1789 he abandoned the stage and became a lawless Indian trader. By his shrewdness and boldness he managed to smuggle cargo after cargo of "contraband" goods through the Spanish dominions of Florida and into Georgia, where he sold them to the Creek Indians at enormous profits. The Spanish Government offered a reward of seven thousand dollars for his capture, and pursuers got so hot on his trail that he abandoned the smuggling business and went back to live among the Creek Indians in Georgia. He settled on the Chattahoochee River, where he was at once made chief of one of the Indian tribes, and he rapidly acquired great influence with the savages. McGillivray, hearing of him and knowing his character, threatened to arrest him and cut off his ears if he did not leave the Creek Nation in twenty-four hours. Bowles, knowing that McGillivray would carry out his threat, left immediately and went again to the Bahama Islands, where he was soon followed by a number of Creek and Cherokee chiefs, who idolized him.

By his personal magnetism (for, like most successful scoundrels, he was a man of attractive personality) he won the favor and confidence of Lord Dunmore, the English governor of the Bahamas; and Dunmore gave him a strong letter of recommendation to the leaders of the British Government in London. Bowles, accompanied by his Creeks and Cherokees, took ship and sailed for London, where, with his painted savages, he appeared before the leaders of the Government, and made them a speech like this: "I come as the ambassador of the united nations of the Creeks and Cherokees. These great Indian nations are anxious to break with Spain and the United States and to renew their old allegiance to England, if she will aid them in their enterprise. I am authorized to make you this offer by the unanimous voice of twenty thousand warriors, ready to hazard their lives at the command of myself, their beloved brother and supreme chief!"

Of course, there was no truth in the statement, but Bowles was a great liar, and by his personal magnetism he usually got his lies believed; but fortunately some of the leaders were clear-headed enough to see that he was a humbug, so he was very politely but firmly turned down and dismissed. Nevertheless, he and his Indians received a great ovation and many rich presents from the people of London.

Having failed in his schemes, he returned to the Bahamas. With the money that he had made from his smuggling trade he bought a strong, swift-sailing little ship, which he armed with four cannon and manned with an Indian crew trained by himself in the art of navigation. Thus equipped he entered boldly on the career of a pirate. He went to Apalachicola Bay, Florida, where for a year he played havoc with the Spanish merchant ships, destroying many of them and securing an immense booty. Again Spain offered a big reward for his capture; so, finding that he was about to be taken and hanged, he sold his ship and returned once more to his beloved Creeks in Georgia. The Indians made a greater hero of him than ever, and he rapidly acquired a powerful ascendency over them. They dubbed him "General," and declared him commander-in-chief of all the armies of the Creek Nation.

Bowles saw that now was his opportunity to be avenged on McGillivray, who had threatened to cut off his ears. That chieftain had just made his wise but unpopular Treaty of New York. Bowles poisoned the minds of the Indians against him, and made them believe that he was a traitor and had sold them first to Spain and then to the United States, all for his own selfish gain. Unfortunately there was some truth, or at least semblance of truth, in these charges. The Indians believed Bowles's accusations. They turned against their great chieftain, whom they had idolized for so many years, and he rapidly fell into disfavor.

Poor McGillivray seems not to have had much courage or "backbone"; for he gave way without a struggle before the strong tide of unpopularity, and, abandoning the Indians and Indian affairs, left the field to Bowles, and spent the two remaining years of his life in looking after his commercial interests.

As for Bowles, he continued to work his rascally schemes in Georgia and Florida for several years, and became an intolerable annoyance both to Spain and the United States. Spain, now for the third time, offered a big reward for his capture, but for a long time no one could lay hands on him. Finally, however, some Indians set a trap for him, and caught him for the sake of the rich reward offered. While they were on their way to Florida, they camped in the woods one night, setting a guard over their prisoner. During the night the guard fell asleep, and Bowles gnawed apart the rope that bound him and made his escape. The astonished Indians awoke and found him gone. They soon got track of him, however, and after a long pursuit caught him nearly starved to death in a swamp. The Spanish Government sent him to Havana, Cuba, and threw him into the dungeon of Morro Castle, where, after languishing a few years, he died.

VI. PASSING OF McGILLIVRAY.

Alexander McGillivray, while possessing some noble traits of character, was crafty, scheming and avaricious. We have seen his double-dealing in politics, but we should not judge him too harshly on this account; for he was protecting a weak people against a strong, and in such cases cunning and deceit are sometimes the only weapons that avail. He loved money, and his methods of obtaining it were not entirely above reproach. He managed always to get well paid by one or another of the great governments of the world for his influence over the Indians. He was first a British colonel, then a Spanish colonel, and finally an American brigadier-general, getting in each instance a high salary. By his shrewdness he succeeded in securing these offices. He entered into partnership with a Scotch merchant by the name of Panton, and, in a way that was not altogether honorable, he used his position as head of the Creek Nation to further his commercial interests. He was undoubtedly true to the Indians, but not in a pure and unselfish way like old Tomo-chi-chi. While serving the cause of his oppressed people with sincere and deep devotion, he managed also, in an incidental way, to enrich himself. When he died he owned a number of slaves and two well-stocked plantations in Georgia, one in Cherokee County and one on Little River, in Putnam County.

That he was a man of very high order of ability there can be no doubt. He was a born leader of men. For many years by sheer force of intellect and character he held a great nation of fickle, unstable savages, scattered over a vast region of country, absolutely obedient to his will. No other man ever succeeded in so governing the Indian race.

He was a great diplomat. For years he baffled the utmost efforts of the statesmen of Georgia and the United States to make terms with the Creek Indians. In the fine game of politics he played off Spain, the United States, and Georgia against one another. He induced the Federal Government to abrogate a treaty made by Georgia, thus causing the first "State Sovereignty" quarrel that ever arose in the United States.

He was a strong, vigorous writer. His classical education gave him a fine command of language. His political letters are said by competent critics to be among the ablest documents to be found in the huge volumes of "American State Papers." He impressed every one who met him personally as a man of rare intellect and of great force and dignity of character. He had a large head, expanded above the ears, with a broad and lofty forehead.*

He seems to have possessed but little courage, either physical or moral. Though for years a promoter and instigator of war, he was never in a battle. This does not necessarily imply cowardice; but if he had possessed the fighting instinct in any degree, he would scarcely have been so careful to keep away from the smell of gunpowder. If he had been a warrior or a man who was ready to fight, he would not have allowed himself to be so completely displaced by that brazen-faced adventurer, Bowles.

* For a masterful sketch of this remarkable man and the Oconee War the reader is referred to Absalom H. Chappell's little volume, "Miscellanies of Georgia," where these and a number of other subjects in our State history are treated with classic beauty.

His last days on earth were passed under a cloud. He had fallen into disfavor with his own people, whom he had served so long, so faithfully and so well; Spain regarded him as a time server and turncoat, and even the United States had begun to mistrust him. He had been in bad health for more than a year; and while on a visit to his Scotch friend and business partner, Panton, at Pensacola, he died, in February, 1793. The Spanish Catholic priest at Pensacola, out of spite perhaps, refused him Christian burial; but his funeral was attended with imposing civic and Masonic ceremonies. He was laid to rest in the beautiful flower garden of his friend. Thus the great chieftain of the Creeks was buried in the sands of the Seminoles; and there to-day his bones lie in an unmarked and unknown grave, while his very name (once "a name to conjure with") has passed almost into oblivion.

When the Creek Indians heard of his death, their old love for him came back in full force, and from all their forest homes throughout Georgia and Alabama there went up a mighty wail and lamentation, and many savage ceremonies and funeral rites were performed in honor of Alexander McGillivray, son of the beautiful Sehoy, of the Tribe of the Wind of the great Creek Nation.

CHAPTER XVI.

THE YAZOO FRAUD.

I. THE YAZOO COUNTRY AND THE SPECULATORS.

Take a map of the Southern States or of the United States and find where the Yazoo River empties into the Mississippi. From this point draw a line due eastward until it strikes the Chattahoochee River about where the town of West Point (Ga.) now stands. Many years ago this line was known as the "Yazoo Line," and the region above and below it, for an indefinite distance, was known as the "Yazoo Country." This region, like all the rest of what is now Alabama and Mississippi, was claimed by Georgia. The part below the line was claimed also by Spain, and for many years the ownership was in dispute between the two countries. This immense region was at that time one vast wilderness, inhabited only by scattered tribes of Indians, but the lands were among the richest and most desirable on the American Continent.

At that time, soon after the Revolutionary War, there prevailed throughout the United States a sort of mania for speculating in "wild lands," as the extensive unusued territory of the different States was called.

In the year 1789 a combination of speculators from several different States in the Union tried to buy the Yazoo Country, or a large section of it, from Georgia. Owing to Spain's counter claim to this region, Georgia's title to it was in doubt, and therefore the commercial value of the lands was greatly depreciated. The speculators offered a half-cent an acre for five million acres, agreeing, of course, to take all the risk of Georgia's doubtful title. Georgia was at that time sorely in need of money to pay off her Revolutionary soldiers, who were clamoring strongly for their wages, long past due. So the State Legislature, by a unanimous vote, agreed to sell to the speculators five million acres of the Yazoo Country for two hundred thousand dollars.

But before the sale was consummated, President Washington issued a proclamation declaring it to be illegal and unconstitutional; because, in the first place, negotiations were now going on between Spain and the United States in regard to the ownership of this region, and during the negotiations, of course, neither party had a right to sell the lands; and because, in the second place, according to the Federal Constitution no state could sell or occupy its wild lands until the Indian claims thereto had been "extinguished" by the United States Government by fair and legal treaty, and this had not yet been done in regard to the Yazoo Country. So Georgia's sale to the speculators was declared void, and was not carried into effect. This transaction was but the preliminary to the famous "Yazoo Fraud."

II. "THE YAZOOISTS."

In 1793 a new and powerful combination of speculators was organized for the purpose of buying the Yazoo Country from Georgia. It was composed of men from nearly every State in the Union. They were formed into several different "companies," but practically they were united into one mighty combination, acting together under one leadership. They offered to pay Georgia in cash about one and a half cents an acre for twenty million acres of the Yazoo Country. The Legislature of 1793 rejected their proposition by an almost unanimous vote. Bitterly disappointed, but nothing daunted by this rebuff, the Yazooists, as this cohort of speculators came to be called, determined to try again. They knew perfectly well now that they could not buy the lands by fair and open means; but, being unscrupulous men, they were willing to resort to unprincipled methods to accomplish their purpose.

The leader and business manager of the whole scheme was a James Gunn, or General Gunn, as he was commonly called. He was a man exactly suited to the base purposes of the Yazooists. He came to Georgia from Virginia towards the latter part of the Revolutionary War, as captain of a company in General Nathaniel Greene's army. Soon after reaching Georgia, General Greene reprimanded him severely for some dishonest and disgraceful conduct. When the war ended, he settled in Georgia. He was guilty of a number of disreputable acts that should have disgraced him. He was a coarse, brutal, blustering fellow, utterly unprincipled, but very shrewd and full of energy, and possessing in a high degree the "gift of gab." He managed, as bad men frequently do, to make himself exceedingly popular with the masses of the people, and even acquired great influence over many of the leading men of the State. Undeserved honors were heaped upon him, and he was made a brigadier-general in the State militia. Finally he was elected to the exalted station of United States Senator from Georgia.

After a miniature on ivory.
General Nathaniel Greene.

The Yazoo Fraud.

Immediately after their failure with the Legislature of 1793 the Yazooists set about strengthening themselves for another effort. Their first step was to enlist the interest of leading men of Georgia in their enterprise. The wily Gunn and his assistants moved quietly over the State, trying to induce prominent and influential people to "take stock" in their rascally scheme. In this they met with great success. Here seemed an opportunity to make a fortune at one easy stroke! A number of men who were of high standing and who had always had reputation for uprightness and integrity fell before the temptation, for nothing so blinds the conscience as lust for gold. The scheme now had the "moral backing" of many of the most reputable and influential men in Georgia, which was a great point gained for the Yazooists. The Yazooists tried also to influence the elections in nearly every county in the State, securing as representatives to the Legislature, as far as they could, men who they believed could be *bribed;* for already they saw that bribery must play a very important part in their game.

One of the most energetic and most corrupt of the Yazooists was Judge Henry Wilson, of Pennsylvania, one of the most distinguished men in America. Few men stood higher in the esteem of the people or had been more greatly honored. He was one of the signers of the Declaration of Independence, had been a member of the Constitutional Convention of 1787, and for many years a leading member of the Congress, and at this very time occupied the exalted position of Associate Judge of the Supreme Court of the United States; but he had become a greedy land speculator and had lost all sense of honor. From the beginning he was most active in this Yazoo business, for he was a very large owner of its stock. It was his brain mainly that planned the operations of the company, though their practical execution was left chiefly to James Gunn.

As has already been stated, Georgia's title to the Yazoo region was clouded by Spain's counter claim, which greatly depreciated the commercial value of the lands; and that is why the Yazooists thought they could buy them at so small a price as a cent and a half an acre. In the summer of 1794 James Gunn, from his place in the United States Senate in Washington, wrote to the leading Yazooists in Georgia and in other states a stirring letter like this (we do not pretend to give the words, for the letter was never published) :—

"I have secret but perfectly reliable information that Spain will before long conclude a treaty with the United States, by which the Yazoo region will be the property of Georgia. Of course, these lands will at once enhance enormously in value. Hence it is a matter of vital importance to make the purchase before the people of Georgia know about the treaty with Spain. Now is the time to strike. Be prepared to make the purchase and close the transaction immediately on the meeting of the next Legislature. Be supplied with plenty of money to use on the members. Remember, 'Every man has his price!'"

III. PASSAGE OF THE YAZOO ACT.

On the 1st of January, 1795, the Georgia Legislature met at Augusta, which was then the capital. James Gunn and a choice gang of conspirators were present. They were supplied with $25,000 in cash and a great quantity of Yazoo "land shares" to be used in buying votes for the Yazoo sale. Every member was approached and "sounded," and those that were corrupt enough were bribed to vote for the sale. The price offered was five hundred thousand dollars for twenty-five million acres of land, or two cents an acre. The price was ridiculously small. By waiting two or three years the State could easily sell the lands at from ten to twenty times as much. Besides, there were at that time other strong reasons why they should not sell this vast territory.

The Georgia Legislature was then a small body,

consisting of scarcely more than fifty men, Senators and Representatives all told. At length, on February 7th, 1795, after a long discussion, the infamous Yazoo Act came to a vote. It was passed by the House of Representatives by a vote of nineteen to nine and by the Senate by a vote of ten to nine. It was afterwards proved that every man that voted for the act (except one, Mr. Robert Watkins) owned large shares of the stock of the Yazoo Land Company—proof positive that "undue influence," or, in other words, bribery, had been used to obtain their votes.

But before the Act could become a law, it had to be signed by the Governor of the State. By refusing to sign it he could defeat the whole project. The Governor at that time was Mr. George Mathews, a brave, rough old soldier, who had been a great hero in the Revolutionary War. He was an honest man, but weak both in understanding and in character. It was well known that in his heart he was opposed to the Yazoo Act, but he had not the moral strength to stand by his convictions. He was overawed by the great number of prominent and influential people in the State who were strongly in favor of the Act, and in an evil moment he signed the document. The deed was done! A foul blot was placed on Georgia's escutcheon.

Georgia's legislators had sold their birthright of honor for a mess of pottage!

It is the strangest instance of the wholesale corruption of public officials in American history. For these men were no worse, but rather better than the average man. Most of them belonged to the best families in Georgia, and they had hitherto maintained a pure character and an unblemished reputation. Love of money and the wiles of the tempter had for the moment blinded their moral sense, and they stumbled and fell.

No sooner was the sale consummated than the Yazooists set about realizing on their investment. They were fearful that when the people of Georgia should find out the great fraud that had been practiced they would rise in indignation, have the Act repealed, and the lands returned to the State; hence the speculators lost no time in dividing their immense territory into small parcels and selling them out at from five to ten times the price they had paid. They sent agents all over the United States, and even to Europe, to push the sales. Purchasers were found without difficulty. The Yazooists were doing, both literally and figuratively, "a land office business," and if it had continued long every one of them would have made big fortunes; but their prosperity was short lived, for a cloud was gathering that was soon to burst in terrific fury on their doomed heads!

IV. JAMES JACKSON AND THE DAY OF WRATH.

From the first this Yazoo sale had been strongly opposed by several leading men of Georgia; but in those days, when there were few newspapers, no railroads, no telegraph, and slow mails, it was very difficult to reach the ear of the public. The Yazooists had worked so secretly and rapidly that the deed was accomplished before the people knew what was being done. The Act was now passed and had become a law, and seemed irrevocable. Undoubtedly it would have gone fully into effect without further opposition if it had not been for one man. That man was the brave and fiery General James Jackson, of whose splendid record in the Revolutionary War you have read in another part of this book. Jackson was now United States Senator from Georgia. He had always been a bitter opponent of the Yazoo sale. The speculators had secretly offered him a half-million acres of land without the payment of a dollar if he would use his powerful influence in favor of their scheme, but he indignantly replied: "I have fought for the people of Georgia; that land belongs to them and their children; not for all the world would I defraud them of it. On the contrary, I will do all in my power to thwart your scheme!"

In spite of Jackson's efforts, the Act was passed and made a law of Georgia; but even then he would not let the matter alone. In a speech in the United States Senate, in the presence of James Gunn himself, he denounced the sale as "a speculation of the darkest character and of deliberate villainy!" With fiery vehemence and determination he declared *"the infamous act must be repealed by the next Georgia Legislature!"* He was not content to fulminate against the outrage from a distance. He resigned his place in the United States Senate and came back to Georgia and "bearded the lion in his den." He devoted his whole time to stirring up the people on the subject. By pen and by speech he exposed the deep-dyed villainy of the whole Yazoo transaction. He filled the columns of the only two newspapers in the State with able and severe articles of denunciation. He traveled over the State, and in speeches and talks fired the minds of the people. In pursuing this course Jackson had everything to lose and nothing to gain for himself. Most of the rich and influential people of Georgia were in favor of the Yazoo sale, because either they themselves or members of their family were financially interested in the enterprise. In defying these powerful people and publicly charging them with corruption and villainy, Jackson took his life in his hands, and well he knew it. History furnishes no finer example of physical and moral courage, nor any more splendid illustration of pure patriotism. The Yazooists, some of whom were desperate men, plainly saw that Jackson was bringing ruin and disgrace upon them, and the wonder is that he was not assassinated; but he seemed to "bear a charmed life," as often seems the case with brave and heroic souls.

He soon had the masses of the people all over Georgia wrought up to a pitch of furious indignation. It was not merely the fact that they had been so badly cheated as to the price of the lands that angered the people, but that the State had been disgraced by the wholesale corruption of its prominent men and law makers. The very name Yazooist became a synonym of infamy, and the members of the Legislature who had voted for the Act were branded with disgrace. So incensed were the people against them that their lives seemed to be in danger. They trembled for their personal safety, as well they might. A number of them left the State until the storm would blow over, some of them never to return. Others skulked in hiding about their homes for months, afraid to show their faces in any public place. The member from Oglethorpe County came near being lynched by a furious mob of his fellow citizens, headed by a man with a rope in his hand; but being warned by a friend he jumped from a back window and made his escape on horseback. The Senator from Hancock County fled in terror into South Carolina, where he was shot to death in his hiding-place by an unknown assassin. It has always been believed that the deed was done by some one who followed him from Georgia, being chosen by lot for the purpose by a secret organization of the enraged citizens of Hancock County.

As to poor, weak Governor Mathews, the people never forgave him for signing the Act, though they knew he had not been bribed to do it. From the heights of popularity he fell into general disfavor. Wherever he went in Georgia, he fancied that the finger of scorn was pointing at him. His life was made so miserable that he left the State never to return.

The arch scoundrel of them all, James Gunn, was too thick-skinned to mind the disgrace and ignominy that came upon him. With brazen effrontery he continued to live in Georgia, and to strut before the public with his usual swagger and insolent airs; but it was not for long, for early in the year 1801 he died, and went

"Down to the vile earth whence he sprung
Unwept, unhonored, and unsung!"

V. REPEAL OF THE YAZOO ACT.

The only issue in the next State election was the re-repeal of the Yazoo Act. James Jackson was elected as Representative from Chatham County. To accept this lowly place in the political service, he had voluntarily given up the exalted position of United States Senator, simply because he knew he could thus serve the people better. The rich and influential people of Georgia were mostly, for reasons already given, opposed to the repeal of the Yazoo Act, but the honest masses were ardently in favor of it.

The Legislature met at the little town of Louisville, to which the capital had just been moved, in January, 1796. A bill was introduced declaring the Yazoo Act null and void: first, because it was unconstitutional; second, because its passage had been obtained by fraud and bribery. The bill was passed on the 17th of February by a large majority of both houses of the Legislature and received the signature of Governor Erwin. Thus the infamous deed was undone, and the foul blot was wiped from Georgia's escutcheon!

To make the expunging of this disgrace from the archives of Georgia more impressive, a resolution was passed that the official record of the Yazoo Act should be publicly burned in the presence of the Governor, the

State House officers, and members of the Legislature. At high noon the Governor, the State House officers, and the whole Legislative body marched out of the Capitol in solemn order and formed in a circle around a pile of fat lightwood that had been placed in the middle of the square in front of the Capitol building. The procession was headed by the Secretary of State, who bore in his hand a great roll of paper, on which was engrossed the Legislative record of the Yazoo Act. He passed it to the President of the Senate, who looked at the caption to be sure that it was the right document, and then passed it to the Speaker of the House, who, after glancing at the caption, passed it in turn to the Clerk of the House. That officer read the caption aloud, so that all present might hear it and know that this was certainly the right paper. A man stooped down and was about to kindle the fire with a "flint and steel" (for there were no matches in those days), when he was stopped by an old, gray-haired preacher, a member of the Legislature, who, stepping forth, said in a deep, impressive voice: "My fellow countrymen, the fire that consumes that infamous deed should be drawn directly from heaven!" Then, drawing a burning-glass from his pocket, he focused the rays of the sun on the fuel, which was soon kindled into a blaze. The clerk of the

House stepped up and threw the accursed document into the flames, at the same time crying out in a loud voice, "God save the State and preserve her rights, and may every attempt to injure them perish as these corrupt acts now do!" In a few seconds the notorious Yazoo Act had gone up in smoke and ashes.

The story had a long, tiresome aftermath. Of course, the State of Georgia returned to the Yazooists the $500,000 that they had paid, but the innocent victims who had bought parcels of land from these speculators before the business was stopped seemed left in the lurch. The State of Georgia was in no way bound to reimburse them, and it seems there was no law by which the Yazooists could be compelled to do so. In the year 1802 Georgia ceded to the United States the whole Yazoo region, along with the rest of lands which are now Alabama and Mississippi. After many suits in the Supreme Court, petitions to Congress, et cetera, the United States, by act of Congress, finally returned to the said innocent victims the amount of money that they had paid to the speculators for the baleful Yazoo lands. It was about 1815 before the last of these claims were adjusted, and it was years later than that before the echoes of the great Yazoo Fraud* died out in Georgia.

*See masterful account in Absalom H. Chappell's "Miscellanies of Georgia."

CHAPTER XVII.
TROUP AND THE TREATY.

I. STATUS OF INDIAN AFFAIRS IN GEORGIA IN 1823.

By the old grant from England, Georgia claimed all the country lying between the Savannah River and the Atlantic Ocean on the east and the Mississippi River on the west. This included not only the present State of Georgia, but also that region which is now included in Alabama and Mississippi. After the Revolutionary War, Georgia realized that this immense region was far more than she could use to any profitable purpose; so in the year 1802 she ceded to the United States all of the country lying between the Chattahoochee and Mississippi rivers, including the present states of Alabama and Mississippi. She retained for herself only the State of Georgia precisely as it stands to-day. Thus by one act of her Legislature, Georgia was cut down to one-third her original size.

The terms of the cession to the United States were as follows: First: The United States was to pay Georgia $1,250,000 in cash. Second: The United States was, for the benefit of Georgia, to *extinguish*, at the expense of the Federal Government, all Indian titles to lands in Georgia. This meant simply that the United States was to purchase from the Indians, from time to time, as opportunity offered, by fair and legal treaty, their Georgia lands and turn them over to the State. In accordance with this provision, the United States did within the next fifteen or twenty years extinguish the Indian titles to large areas of land in middle and southeast Georgia, pushing the red man further and further to the west.

In 1733, when Oglethorpe landed at Savannah, the Indians possessed and occupied the whole of what is the present State of Georgia; but the resistless hand of the white man pushed them back, back, until in the year 1822 they were confined to a comparatively narrow belt in the extreme western part of the State. The long strip between the Flint and the Chattahoochee rivers was occupied by the Creeks, and the extreme northwest corner of the State was held by the Cherokees.

For several years the white man, with his insatiable land greed, had been looking with longing eyes on this rich and desirable western belt. Throughout the State the feeling was very strong that the Indians should be required to give up all of their remaining Georgia lands to the whites and move away to the Far

West to a reservation to be set aside for them by the United States. On the other hand, the feeling among the Indians was equally as strong not to budge another inch nor cede nor sell another foot of ground to the whites on any terms. Among the Cherokees in northwest Georgia this feeling was specially strong and absolutely unanimous. The Creeks were somewhat divided on the subject. They were the most numerous, most powerful, and most warlike of all the southern Indian nations. In 1822 comparatively few of them lived in Georgia, not more perhaps than seven or eight thousand all told, occupying the western belt, between the Flint and the Chattahoochee rivers, as mentioned above. The great mass of the nation lived in Alabama.

The Georgia Creeks (or Lower Creeks, as they were generally called) were under the leadership of an able and powerful half-breed chief by the name of William McIntosh. His father was a Scotchman and a colonel in the British army. His mother was a full-blooded Creek Indian. He was an intelligent, well educated man of sound judgment and excellent practical sense. He sincerely believed that it would be best for his people to yield their Georgia lands to the whites and to move beyond the Mississippi to a reservation set aside for them by the United States Government.

By his dominating influence he brought most of the Georgia or Lower Creeks to agree with him on this subject; but the Alabama or Upper Creeks, under the leadership of their two principal chiefs, Big Warrior and Little Prince, were strongly opposed to the movement. There existed among the Creeks at this time a law of recent origin that no tribe, or part of the Creek Nation, should be allowed to cede or sell to the whites any part of the Creek lands without the consent of the whole Creek Nation, through their chiefs in grand council assembled. Such a council was called to meet at Broken Arrow, Alabama, early in 1824, with a view to getting the nation to consent to the Georgia Creeks' ceding their lands to the whites and moving to a reservation beyond the Mississippi. McIntosh

William McIntosh.

was present, and urged the measure in a powerful speech, but he met with the bitter and nearly unanimous opposition of the Alabama Creeks, so the meeting was a failure.

Shortly after this grand council, Big Warrior, Little Prince, and a number of other hostile chiefs met at Pole Cat Spring, in Alabama, and, in the usual irregular, loose, savage fashion, passed a law or decree that any Creek chief who should hereafter cede or sell to the whites any part of the Creek lands without the consent of the whole Creek Nation should be adjudged a traitor and put to death. This bloody decree was ever afterwards known among the Indians as the "Law of Pole Cat Spring."

Governor George M. Troup.

II. THE INDIAN SPRING TREATY.

Such was the condition of Indian affairs in Georgia in 1824, when George M. Troup was elected Governor of the State.

Troup came of a fine old English family, and he

was an aristocrat in every fiber of his being, though in political convictions an ardent Democrat. He had been reared in wealth and luxury, and amid the finest social surroundings. He was splendidly educated, having been graduated with high honors from Princeton University at the age of nineteen years. When he was barely twenty-one years old he was elected to the State Legislature from Chatham County. As soon as he had reached the eligible age of twenty-five years he was elected to the United States Congress. He had served a number of terms in Congress with great ability and distinction.

He was a man of fine intellect, of perfect integrity of character, and possessed a fiery temper and an iron will. A truer and purer patriot never lived in Georgia. In politics he was a most ardent supporter of the "States' Rights" or "State Sovereignty" doctrine.

Governor Troup was strongly in favor of clearing all of the Indians out of Georgia and turning the vacated lands over to white settlers. In his first message to the State Legislature he spoke with great emphasis and force on this subject. He also wrote to President Monroe demanding that the United States Government proceed without delay to fulfil its obligation to "extinguish all remaining Indian titles to lands in Georgia." President Monroe replied, "The United States stands ready to carry out her agreement to extinguish the Indian titles whenever it may be done *peaceably* and on *reasonable terms,* but she will not use force or compulsion to dispossess the Indians of their lands."

At the request of the Georgia Legislature, President Monroe summoned, or "invited," all the chiefs of the Creek Nation to meet at Indian Spring early in February, 1825, to consider a treaty looking to the sale of all their remaining Georgia lands to the whites. The President appointed Duncan G. Campbell and J. Meriwether as commissioners to represent the United States in negotiating the treaty.

President Monroe.

The convention met at Indian Spring on February 8th, 1825. There were nearly four hundred chiefs and head men present. Most of them were Georgia, or Lower Creeks, under the leadership of McIntosh, but there was also a considerable delegation of Alabama or Upper Creeks under the leadership of Big Warrior and Little Prince.

A very important personage at this meeting was

Colonel John Crowell, United States Agent to the Creek Indians. He had held this position for several years, and, in the main, had discharged its difficult duties with great efficiency, though he seems not to have been a man of high principles. He was the bitter political enemy of Governor Troup. He was a shrewd man, and knew how to keep his own counsel; but it was generally known that in his heart he was opposed to the proposed treaty, and that for weeks he had been secretly using his influence with the Indians to prevent its consummation. On this account Governor Troup had written to the President of the United States requesting that Crowell be discharged from office and that some one else be appointed in his place; but the President refused to grant the request. At the Indian Spring meeting Crowell deported himself very quietly; but he was a wily fellow, and it was strongly suspected that in an underhand way he was doing all in his power to stir the Indians to oppose the treaty.

On the afternoon of the 9th of February the commissioners read to the assembled chiefs the terms of the treaty, which were as follows: That all Creek Indians now living in Georgia should move west of the Mississippi River, where they would receive from the United States, acre for acre, the same quantity of land that they had relinquished in Georgia—land of as good or better quality. The United States was to give them also $5,000,000 in money to pay for the improvements on their Georgia lands and to defray the expenses of their removal. They were to be allowed a year and a half to get ready for the removal, and during the time were to remain in peaceful possession of their Georgia homes and to be protected from all intrusion and molestation on the part of the whites.

The chiefs were instructed to sleep on the proposition over night and be ready to give their answer the next morning. During the afternoon Big Warrior (his Indian name was Tustennugee Thlucco) gathered around him his adherents and all others who wished to listen to him and made a fiery, eloquent speech against the treaty. The great rock on which he stood while making his speech is still at Indian Spring and is pointed out to visitors to that popular health resort. During that night Big Warrior, Little Prince, and several other chiefs, mainly Alabama Creeks, left the convention and journeyed homeward, but they constituted only a very small minority of the assembly. The next morning all of the others, mostly Georgia Creeks, who were alone immediately concerned in the provisions of the treaty, gave their full and free consent to its terms without a word of objection or a dissenting voice. The document was signed by McIntosh and fifty-one other chiefs on the part of the Indians, by Duncan G. Campbell and James Meriwether, commissioners, on the part of the United States, and by John Crowell, United States agent, as witness for both parties. Throughout the proceedings Crowell had uttered no word of protest, or objection.

The treaty was immediately forwarded to Washington City to receive, as the law required, the approval and confirmation of the President and the United States Senate. The same mail carried a letter secretly written by Agent Crowell to the President urging that the treaty be *not* confirmed, and stating that it had been obtained by unfair and fraudulent means; that, with the exception of McIntosh and two or three others, the Indians who had signed it were either chiefs of low grade or no chiefs at all; that an enormous majority of the Creek Nation were opposed to it, and that it could not be carried out without a bloody Indian war. Strange to say, as if placing little confidence in their agent, the Federal authorities paid no attention whatever to this protest. The treaty was confirmed by an almost unanimous vote of the Senate and received the President's approval and signature.

The deed was done! The Indian titles had been fairly and legally extinguished, and the lands had been fully vested in the State of Georgia. The people of Georgia were delighted at the success of the Indian Spring conference. They supposed, of course, there

From an old print.
Chiefs of the Creek Nation and a Georgia Squatter.

would be no trouble about carrying out the provisions of the treaty.

III. MURDER OF McINTOSH.

In this expectation, however, the Georgians were doomed to disappointment. Scarcely two weeks had elapsed after the treaty was ratified before reports began coming to the Governor that the hostile Creeks were in an ugly mood, were holding big meetings and were vowing that the treaty should never be carried out. On the 5th of March the Governor received from

Chilly McIntosh, son of Chief William McIntosh, a letter like this: "I am reliably informed that the hostiles have planned to murder my father and six other chiefs (naming them), who signed the treaty," et cetera.

The Governor at once wrote to Chief McIntosh, urging him to absent himself from home and from the vicinity of the hostiles until proper arrangements for his protection could be made, but McIntosh was a brave man, and knew no fear. He was a very wealthy man for those times, for he owned two large plantations and a hundred negro slaves and had three wives, all full-blooded Indian women. He lived on one of his plantations on the banks of the Chattahoochee River, in what is now Carroll County. Not far away was the Tallapoosa Country, where dwelt the fiercest of the hostiles and his bitterest enemies. He must have known, or should have known, that his life was in danger, but he seemed to give the matter no thought. He remained quietly at home attending to his farming interests.

Governor Troup was very anxious that the ceded lands should be surveyed as soon as possible, so that when the Indians should leave a year hence the white settlers might move in without delay. The survey would be a tedious process requiring a full year, and it would not be possible for the whites to move in until the work was completed. So the Governor wrote McIntosh asking permission to begin the survey at once, guaranteeing that the Indians should not suffer the slightest molestation or annoyance from the surveying parties. After considerable correspondence on the subject, McIntosh, on the 25th day of April, wrote the Governor, on behalf of the chiefs who had made the treaty, giving free and full permission for the survey to begin immediately. The writing of that letter was the last official act of poor McIntosh!

At daybreak on the morning of April 28th a party of one hundred and sixty carefully picked warriors of the hostile Creeks left the Tallapoosa Country and started on a mysterious expedition to McIntosh's home on the Chattahoochee River. For fifty miles they marched with the utmost secrecy through the thick concealing woods, avoiding roads and paths. At dusk on April 29th they reached the vicinity of McIntosh's plantation. Creeping stealthily through the darkness they formed a cordon around his residence. There they lay concealed in the woods and bushes watching his house until all the lights were out; then they drew the cordon closer. After midnight they crept up to the house and set it on fire, and as the flames leaped heavenward they uttered the blood-curdling war whoop! Mc-

Intosh, aroused from sound sleep, knew at once what it meant, and that he was a doomed man; but, brave to the last, he determined to sell his life as dearly as possible. Rushing to the front door he opened it and let out his two wives, Peggy and Susannah, and an Indian guest, old Toma Tustenuggee, one of the treaty signing chiefs, to make their escape from the flames. Old Toma was shot dead immediately, but the women were spared. McIntosh having barred and barricaded the door, retreated up stairs, and from the upper windows, with the four guns that he had, kept up for some minutes a brisk fire on the Indian fiends that were yelling and dancing around the flaming house, while the two women, with frantic screams, were imploring them not to burn him with the building. Forced at length by the smoke and heat, he started to rush out, pistol in hand; but on the threshold he fell, shot down but not killed. Several Indians rushed up and, catching him by the legs, dragged him out into the yard. While two of the demons took his scalp, a third drove a long knife through his heart. With a low moan he expired.

Near by was an outhouse in which Chilly McIntosh was sleeping. As the Indians made a dash for the building, Chilly jumped through the window and made his escape through the woods. During the night the Indians went to the home of Samuel Hawkins, another treaty signing chief, and a son-in-law of McIntosh, who lived in the neighborhood, and killed him as they had McIntosh, thus making their victims three in number, all treaty signers. They burned all the buildings on McIntosh's plantation, shot down his horses and cattle, and took his negroes and carried them off. All the next day they lingered about the place, feasting on McIntosh's provisions and cattle, rending the air with terrific war whoops, and dancing the war dance around McIntosh's scalp raised aloft on a long pole. At dusk that evening they vanished as silently as they had come on the evening before, and returned to the Tallapoosa Country. They carried McIntosh's scalp as a precious trophy with them, and for days through many of their towns and villages they displayed it on a long pole with great popular demonstrations of joy and satisfied revenge. The bloody "Law of Pole Cat Spring" had been executed in true Indian fashion!

The first that Governor Troup heard of this terrible occurrence was on May 2d, when Chilly McIntosh and several other Indians, worn out and bedraggled, rode into Milledgeville on horseback and, proceeding to the

Governor's mansion, told him the story of the dreadful tragedy.

As the news spread through the State it produced intense excitement. The universal belief was that a bloody Indian war was imminent and inevitable. Governor Troup immediately ordered the State militia to get ready to march at a moment's notice to the scene of the tragedy to protect the friendly Indians. But the war did not come. The savages, having executed the sentence of their murderous law, seemed satisfied; they settled down quietly and attempted no further outrages.

President John Quincy Adams.

IV. TROUP'S ALTERCATION WITH MAJOR ANDREWS AND GENERAL GAINES.

Governor Troup jumped at the conclusion, wrongly no doubt, that Agent Crowell had instigated the Indians to the murder of McIntosh and his brother chiefs. He wrote his suspicions to President John Quincy Adams, who had just succeeded President Monroe, and again demanded Crowell's removal. The President appointed Major T. P. Andrews to go to Georgia as special agent to make a thorough investigation of the charges against Crowell. About the same time he also ordered Major-General Edmund P. Gaines, of the United States army, to go to Milledgeville and offer his services and, if need be, the aid of the United States army to the Governor to suppress any outrages that might be attempted by the hostile Indians.

Major Andrews reached Milledgeville in the latter part of May, and at once demanded of the Governor his charges against Crowell. The Governor wrote them out briefly as follows: "I charge the agent superintending the affairs of the Creek Indians with: 1st, Predetermined resolution to prevent the Indians, by all means in his power, from making any cession of their lands in favor of the Georgians, and this from the most unworthy and most unjustifiable of all motives. 2d, With advising and instigating the murder of McIntosh and his friends."

For some reason Major Andrews was very slow about beginning the investigation. Before doing so he, very improperly, wrote to Crowell like this: "You are aware that I have been appointed by the United States Government to investigate the charges made against you by the Governor of Georgia. While the investigation is going on I am compelled to suspend you from your office. I apologize to you for this indignity. From all that I have been able to learn, I am inclined to believe not only that you are innocent of the charges but that you are a wronged and persecuted man." This most improper letter was published in the leading newspaper of Milledgeville, where it met the eye of Governor Troup. He immediately clipped it out and sent it in an envelope to Major Andrews with this note: "If the enclosed letter be authentic, you will consider all intercourse between yourself and this government suspended from receipt of this." He also sent a copy of Andrews's letter to President Adams, saying that since the agent of the United States had already fully *prejudged the case* which he was sent to Georgia to investigate, he was therefore incompetent to conduct the investigation fairly, and that another should be appointed in his place. The President, however, paid no attention to the complaint or the suggestion. After considerable delay Andrews went into a consideration of the charges against Crowell. Perhaps the investigation was thorough and honest. It ended in a verdict completely vindicating Crowell; and this, Andrews reported to the President. Of course, Crowell was acquitted and was retained in his position,

About the middle of June General Gaines, in accordance with the President's instructions, reported to Governor Troup at Milledgeville. Gaines was a grand old soldier, and had won great distinction in the War of 1812 and in Indian wars. Troup had a warm admiration for him, and the conference between them was sympathetic and cordial.

Gaines and Andrews, after attending to the special business for which each had been sent to Georgia, were assigned by the President to the further duty of making a thorough inquiry into the whole state of Indian affairs in Georgia.

General Edmund P. Gaines.

Leaving Milledgeville, Gaines went into the Indian country on this investigating mission. Soon he wrote Governor Troup a long letter, the substance of which was this: "I find that the Indians are bitterly opposed to your survey of the ceded lands while they are still occupying them. They regard it as an intrusion and molestation, and therefore a flagrant violation of the express terms of the treaty. You will therefore abstain from beginning the survey until the time stipulated in the treaty for the removal of the Indians has fully expired."

Troup replied in a strong, manly letter, assuring General Gaines that the same Indians who had made the treaty had given him full and free permission to begin the survey at once; that it would not be in any sense an intrusion or molestation; that this seeming opposition of some hostiles to it was mere bluster, and that they had doubtless been instigated to it by Crowell and other bad white men living among them. He further asserted that the State of Georgia had a perfect constitutional right to make the survey, and that the United States had no right whatever to interfere. Holding these opinions, the Governor refused to obey the mandate of General Gaines, and began the survey at once, as had been planned. The letter, though firm and positive, was couched in terms of the utmost courtesy. In reply, General Gaines wrote to Troup a long, weak, childish effusion, in which he berated the Governor soundly and read him a severe moral lecture. The whole tone of the letter was grossly insulting. Before mailing the original to the Governor he sent a copy of it to the Milledgeville *Patriot*, in whose columns it appeared, and there Troup first saw it. Troup at once wrote General Gaines: "On reading your letter, published in the Milledgeville *Patriot,* I lose no time in directing you to forbear further communication with this government."

General Gaines, thus cut off from direct communication with the Governor, vented his spite by publishing open letters in the newspapers criticizing and abusing the Governor fearfully. In conversation on the streets and in public places he was also very abusive, and declared that, if the Governor persisted in carrying on the survey, he would be guilty of treason, for which he would be arrested and thrown into prison. Governor Troup wrote to President Adams informing him fully of Gaines's outrageous conduct and demanding that he be arrested and court-martialed. This the President refused to do, but he did adminster a rebuke to Gaines and warned him to be more guarded in his utterances.

V. TROUP'S CONTROVERSY WITH THE FEDERAL GOVERNMENT.

Shortly after this altercation with General Gaines, Governor Troup received from the President of the United States, through the Secretary of War, a communication ordering Troup politely, but positively, not to begin the survey of the ceded lands until the time allowed in the treaty for the Indians to leave had fully expired.

Governor Troup replied to the President in a letter of the same tenor as that in which he had already written to General Gaines. Among other things, he said, in effect: "I deplore extremely the unfortunate controversy between Georgia and the United States; but I cannot consent, especially in an issue so grave as this, to compromise a principle for the sake of expediency. Such weakness, carried to its logical conclusion, would result in the speedy destruction of all State rights and in the ultimate destruction of the Union itself. The survey of the ceded lands will be begun in a few days."

But before the survey was actually started, Agents Gaines and Andrews had sent to the Federal Government their full reports on the whole state of Indian affairs in Georgia. They were voluminous documents, but the gist of it all was about this:

1st. Agent John Crowell is innocent of the charges against him.

2d. The murdered McIntosh was a traitor to his people.

3d. Governor Troup never received permission from the Indians to survey the ceded lands before the expiration of the time allowed them to leave.

4th. The Indian Spring Treaty was obtained by unfair and fraudulent means. It is bitterly opposed by forty-nine fiftieths of the Creek Nation, and it cannot be carried into effect without great risk of a horrible Indian war.

President Adams sent a copy of these reports to Governor Troup, stating that he would at once enter into a thorough investigation as to the validity of the Indian Spring Treaty. Pending this investigation Governor Troup decided to postpone the survey; for not the survey, but the much more serious matter of the validity of the treaty itself was now the issue.

President Adams summoned to Washington City a number of leading chiefs of the hostile party of the Creeks, and from their evidence, taken in a secret, or "executive," investigation, he decided that the Indian Spring Treaty had been obtained by unfair and illegal means, and should therefore be annulled. Also, acting under the authority given him by the Constitution of the United States, he proceeded to make a *new* treaty with the thirteen Indian chiefs present in Washington.

This new, or Washington, Treaty, did not differ greatly from the Indian Spring Treaty. The only points of difference were:

1st. By the Washington Treaty the Indians were

allowed two full years to leave the ceded lands instead of only a year and a half, as stipulated in the Indian Spring Treaty.

2d. By the Washington Treaty a considerable section of country contained in the cession of the Indian Spring Treaty was given back to the Indians.

Take a map of Georgia, draw a line from the little town of Roswell on the Chattahoochee River due west to the Alabama boundary. The triangle of country bounded on the north by this line, on the east and south by the Chattahoochee River from Roswell down to West Point, and on the west by the Alabama boundary line, indicates about the section given back to the Indians by the Washington Treaty. It embraces several hundred thousand acres of land. In April, 1826, this new or Washington Treaty was ratified by the United States Senate, and the Indian Spring Treaty was thereby annulled.

Governor Troup was officially notified of all these proceedings, and in a polite communication President Adams said to him, in substance: "You must not begin the survey of the ceded lands until the expiration of the time allowed by the *new* treaty; and when the survey is made, the lines must be run according to the new, or Washington, Treaty, and not according to the

Indian Spring Treaty." Governor Troup, in reply, practically said: "The Indian Spring Treaty was perfectly fair, legal and constitutional. It was approved and confirmed by the President and the Senate of the United States. From that moment, the Indian titles were extinguished and the lands were transferred to the State of Georgia, as a vested right, and henceforth could not possibly be under the jurisdiction of the United States. The Washington Treaty is unconstitutional, and therefore null and void. The Indian Spring Treaty is valid, and the rights of Georgia demand that its terms be carried out. I shall see to it that it is carried out. I shall begin the survey of the ceded lands at once. I shall run the lines according to the Indian Spring Treaty, and *not* according to the Washington Treaty; and on the 26th day of September, 1826, we shall begin the actual occupancy of these lands, as allowed by the Indian Spring Treaty."

Up to this time, while a majority of the people of Georgia warmly approved the Governor's course, yet a respectable minority, composed largely of conservative, well-balanced men, thought that he was acting unwisely, and that he should yield as to the *time* of beginning the survey, rather than involve Georgia in a serious controversy with the United States; but now that the

United States had gone so far as to annul the treaty itself, well-nigh the whole people of Georgia rallied to Troup's support; and the State, throughout its length and breadth, rang with the popular cry, "Troup and the Treaty! Troup and the Treaty!"

True to his word, Troup at once began the survey of the ceded lands in the face of the President's order to the contrary. For a while everything went on peaceably and without any disturbance from the Indians, while President Adams, anxious not to go to extremities, quietly allowed it to proceed, but warned Troup to "let the lines be run according to the Washington Treaty and not according to the Indian Spring Treaty."

The survey began in the southern part of the ceded territory and progressed northward. Everything went smoothly until the surveyors reached the bend in the Chattahoochee River where the town of West Point now stands, and where the stream deflects sharply to the northeast. From this point the surveyors should, according to the *Washington Treaty,* have proceeded along the *east* side of the Chattahoochee; but instead of doing so, they continued straight northward along the Alabama boundary to the *west* of the Chattahoochee, according to the *Indian Spring Treaty.* Then the trouble began; for the Indians, holding to the

Washington Treaty, considered this as a hostile invasion of their domains. They raised a great howl and made violent threats. A band of them pounced down upon a party of surveyors, took their instruments away and drove them off. Little Prince and several other chiefs hastened to Washington City and made a furious protest to the United States Government, and called on the President for protection. President Adams ordered the officers of the Federal Court in Georgia to arrest and imprison any surveyors who should persist in invading the Indian domains, as defined by the Washington Treaty. Governor Troup retorted by ordering the State Courts to liberate by legal process any persons that might be so arrested. But this issue between the Federal Court and the State Court was never brought to a test, for no arrests were actually made.

VI. DECLARATION OF WAR.

On the 16th of February, 1827, a young man, Lieutenant J. R. Vinton, of the United States Army, arrived in Milledgeville from Washington City. He was dressed in citizen's clothes, and he had come on a *secret* mission from the President of the United States to the Governor of Georgia. Entering the executive office, he introduced himself and gave his rank and position; then, drawing a letter from the inside pocket of his coat, he handed it to Governor Troup. It was a communication from the President of the United States, through the Secretary of War, to the Governor of Georgia, announcing in unmistakable terms that if the Georgia surveyors did not cease from invading the Indian domains, as defined by the Treaty of Washington, the United States Government would use force of arms to protect the Indians in their rights. This was an *ultimatum,* or tentative declaration of war. Governor Troup's reply is the most remarkable communication ever sent by the Governor of a State to the President of the United States. While preserving perfectly the form of official courtesy, it was full of spirit, fire, and bold defiance, saying, among other things: "I give your threat the defiance that it merits. Understand distinctly that I will resist by force of arms to the utmost any military attack that the Government of the United States may make on the territory, the people or the sovereignty of Georgia; and all the preparations necessary to the performance of this

State House at Milledgeville.

duty, according to our limited means, will be made immediately. You who are constitutionally bound to protect us from invasion are yourselves the invaders. You have espoused the cause of savages against the rights of Georgia. From the first decisive act of hostility, you will be considered and treated as a public enemy. The argument is exhausted; Georgia will stand by her arms." To show that he meant what he said, Troup immediately ordered the different militia generals throughout the State to collect arms, provide depots of supplies, and have their commands ready to march at a moment's notice to the threatened frontier to repel any attempt of the United States forces to invade Georgia soil.

The controversy had now reached its crisis. Georgia was in open, armed rebellion against the United States! Intense excitement prevailed throughout the State. The people, almost to a man, enthusiastically approved Troup's course, and almost to a man perhaps they would have joined his army to fight any invading Federal forces. More than ever the State rang with the cry, "Troup and the Treaty! Troup and the Treaty!" A bloody civil war between Georgia and the United States seemed almost inevitable.

VII. "ALL'S WELL THAT ENDS WELL."

Happily, however, wiser counsels prevailed in

Washington. President Adams and the other Federal authorities were extremely anxious to avoid an armed conflict with Georgia. Therefore they had for weeks been carrying on secret negotiations with the disaffected Indians, trying to induce them, for a moneyed consideration, to transfer to the United States for the benefit of Georgia the tract of country in dispute between the Indian Spring Treaty and the Washington Treaty. It now seemed, quite suddenly, that these negotiations would almost certainly be successful. President Adams wrote to Governor Troup announcing the gratifying fact. The news followed quickly on the heels of the "declaration of war," and filled Troup's heart with joy. His reply to the President is one of the noblest of his noble letters. It breathes the spirit of purest and loftiest patriotism, and as a splendid expression of the "States' Rights" doctrine, it has never been surpassed. Pending the negotiations, he withdrew the surveyors from the field.

In November, 1827, it was announced that the negotiations had been completely successful. The Indians had agreed, for a moneyed consideration, to give up the disputed lands to the United States for the benefit of Georgia, and also to make no further objection to the immediate prosecution of the survey. In other words, they had agreed *to rescind the Washington Treaty and to abide by the Indian Spring Treaty* in its stead! The ease with which this concession was obtained seems to show conclusively that the hostiles never were seriously rebellious against the Indian Spring Treaty, and that there would have been no real trouble about the matter if it had been left to Georgia, as it should have been. Either the United States authorities had been greatly misled (as Troup all along had insisted) as to the real temper of the Indians, or else their actions had been governed by sheer obstinacy and a determination to have their own way.

The cause of war having now been entirely removed, the trouble between Georgia and the United States was quickly and amicably adjusted. The war cloud vanished, the drawn swords were sheathed, excitement rapidly subsided, and soon everything was serene and lovely. The long and heated controversy was over, and "States' Rights" had come out gloriously triumphant In a year or two all of the Creek Indians had moved from Georgia to Mississippi, and the vacated lands were quickly occupied by sturdy white settlers.

It is impossible for any fair-minded person to read Governor Troup's correspondence with the United States authorities during this controversy without being convinced that throughout the affair he was governed by no motive but the purest and most courageous patriotism, and that in the whole proceeding he was *right* and the United States was *wrong*. His messages and letters on the subject would fill a good-sized volume. They are masterpieces of English. In clearness, conciseness and force of expression, and in simple, unaffected eloquence they are unequaled by the official utterances of any other governor of Georgia.

VIII. LAST DAYS OF TROUP.

In the fall of 1827 Troup retired from the gubernatorial chair, a position which he had held for two terms (four years). Declining a number of banquets and ovations with which his admiring fellow-citizens in different towns in Georgia were anxious to honor him, he withdrew at once to his elegant country home "Valdosta," in what is now Laurens County. His earnest wish was to spend the rest of his life there in quiet and domestic tranquillity, but he was not permitted to do so.

One year later, in November, 1828, the Georgia Legislature, without giving him the slightest intimation of its intention, unanimously elected him United States Senator for the long term of six years. As soon as he heard the rumor that this would probably be done, he hastened as rapidly as possible from Laurens County to Milledgeville for the purpose of positively forbidding his nomination; but travel was slow in those days, and he reached Milledgeville just two hours after the election. Under the circumstances he felt that he ought not to refuse the office that had thus been thrust upon him. With unfeigned reluctance he went to Washington City and took his place in the United States Senate. Owing to bad health, in the form of a distressing throat trouble, he was unable to take any prominent part in the debates and discussions. After serving two or three years he resigned on account of his health, and again withdrew to his Laurens County plantation, where he spent the remaining twenty-odd years of his life in quiet retirement, though many efforts were made to drag him back into public life.

In April, 1856, at the age of seventy-three years, he died rather suddenly of hemorrhage of the lungs while on a visit to his Montgomery County plantation. He was buried in the family burying ground in the same county, and a handsome granite shaft was erected over his grave. Although he had been out of public life for so many years, the people had not forgotten him. He was still dear to their hearts, and all over Georgia impressive memorial services were held in his honor. Troup County was named for him.

He was one of the greatest men that Georgia ever produced. He will go down in history as Georgia's doughty champion of "States' Rights."

CHAPTER XVIII.

GEORGIA AND THE CHEROKEES.

I. EARLY RELATIONS.

The dealings of the State of Georgia with the Cherokee Indians is a subject replete with interest for the student of American history. It makes a peculiar and unique story. It is a case without a parallel. Volumes have been written on the subject, but these books are now out of print and are rarely if ever read. In the following condensed statement of the leading facts in the case the author hopes that he may help to rescue this remarkable story from the oblivion into which it seems likely to fall.

The Cherokees were a nation of Indians that had their homes in northern Georgia and in adjoining parts of Tennessee, North Carolina, and South Carolina. Compared with the Creeks, the Cherokees were a weak people, not nearly so numerous and not so fierce and warlike. Their nearest town or village was two hundred miles away from Savannah and vicinity, where Oglethorpe planted his first colonies. On account of this great separating distance there was, during the Colonial period, little intercourse between the Cherokees and the whites of Georgia; they were almost strangers to each other.

During the Revolutionary War the Cherokees, like the Creeks, espoused the cause of the British against the Americans; and in the campaigns in Georgia they took, under the leadership of the Tories, quite an active part against the Patriots. When the war was over they had, of course, to accept the fate of the conquered and submit to such terms as the victors might choose to impose. Accordingly, in May, 1783, at what was called the Treaty of Augusta, the Cherokees were required by Georgia to cede to her quite a large tract of their country lying about the head waters of the Oconee River, in the northeastern part of the State. The tract included the whole or parts of what are now Franklin, Hart, Banks, Jackson, Hall and Madison counties. After this treaty, for the next thirty-five or forty years the Cherokees were, in the main, left alone by the whites of Georgia.

During all these years Georgia was acquiring from the Creek Indians by a successive series of treaties (as will be fully shown in the next chapter) great strips of territory throughout middle, west, and south Georgia; and as each strip was obtained, it was rapidly settled up by the whites. This Creek country was nearly all well adapted to the cultivation of cotton, which was then the great industry, and we might say the only money-making industry, in Georgia; hence these lands were much sought after. The people at that time cared little for lands that would not produce cotton. The lands of north Georgia were not suited to this purpose; and that is why during all these years, while the Creek Indians were being pushed out of middle, west and south Georgia by the resistless hand of the white man, the Cherokees were left unmolested in their beautiful mountain valleys in the northern part of the State.

From 1802 to 1823 the United States Government, of its own motion, and in pursuance of a general policy that it had adopted in regard to the Indian race, made repeated efforts to persuade the whole Cherokee Nation, not only those that lived in Georgia, but in other states, to remove to a rich reservation set aside for them beyond the Mississippi River. They were offered liberal inducements to make this removal, but the efforts of the Government were almost entirely futile. Several hundreds did move to the West, but the bulk of the nation clung persistently to their Eastern homes. Those that lived in Georgia were especially firm in their determination not to move.

In the year 1819 the United States Government

purchased from the Cherokees, for the benefit of the State of Georgia, by fair and legal treaty, quite a large tract of country in the northeastern part of the State and lying adjacent to the tract that had been ceded by the treaty of 1783, already mentioned. The Cherokees now occupied only the northwestern portion of Georgia, embracing about one-sixth of the entire State.

In a general way it may be said that from 1783 to 1824 the Cherokees were unmolested by the Georgians.

II. CIVILIZING OF THE CHEROKEES.

During these long years of tranquillity great changes were being wrought in the social and political condition of the Cherokees. Many white men, mostly Scotch, or Scotch-Irish, were accustomed as licensed Indian traders to go to and fro in the nation plying their vocation. A number of them married dusky damsels of the race, the daughters of chiefs and head men, and settled down in the Indian country. They were shrewd fellows, with a keen eye to business. They established themselves on the choicest lands in the rich valleys, and by industry, thrift, and cunning accumulated fortunes. From these mixed marriages there sprang, of course, numerous half-breeds, and in the next generation a number of these became chiefs of the principal tribes of the Cherokees. By sheer force of superior intellect, character, and intelligence, these half-breed chiefs gained complete ascendency over the nation and exercised a dominating influence in all of its affairs. Some of the most noted of these chiefs were John Ross, Major Ridge, and his son, John Ridge, Elias Boudinot, Charles Vann, George Waters, and John Gunter. There were also a number of others.

Major Ridge.

These mixed-breed leaders were generally men of education and force of character. They were energetic and enterprising, and very ambitious for the elevation of their race. They threw open the Cherokee Nation to civilizing influences. Under their encouragement Christian missionaries, most of them from the Northern States, swarmed into the country and went up and

John Ridge.

down in the land preaching the gospel with great zeal. Nearly all of the Cherokees in Georgia were converted to Christianity, such conversion as it was. Numerous churches were built and were well attended and supported. Schoolmasters were imported, and a number of schools were established. A Cherokee alphabet was invented, and books were printed in the language. A newspaper devoted entirely to the interests of the nation was published at the capital, New Echota. Several quite large towns arose in the valleys. Agriculture was pursued with steadiness, intelligence and success. Many of the half-breed chiefs and a number of white men who had married Indian women ("squaw-men" as they were called) owned large, well-conducted plantations and gangs of negro slaves. Indeed, nearly all of the wealth and practically the whole political power of the nation were in the hands of these two classes of men. On account of their wealth and comfortable homes, they were indeed loath to leave Georgia. The masses of the nation seem to have been a dull, inert, poverty-stricken people, living in a half-civilized state which, though it may have been better, was not nearly so interesting as out-and-out savagery. Still to a man they were devotedly attached to their Georgia homes, and to a man they were firmly resolved not to budge a peg nor to cede another foot of land to the whites.

III. POLITICAL STATUS OF THE CHEROKEES.

As the Cherokees advanced in civilization they grew more and more ambitious, aggressive and arrogant in regard to their political standing. In 1823, when President Monroe once more made an earnest effort to persuade them to move west, they thus replied: "It is the fixed and unalterable determination of this nation never again to cede one foot of our land. The Cherokees are not foreigners, but the original inhabitants of America; and they now stand on their own territory, and they will not recognize the sovereignty of any state within the limits of their territory." You may be sure that this was not the language of any simple Indian, but of the educated, sophisticated half-breed chiefs. He who runs may read the significance of the utterance. It was tantamount to saying: "We, the Cherokees, are here in Georgia to stay. We claim absolute ownership of the lands and absolute sovereignty within the territory which we now occupy, and we will brook no interference from any other power. The State of Georgia can exercise no sort of authority over us, nor has it any claim to our lands." Strange to say, the United States, under the administration of President

Monroe and afterwards of President Adams, upheld the Cherokees in this claim of absolute, fee simple ownership of the lands and of independent sovereignty. Georgia protested vigorously against it, urging that the State of Georgia alone had the sole right to the lands, and denying that the Indians had a right to refuse when a cession was demanded on fair and reasonable terms. President Monroe, speaking for the United States Government, replied: "We have done our best to persuade the Cherokees, by the offer of liberal terms, to cede their lands to the State of Georgia, but we have entirely failed to get their consent. We have no authority and are under no obligation to use force or compulsion to accomplish this result." Here the matter was dropped for two or three years. During this time the attention of Georgia was absorbed in acquiring from the Creek Indians, by the famous Treaty of Indian Spring (a full account of which was given in the last chapter), the last remaining strip of their Georgia lands.

During these two or three years the Cherokees were allowed to go their own pace, and they went it in a gallop. In July, 1827, the Cherokees held a national constitutional convention at their capital, New Echota, situated in what is now Gordon County, near the present town of Calhoun. They framed and adopted an elaborate constitution, modeled largely after the Constitution of the United States. It asserted that the Cherokee Indians constituted one of the sovereign and independent nations of the earth, having complete jurisdiction over its territory, to the exclusion of any other state. It provided for a representative system of government much like that of the United States. It is needless to say that the making of this constitution was wholly the work of the educated mixed-breed chiefs. All arrangements were made for organizing the government under this constitution and for putting its provisions into full operation.

In November, 1827, Georgia completed her final deal with the Creek Indians, and the last red man of that great nation left the State forever and journeyed towards the setting sun. The only Indians now left in Georgia were the Cherokees, who occupied about one-sixth of the entire State, the most beautiful and in many particulars the choicest part. To these Georgia now turned her attention, with the full determination that they, too, must be required to leave the State forever and yield their lands to the whites. On the other hand, the Cherokees were, to a man, equally as determined not to budge a peg.

The Cherokees' contention was: "We are an independent and sovereign nation, owing neither allegiance nor obedience to any other power on earth. The lands that we occupy belong to us by the most absolute and unquestionable title known to man. We shall never surrender nor leave them. We are here to stay." The Georgians' contention was: "The lands now held by the Cherokees belong solely to the State of Georgia. The Indians are only tenants at will; they have been allowed to occupy these lands thus long only by sufferance. They must now be required to surrender these lands to the State of Georgia, by peaceful means if possible, by force if necessary. The Cherokees must go." Plainly a battle royal between these two powers was inevitable and imminent. In the winter of 1828 Georgia struck the first blow, and the contest was on!

IV. GEORGIA AND THE CHEROKEES LOCK HORNS.

In December, 1828, the Georgia Legislature passed a bill enacting that the Cherokee country should be put under the jurisdiction of the laws of Georgia. The act was passed on the ground that, as the Cherokee country was part and parcel of the State of Georgia, it should be governed by the laws of Georgia. The real object of Georgia in passing this act was to move the Cherokees to leave the State, for it was supposed that when they were convinced that they would not be allowed self-government in Georgia, they would be much more willing to cede their lands to the whites and move away. In order to give them plenty of time to make up their minds to do this, the Act was not to go into effect until June 1, 1830.

Of course, the effect of this Act was to abolish the Cherokee government and to render null and void the constitution that the nation had so recently made. The Cherokees felt deeply outraged at the Act, the purpose of which was to destroy their government, to snuff out their constitution like a candle, and to render their boasted sovereignty utterly meaningless. But instead of resenting the wrong in savage fashion, instead of defending their rights with the tomahawk, knife and rifle, as Indians are wont to do, they resorted to the more civilized but tamer method of appealing to the courts. They determined at the first opportunity to test the validity of the Act of the Georgia Legislature before the Supreme Court of the United States. They had good reason to feel assured that the Federal tribunal would decide the case in their favor.

An opportunity to test the matter soon occurred. In the summer of 1830, very soon after Georgia's obnoxious act of jurisdiction had gone into effect, a halfbreed Cherokee by the name of George Tassel committed murder in the Cherokee country. He was arraigned before the Georgia State Superior Court then sitting in Hall County, and was duly tried, found guilty and sentenced to be hanged. His attorneys appealed the case to the United States Supreme Court, asking that the verdict be set aside, on the ground that the act of the Legislature giving the State of Georgia jurisdiction over the Cherokee country was a violation of the Federal Constitution, and was therefore null and void. The case, George Tassel *vs.* the State of Georgia, was duly entered on the Supreme Court docket. Governor Gilmer was officially notified of the action, and was instructed to appear before the court for Georgia as defendant in the case. The Governor replied with spirit that the United States Supreme Court had no jurisdiction in the case, and that the State of Georgia would scorn to compromise itself by appearing before that tribunal as defendant in the case. The Governor knew that it was a foregone conclusion that the court would

Governor George M. Gilmer.

decide the case against Georgia and in favor of the Cherokees. To prevent this he resorted to the extraordinary measure of dispatching a special messenger to the sheriff of Hall County, with instructions to hang George Tassel immediately, before his case could be reached on the Supreme Court docket. The Sheriff obeyed the order promptly, so poor George Tassel was precipitately hanged while his case was pending in the Federal Supreme Court. Thus ended the case, an end which, we must admit, was brought about by a rather high-handed measure on the part of the State of Georgia. Georgia's action was severely criticized in the halls of Congress; it was furiously condemned by the Cherokees themselves, and it was violently censured by a large part of the people in the North. But these protests and howlings had no effect on Georgia, for she went sturdily ahead executing her laws over the Cherokee country. The Cherokees resented it bitterly in their hearts, but they used no force of arms to stop it, and they struck no blow from the shoulder out. They were determined at the first opportunity to appeal again to the Supreme Court of the United States. They hoped that that high tribunal might be the means of freeing them from the grasp of Georgia, and of confirming them in the fee simple possession of their lands.

V. GEORGIA AND THE GOLD DIGGERS.

In the year 1829 gold in moderate quantities was discovered in the Cherokee country, especially in that section which is now included in Lumpkin, Gilmer and Union counties. As the news spread through Georgia and the neighboring states it caused much excitement, and there was an immediate rush of adventurers to the Cherokee country. By the summer of 1830 there were upwards of three thousand of these interlopers in the alleged gold regions. They did not find any great quantity of gold, but enough perhaps to pay them better than ordinary labor would have done, and the free and easy life was exactly to their liking. During the day they would dig and wash for gold after the crudest methods, and would spend the greater part of the night in drinking, carousing, gambling and fighting. In intruding on the Indian lands without leave, license or title from any one, they were violating the laws of three governments—the law of the Cherokees, the law of the United States and the law of Georgia. The Cherokees were too weak or too spiritless to drive them away, although they must have been a sore annoyance to them; the United States was too indifferent to undertake it; so the task was left to Georgia. Governor Gilmer, by instructions from the State Legislature, sent numerous proclamations to the intruders to leave on pain of severe punishment, but they gave no heed to these orders. Indeed, the Governor's "paper bullets," as they were called, got to be the subject of ridicule, not only among the gold diggers themselves, but throughout Georgia. Convinced at length that he would have to use strong measures, the Governor braced himself manfully to the job. He sent into the region a company of seventy-five Georgia soldiers, under the command of Major Wager, of the United States army, with orders to oust the intruders at any cost. The soldiers broke up the miners' camps, destroyed their implements, and escorted many of them at the point of the bayonet across the border with fierce warnings never to return. Thus, in the course of two or three months the lawless gangs were cleared out of the Indian country. It is not recorded that the Cherokees urged any objection to this exercise of Georgia's authority in their country.

In December, 1830, the Legislature passed a law that no white person should reside in the Cherokee country without a special license from the Governor of Georgia. The Governor was empowered to grant such licenses, in his discretion, to those who would take an oath to support and defend the Constitution and laws of Georgia, and to demean themselves in all ways as loyal and faithful citizens of the State. Persons violating this law would be guilty of a high misdemeanor, the penalty for which should be not less than four years' imprisonment in the State Penitentiary. This law, though aimed primarily at the intruding gold diggers, was also intended for another class of persons very different from the gold seekers. These were the Christian missionaries, who for a number of years had been preaching the gospel to the Cherokees. These men were all from the North, sent thither by the rich missionary societies and organizations of that section. Not content with discharging their high function of preaching Christ and Him crucified, they began to take a part in Indian politics. They sympathized ardently with the Cherokees in their struggles with Georgia, and they expressed their views and feelings on the subject without restraint. They openly and publicly condemned the action of Georgia in extending her jurisdiction over the Cherokee country, and they encouraged the Indians in their obstinate and unwise attitude toward the whites. To exclude such a class, the Legislature, in large measure, enacted the above-mentioned law.

VI. THE CHEROKEE NATION VS. THE STATE OF GEORGIA.

Early in the year 1831, John Ross, head chief of the Cherokees, acting for the nation, brought suit in the

United States Supreme Court against the State of Georgia. The suit was in the form of a bill of injunction praying the court to restrain the State of Georgia from executing its laws in the Cherokee country, on the ground that the Act of the Legislature extending the jurisdiction of Georgia over this country was a violation of the Constitution of the United States, and therefore null and void.

The first difficulty with which Ross met was to get a proper plaintiff for the suit. To bring a suit like this before the Supreme Court the plaintiff must be either some individual person or some state in the Union or some foreign state. No favorable personal or individual case on which a suit might be based had occurred since the precipitate hanging of poor George Tassel, and John Ross was too impatient to wait for another to occur. The Cherokee Nation was not a "state in the Union"; so, in order to bring suit, there was nothing to do but to claim that it was a "foreign state," using the word "foreign" in its purely political sense, of course. Ross carefully consulted some of the most eminent jurists in America on this point, and he was assured by them that the Cherokee Nation was "a foreign state" within the meaning of the Federal Constitution, and therefore a competent plaintiff in the proposed suit. So the case was duly entered on the Supreme Court docket under the caption "The Cherokee Nation *vs.* the State of Georgia." The Cherokees employed William Wirt, one of the most eminent and eloquent lawyers in America, at a fee of twenty thousand dollars, to represent their case. Mr. Wirt associated himself with Mr. Sergeant, another lawyer of great ability. The Governor of Georgia was cited to appear as defendant in the suit, but, as in the case of George Tassel, he scornfully declined, stating that the Federal Court had, under the Constitution, no jurisdiction in the matter.

The case came up for trial in January, 1831. Messrs. Wirt and Sergeant made able and exhaustive arguments in behalf of the Cherokees. Their speeches were masterpieces of eloquence. No counsel appeared for Georgia, as the State had purposely ignored the suit. Chief Justice John Marshall, speaking for a majority of the court, rendered the decision. The gist of it was this: "It has been established to the satisfaction of this court that the Cherokees are an independent and sovereign state, subject to the authority and laws of no other state, nation or power on earth; but they are a sovereign state under peculiar and unique conditions. They are certainly not a state in the United States; neither are they, in the opinion of this court, 'a foreign state' within the meaning of the Federal Constitution. Not being 'a foreign state,' they cannot be competent plaintiffs in this case; hence the injunction asked is denied." The decision was seemingly a triumph for Georgia, but, as any one who would read between the lines might see, it was only a temporary triumph. It was almost as if the Chief Justice had said: "In assuming jurisdiction over the Cherokee country, the State of Georgia has plainly violated the Constitution of the United States. If a suit involving the same principles as are contained in this case should be brought by a competent plaintiff, by some person or individual, for instance, the decision of the court would be for the plaintiff and against the State of Georgia." So there was nothing for the Cherokees

John Marshall.

to do but to wait for some favorable personal case to occur. Such a case did occur very soon. It was a notable and striking case, and exactly suited to the purpose of the Cherokees.

VII. WORCESTER AND BUTLER VS. THE STATE OF GEORGIA.

The Act of the State Legislature, passed in 1828, forbidding any white persons except those specially licensed by the Governor to reside in the Cherokee country, went into effect on June 1, 1830. A small number of persons openly defied this law by refusing either to leave the territory or to accept the alternative of taking the required oath of allegiance to the State of Georgia in order to secure license to continue to reside there. Among these were three Northern missionaries—Rev. Samuel A. Worcester, Rev. Elizur Butler and Rev. James Trott. Governor Gilmer was sincerely anxious not to arrest these preachers; so he wrote them a kindly note earnestly urging them to obey the law, and warning them that if they still refused, they would have to suffer the consequences. Since they did not heed the warning of the Governor, they and eight other persons were arrested and tried by the Georgia Superior Court, and were found guilty and sentenced to four years' imprisonment in the State Penitentiary at Milledgeville. At the penitentiary gates a proposition was read to them

Georgia and the Cherokees.

from the Governor offering to set them free at this last moment if they would agree to obey the law. Nine of them accepted the offer and were turned loose, but Revs. Worcester and Butler refused to yield. The prison doors closed behind them, and they were put to hard labor like common criminals. Their deed of self-sacrificing heroism was tremendously applauded by their friends at the North. The principal object of Messrs. Worcester and Butler in accepting imprisonment was to furnish the Cherokee Nation with a suitable test case to carry to the Supreme Court. The case was accordingly appealed to that court under the caption "Worcester and Butler *vs.* the State of Georgia." Of course, the main object of this suit was not to secure the release of Worcester and Butler, but to get from the Supreme Court of the United States a declaration that the Act of the Georgia Legislature in extending the jurisdiction of the State over the Cherokee country was a violation of the Federal Constitution, and therefore null and void. Messrs. Wirt and Sergeant were again retained as counsel by the Cherokee Nation. Georgia again, now for the third time, refused to appear as defendant. The line of argument for the plaintiffs was necessarily much the same as had been presented in the case of "The Cherokee Nation *vs.* the State of Georgia."

As every one expected, the decision of the court was in favor of the plaintiffs and against the State of Georgia. Chief Justice Marshall, in delivering the decision, went into quite an extensive historical argument; but the main point of it was that the Cherokee Indians were an independent and sovereign nation, and that no other state, people or power had any right to interfere with their government or to dispossess them of their lands; that the Act of the Georgia Legislature extending the jurisdiction of the State of Georgia over the Cherokee country was a violation of the Constitution of the United States, and was consequently null and void; and that, therefore, Messrs. Worcester and Butler, who had been convicted under the operation of this Act, had been illegally convicted, and were now illegally imprisoned and should be released.

The Cherokees were overjoyed when they heard of this decision. They believed it would lead to securing them in the permanent possession of their lands, and in absolute sovereignty in their own territory. The news also gladdened the hearts of Messrs. Worcester and Butler in the penitentiary; for they supposed, of course, that their prison doors would now fly open and that they would walk forth free men, to be lionized and glorified by the Cherokee Nation, and by their hosts of admiring friends in the North. But both Indians and martyr preachers were doomed to bitter disappointment. Andrew Jackson was now President of the United States, and his views about dealing with the Indians were the reverse of those of his two immediate predecessors, Monroe and Adams. He had for years been known as a strong advocate of clearing the Indians out of the way of the white man and removing them to Western reservations, by peaceful means if possible, by force if necessary. Georgia could count on his helping her, as far as he could, in getting rid of the Cherokees. Now, in this crisis, he helped her with a daring hand. He simply refused to execute the judgment of the Supreme Court. When approached on the subject by friends of the Cherokees, he curtly replied: "John Marshall has pronounced the judgment; now let him execute it!" But, of course, John Marshall had no power to execute it. So this famous decision of the Supreme Court of the United States amounted practically to nothing. Georgia went steadily ahead executing her government in the

President Jackson.

Cherokee country, and Revs. Worcester and Butler still languished in the penitentiary at Milledgeville.

A year later Governor Lumpkin, who had succeeded Governor Gilmer, notified the two prisoners that if they would comply with the same conditions that had been offered them as they stood at the penitentiary gates sixteen months before, and which they had then rejected, he would pardon them. Concluding that their martyrdom had now been sufficient, they accepted the conditions and were pardoned and set free. For this gracious act Governor Lumpkin was severely criticized by many people in Georgia.

Governor Wilson Lumpkin.

VIII. GEORGIA'S AGGRESSIONS.

In 1831 the Georgia Legislature instructed the Governor to have the whole of the Cherokee country surveyed and marked off into counties. Of course the Indians understood that this was only a preliminary step towards an attempt to dispossess them of their lands. They uttered bitter protests and gnashed their teeth in rage, but they made no warlike movements to prevent the enforcement of the Georgia law. They offered no act of violence to the parties of Georgia surveyors, who went quietly through the country prosecuting their work. In the course of a year the survey was completed and the territory was divided into ten new Georgia counties. The State of Georgia, by advice of Governor Lumpkin, paused here for a while before taking another aggressive step, hoping that the Cherokees would now come to their senses and make a treaty ceding their lands to the whites. President Jackson made an earnest effort to persuade them to do so, but without success, though some of the leading half-breed chiefs did show signs of yielding to the inevitable and of coming to terms.

In the latter part of 1832 Georgia took another aggressive step. The Legislature passed an act instructing the Governor to distribute the lands of the Cherokee country among the people of Georgia by the land lottery system.* It was a tedious process, but in the course of a year it was finished, and the lands of the Cherokees were distributed among the citizens of Georgia. The Indians, however, were not to be ousted for the present. A law was passed allowing the whites to move and settle on the unoccupied lands, of which there were great

*This system is fully described in Section III of the next chapter.

quantities; but they were forbidden by stringent regulations to intrude on those in actual possession of the Indians, or to molest them in any way in their homes. Many whites did move in and establish themselves on the vacant lands in the rich valleys. They must have been odious neighbors to the Indians, but the poor creatures raised no hand of violence against them. This meek behavior, so contrary to the true Indian character, shows how spirit-broken the Cherokees must have been.

In all these procedures Georgia was openly violating the Constitution of the United States as interpreted by the Supreme Court in its recent decision; but her action was countenanced, not to say encouraged, by President Andrew Jackson, who was in hearty sympathy with the Georgians in their desire to get the Cherokees out of the State. He sincerely believed that it would be best for the Indians, as well as the whites; and his strong common sense taught him that it was a case in which it would not do to be too squeamish in regard to the technicalities of the law.

IX. TREATY FACTIONS.

By this time a number of leading chiefs of the Cherokees had come to realize the utter hopelessness of their struggle with Georgia, and were in favor of making a treaty with the Federal Government looking to the cession of their lands and removal to the western reservations; but a large majority of the nation, under the leadership of other chiefs, were as violently opposed as ever to considering any such proposition. Thus the nation became divided into two factions, the treaty party and the anti-treaty party.

In February, 1835, rival delegations from these two factions visited Washington City for the purpose of conferring with the United States Government. John Ridge headed the treaty delegation and John Ross headed the anti-treaty delegation. Ross was given the first hearing. He intimated that the Cherokee Nation might agree to cede their lands and move west on certain specified terms and conditions; but these "terms and conditions" were so thoroughly and absurdly unreasonable that the United States Government refused to consider them for a moment, so Ross was politely dismissed. John Ridge was then heard. He and his fellow delegates remained some days in Washington, and agreed with the United States commissioners upon a treaty that was satisfactory to both parties, but according to Indian law this treaty would have to be accepted by the whole Cherokee Nation before it could become effective. Through the influence of Ross and other chiefs it was rejected by the overwhelming sentiment of the nation; so all of these negotiations came to naught. Many were the maneuverings, contentions, charges and counter charges of the two factions during the next few months. The anti-treaty party grew turbulent. Several leading men of the treaty party were murdered or assassinated on account of the stand they had taken. The whites living in the Cherokee country became alarmed for their own safety, and called on Georgia for help against the threatened danger. Georgia sent a body of troops, known as the Georgia Guard, into the country to protect the whites and friendly Indians. But the hostiles offered no open acts of violence and no armed resistance. They seemed to have lost entirely their old fighting spirit. But still they remained unmoved in their determination to stay in Georgia.

There was but one more step left for Georgia to take. In the fall of 1835 she said in effect to the Federal Government: "If you do not use the power vested in you by the Constitution and laws of the United States and clear these Indians out of our State, as it is your bounden duty to do, we will do it ourselves, even if it has to be done at the point of the bayonet!" The Federal Government knew that Georgia meant what she said. The situation had reached its crisis. Something must be done, and that speedily. Andrew Jackson, President of the United States, saw but one way out of the difficulty, and with characteristic independence he adopted that way, although he knew it was open to severe criticism.

Under the Constitution of the United States only the Federal Government can make treaties with Indians. In the latter part of 1835, Jackson, as Chief Executive of the Federal Government, called on all the chiefs of the Cherokee Nation to meet at their capital, New Echota, for the purpose of making a treaty. A Mr. Schermerhorn was sent as commissioner to represent the Federal Government. The convention assembled at New Echota on the 21st of December, 1835. Only the chiefs of the treaty party, a comparatively small number, attended the meeting; the chiefs of the anti-treaty party purposely absented themselves. Nevertheless, the commissioner went ahead and made a treaty with those that were present, as he had been instructed to do. The terms of the treaty were as follows:

1. The Cherokees were to surrender all of their lands east of the Mississippi River, and were to receive from the Federal Government in lieu thereof 7,000,000 acres of land in the Indian Territory, whither the whole Cherokee Nation was to remove within two years from the date of the treaty.

2. They were to be paid $5,000,000 in money for the improvements they had made on the ceded lands.

3. All the expense of their removal to the Indian Territory and a full year's support after they reached there was to be borne by the United States Government.

4. The Indian Territory was never to be annexed to any other state, nor was any other state ever to exercise any authority over it. The Indians were to be guaranteed the perpetual possession of the lands within their territorial limits to the exclusion of all white persons.

5. The United States was to afford the Indians protection from all intrusion by the whites and against all foreign and domestic enemies.

The treaty was agreed to and signed by all the chiefs present at the meeting. Two months later it was duly confirmed by the United States Senate and received the signature of the President of the United States. Against these proceedings John Ross, head chief of the Cherokees, entered a strong protest, but to no avail.

X. EXPULSION OF THE CHEROKEES.

This Treaty of New Echota was undoubtedly illegal, for it was agreed to by only a handful of chiefs. More than nine-tenths of the Cherokee Nation were avowedly and bitterly opposed to it. But the form of the law had been complied with, and Georgia was determined that the treaty should be rigidly enforced. In this the State was sustained by Andrew Jackson, President of the United States, who with his strong common sense saw that this was the best possible way to settle the Cherokee trouble, which for years had been vexing Georgia and the Federal Government and which was growing every day more and more serious.

According to the terms of the treaty, the Indians were allowed two years to leave, and on the 24th of May, 1838, the State of Georgia was to take possession of the ceded territory. As the time approached and the Indians made no motion to leave, the Secretary of War sent a confidential agent into the country to inquire into the state of affairs. The agent reported back to Washington that practically the whole Cherokee Nation still repudiated the treaty and would positively refuse to abide by it, and that the only possible way to make them move would be at the point of the bayonet.

Throughout this long struggle much public sympathy had been manifested for the Cherokees in nearly all parts of the United States. This sentiment now became stronger than ever. In the halls of Congress such men as Webster, Clay and Calhoun vigorously condemned the

New Echota Treaty, which they declared to be grossly illegal and fraudulent. The people of the North, and especially of New England, poured forth violent tirades of abuse on the Georgians, and, with characteristic meddlesomeness, sent petition after petition to Washington asking Congress to use the United States armies to protect the Cherokees in their rights. Martin Van Buren, who was now President, became so alarmed at this torrent of remonstrance that he urged Governor Gilmer (who after four years' retirement was again in the gubernatorial chair) to allow the Indians two years more; but high-spirited Gilmer very positively and very wisely declined, saying: "They must leave immediately; and if the Federal Government refuses to perform its duty and make them move, we will do it ourselves."

President Van Buren.

Van Buren prudently decided to let things take their course. General Winfield Scott, of the United States army, was sent from Washington to the Cherokee country to superintend the removal. On the 10th day of May he issued a proclamation that every Cherokee man, woman, and child must be on the way to the West within a month; but not an Indian budged. General Scott called on Georgia for two regiments of troops; Georgia responded promptly, for, expecting just such a call, she had the men ready. By the 28th of May sixteen hundred soldiers, composing two regiments, were assembled at New Echota, under the command of General Floyd, of the United States army. Even at this late date John Ross, indefatigable champion of the Cherokees, made a final effort to save his people from expulsion from their homes. He hurried to Washington City, entered a protest, and endeavored to get a stay of proceedings so that he might bring the matter once more before the Supreme Court, but all of no avail. The long struggle was over, and for the poor Cherokees the bitter end had come.

General Winfield Scott.

The two regiments were divided into companies, and these companies were sent to different stations conveniently distributed through the Cherokee country. Then the companies were divided into squads, which marched from home to home of the Cherokees, as they lay widely scattered over valley and hill, and arresting all the Indian families, took them to appointed forts or camps, where the Indians were put into pens, and corralled in great numbers like cattle. It was a heart-rending business, but it was all done in as gentle and as kind a way as possible under the circumstances. The poor Indians would not believe they were leaving their homes forever. They knew that their great chief, John Ross, had gone to Washington in their behalf; and firmly believing that he would succeed, they expected, after being detained a short time, to be allowed to return to their humble homes which they loved so dearly. The arresting soldiers had not the heart to disabuse them of this delusion.

By the middle of June, or a little later, the whole nation was gathered into the various camps and forts, and the journey to Indian Territory, nearly seven hundred miles away, was immediately begun. More than fourteen thousand Cherokee Indians were thus expelled, at the point of the bayonet, from Georgia and contiguous parts of Tennessee and the Carolinas. Their long overland journey occupied four months, and was necessarily full of hardships. Though everything possible was done to lessen their sufferings, it is said that four thousand of the poor wretches died on the route. It was the most pitiful exodus that ever occurred on the American continent. By the 1st of December, 1838, the last Cherokee Indian had left the State of Georgia.

Georgia was much censured in nearly all parts of the United States, and especially by the people of the North, for her conduct towards the Cherokees; but her treatment of them was virtually the same as had been practiced by every state in the Union towards the Indian race. For despite the theories of sentimentalists and the high-sounding opinions of Supreme Court judges, the whites had always acted on the principle that the lands of America belonged to them, and that Indians were only "tenants at will," to be cleared out whenever they got in the white man's way. Self-righteous New England herself, whose fanatical howling against the Georgians had been specially violent and offensive, had acted on precisely this same principle years before; only she got rid of *her* Indians by simply *exterminating* them in heartless wars, instead of by the slow, patient, humane method pursued by Georgia towards the Cherokees.

Throughout this long contention sentimentalism and the strict letter of the Constitution and laws of the United States were all on the side of the Cherokees, but good sense, practical wisdom and real humanity were all on the side of Georgia. The idea that a tribe of Indians should have been allowed to keep perpetual possession of a large portion of the best part of the State of Georgia as an absolutely independent and sovereign power in the very midst of the white man's civilization was absurd. It would have proven a political and social impossibility. It must be borne in mind that these lands were not taken away from the Indians, but were purchased from them. They were forced to sell, it is true; but they were paid a good, fair, full price, as any one who will read the terms of the New Echota Treaty can plainly see.

XI. ASSASSINATION OF THE TREATY CHIEFS.

On the 22d of June, 1839, three of the most prominent chiefs of the Cherokees, Major Ridge, Elias Boudinot and John Ridge, all mixed-breeds and among the most intelligent men of the nation, were cruelly assassinated in the Indian Territory, where they were just establishing themselves in their new homes. Major Ridge was shot dead from his horse in the public road by parties lying in ambush. At almost the same hour Elias Boudinot, twenty miles away, was called from a new house that he was building by several men, who pretended that they wished to speak to him on business. Unsuspecting, he stepped aside with them, and was instantly clubbed to death, the assassins vanishing in the near-by woods. On the night of that same day, John Ridge, thirty miles in another direction, was dragged from his bed and literally cut to pieces with knives. These three men had been the leaders of the treaty party in Georgia, and were therefore very odious to the anti-treaty party. That they were murdered out of pure vengeance by members of the anti-treaty party there has never been the slightest doubt. Thus the civilized and Christianized Cherokees, who through all their persecutions in Georgia had never struck one manly blow from the shoulder out in defense of their rights, showed by these cowardly assassinations that the savage instinct, on its baser side, was still strong in them.

CHAPTER XIX.

EXPANSION OF GEORGIA.

I. GEORGIA'S CONDITION AT THE CLOSE OF THE REVOLUTION.

When the Revolutionary War closed in 1782, the civilized part of Georgia was confined to a long, narrow strip extending along the west side of the Savannah River and along the Atlantic Coast nearly down to Florida. This strip embraced scarcely more than one-eighth the present area of Georgia. It was rather thinly populated by about 35,000 inhabitants—19,000 whites and 16,000 negroes. These people were in a deplorable condition. For more than two years they had been subjected to the havoc and horrors of what had been practically a civil war of the worst kind, a war in which Patriots and Tories, brother Georgians, next-door neighbors, fought each other with bitter hatred and savage cruelty. Murder, theft, wholesale destruction of property, and nearly all conceivable atrocities had characterized this barbarous warfare, and it had left the country ruined. Every family and every individual in the region had suffered severely. Homes had been burned, farms devastated, families scattered, and communities broken up. Savannah and Augusta, the two largest towns, were nearly destroyed. The people were poverty-stricken. There was very little money. Agriculture was badly crippled and commerce was almost suspended.

The morals of the people, too, had suffered seriously. Men had become in a measure brutalized by the hardening experiences through which they had passed. Human life was counted cheap; drunkenness, gambling and profanity were very prevalent; quarreling, fighting and duels were frequent; yet these people were not essentially bad. From the moralist's standpoint there was much wickedness among them, but there was little real depravity, little innate meanness and baseness. Theirs were the sins of passion, provoked by temporary conditions, not the sins of falsehood, which always indicate something radically wrong in character. They got drunk, gambled and swore, quarreled and fought; but they abhorred lying, cheating, deceit, sordid selfishness and all manner of base and dishonorable conduct. The wonderful spirit and energy with which these people set about

The Walton-Hall-Gwinnett Monument at Augusta.

rebuilding their ruined fortunes show that they possessed in high degree the qualities of a sterling and heroic manhood. Their standard of character was high, and there were among them a number of really great men—men who would have been considered great in any age and in any civilized country in the world.

Soon after the war was over the property of all the Georgia Loyalists, or Tories, who had been active against the Americans was confiscated and sold, and the money was put into the State Treasury. It amounted to quite a large sum, and probably saved the State from bankruptcy. Most of the Tories, knowing that they were held in great odium and would probably be bitterly persecuted, left the State immediately after the Revolutionary War. It was, on all accounts, a happy riddance. Some of these Tories were good, high-toned, honorable men; but many of them, especially of the commoner classes, were a base set. Those that remained in Georgia were ill treated by the Patriots and could scarcely get justice in the law courts.

By the side of the civilized strip, above described, lay the uncivilized or undeveloped part of Georgia, stretching far to the westward. It was one vast forest, for the most part trackless and unexplored, and was inhabited only by the scattered tribes of Creek and Cherokee

Expansion of Georgia. 325

Indians. There was not on the American continent at that time any more desirable region for pioneer settlers

Map Showing Expansion of Georgia.

than these wild lands of Georgia. The statesmen of Georgia fully appreciated this fact, and immediately after the Revolutionary War they began to arrange for opening these lands to settlers. The first step was to clear the Indians out of the region, and this was done promptly and vigorously.

II. THE FIRST EXPANSION: FROM THE OGEECHEE TO THE OCONEE.

As you have already learned in the chapter on Alexander McGillivray, the State of Georgia, in the year 1784, under the guise of a so-called treaty, forced the Creek Indians to give up all of their lands lying between the Ogeechee and Oconee rivers and extending up to that section of the Cherokee country which had already been acquired by the whites. Thus an extensive, beautiful and most inviting region was added to Georgia's domain. It was divided into two great counties, Washington County on the south and Franklin County on the north. These two great counties have since been divided up into ten or twelve Georgia counties of the present day.

Every possible encouragement was given by the State to the rapid peopling of this new acquisition. The lands were literally given away. A large portion of them was bestowed as bounties or rewards on Georgia soldiers who had fought in the Revolutionary War. Besides these "military grants," as they were called, the State allowed any new-comer, who was "master or head of a family," to go into the new region and select for himself any parcel of land, not over two hundred and fifty acres, that he might choose, provided it was not already claimed by some one else. He had to bear the expense of the survey himself, and was also required to pay a merely nominal price for the lands. Then the lot was his, and the State issued him a warrant for it, known as "Head-Right," because each head of a family, after complying with the conditions named, had a legal and indisputable right to the property.

Notwithstanding these great inducements and advantages, there was seemingly one very serious drawback to the rapid settling of this choice region, and that was the attitude of the Creek Indians. As you have already learned, these Indians, under the instigation of their supreme chief, Alexander McGillivray, repudiated the so-called treaties by which these lands had been given up. From their homes on the west side of the Oconee they made frequent destructive and bloody forays on the white settlements on the east side of the river. These irregular and fitful, but exceedingly dangerous, forays were kept up for nearly ten years and are known in history as the Oconee War, an account of which you have already had in connection with the story of McGillivray. In spite of this danger many bold pioneers moved with their families into the region; and not a few later paid the penalty of their daring with their property or their lives. For mutual protection they lived close together, formed military companies among themselves, went always armed, and built rude forts, called "block-houses," in which their families could take refuge during a foray or in times of special danger. The remains of a number of these "block-houses" stood in Georgia until recent years, and the location of some of them can be pointed out to this day.

A Block-House.

In 1796 the Indians, as you have been told, were perfectly pacified by the Treaty of Coleraine, and gave no further trouble. The emigration into the new country, which had all along been flowing in a steady stream, was now greatly increased in volume. Many of the settlers came from the older parts of Georgia, especially from Wilkes and Columbia counties; but a large majority of them were emigrants from states other than Georgia. They came mainly from North Carolina and Virginia, with a considerable intermixture of South Carolinians and some Marylanders.

The North Carolinians, who were largely of Scotch-Irish stock, settled chiefly in Franklin, Banks, Oglethorpe, Madison, Washington and Montgomery counties. Most of them were poor people, not poverty-stricken, but of very moderate means, owning few slaves or none. They were not a cultured folk, but they

From an old print.
Family of a Pioneer in the Interior of Georgia.

were robust and wholesome in body and mind, and of sterling character. Many of the ablest men of Georgia came from this North Carolina stock.

The Virginians settled mainly in the section now contained in Hancock and Greene counties. They were wealthier, better educated, and, in a social sense, better bred than the North Carolinians. Most of them were tobacco planters, whose lands in east Virginia had, from long use and careless cultivation, become worn out and unproductive. The opening of the rich, fresh lands of Georgia came as a godsend to these Virginians. They disposed of their Virginia estates and in great numbers moved to "Georgy," as they always pronounced it. The migration of a well-to-do tobacco planter from Virginia to Georgia was a striking spectacle. The family emigrant train usually consisted of

Emigrants and Plantation Wagon.

one or two six-horse plantation wagons, with their great boat-like bodies and arched canvas coverings. Into these huge wagons were stored necessary agricultural implements and the rude belongings of the negro slaves. They were accompanied by two or three two-horse wagons, loaded with provisions for the journey and with the furniture of the white family; and one of these wagons was generally set aside to be used as an ambulance for the weak and feeble negroes and for such as might be taken sick on the journey. The women and children of the white family rode in a vehicle comfortably provided with springs and seats, and known as a "Jersey wagon." The men and youths of the family rode on horseback. The negroes, or all that were strong enough, walked the whole distance, driving the flocks and herds before them. Of course, the outfits of the poorer emigrants were much more modest than the one described, consisting of two or three (or in some cases maybe of only one) two-horse wagons, carrying all their goods and chattels. The journey generally occupied a full month or more. On reaching "Georgy," the emigrants usually found rude, temporary homes already provided for them, prepared by gangs of workmen who had been sent on several months in advance to make a clearing in the forest and erect a few log cabins.

With wonderful energy and rapidity all of the settlers, both North Carolinians and Virginians, cleared away the primeval forest and brought the virgin soil under cultivation. The fresh lands of Georgia, even the uplands, were at that time exceedingly fertile and productive. As some one said: "You had but to tickle the bosom of the earth with a plow and she would laugh an abundant harvest into your lap!" The people devoted themselves exclusively to agriculture. They raised mainly foodstuffs and supplies for home consumption. Corn, wheat, oats, rye, barley, potatoes and pumpkins were produced in great abundance. Flocks and herds of cattle, sheep and hogs were raised. The woods abounded with game, and the streams teemed with fish. There was an overwhelming plenty of the "good things of the earth" for both man and beast. Wool, some flax, and even a little cotton for clothing and leather for shoes were produced and manufactured on the farms. Almost the only "money crop" was tobacco, which these people had learned so well to raise in Virginia and North Carolina.

The principal tobacco market was Augusta; but tobacco growing was not a lucrative business for the planter, barely furnishing him with money enough to buy such necessaries and comforts as he could not make at home. Fortunately, however, these were few. There was never a more independent, self-sustaining, self-respecting people in the civilized world than these pioneer settlers of middle Georgia.

The extreme southern part of the new region (included mainly in what is now Emanuel and Tattnall counties) was one unbroken pine forest, with comparatively sterile soil, and at that time it was supposed to be entirely worthless for agricultural purposes.

Naturally, it was settled up very slowly. By the year 1800, however, a few people, generally very poor, had moved into this uninviting region and established their homes amid the sighing wilderness of pines. Of these people and all the other "piny wood folks" of Georgia, we shall have more to say further on.

In 1783 Georgia had, including whites and blacks, 35,000 inhabitants. In 1790 the population was 82,000, and in 1800 it was 165,000. This increase was owing mainly to the emigrants from other States who had moved into the newly opened country between the Ogeechee and the Oconee. All of the desirable lands in this strip were now occupied, and even the sterile "piny woods" contained a considerable population. The people began to call importunately for more lands. The times were now ripe, the conditions favorable and the demand imperative for another expansion of Georgia. As before, the thing to be done was to make another clearing away of Indians.

III. SECOND EXPANSION: FROM THE OCONEE TO THE OCMULGEE.

In 1802, 1803 and 1804 Georgia acquired from the Creek Indians by fair and legal treaty, or "purchase," as these transactions had now got to be called, all of the lands lying between the Oconee and the Ocmulgee rivers. Thus another beautiful region fully as desirable and nearly as large as the previous one was added to Georgia's domain. So anxious was the State for the rapid peopling of this new acquisition that again she literally gave away the lands. But the method of giving away was entirely different from the old "Head-Right" system. In its stead a new and original device known as the "Land Lottery" was adopted.

The plan was this: The newly acquired territory was thoroughly surveyed by government surveyors, and was marked off into lots of about two hundred acres each. An accurate map of the survey was made, on which the lots were numbered 1, 2, 3, and so on. There were several hundreds of them in all. Numbers corresponding to the numbers of the lots were then written on bits of cardboard, and together with a great many blank cards were placed in a "lottery box" in the Capitol. From this lottery box "every Georgia citizen, every Georgia widow with minor children, and every family of Georgia minor orphans" had a chance to "draw" for a lot. In order that none might miss their opportunity, an alphabetical list of all eligible persons in each county in the State was carefully made. A blindfolded boy stood by the lottery box (which was frequently well "shaken up"), and as each name was called in alphabetical order he drew out a card. Thus every eligible person in the State had his or her chance. A great many drew blanks, of course, but many also drew prizes, a rich prize or an indifferent prize, according to the location of the lot he happened to draw. The drawing was done in the presence of five sworn commissioners, and it was also open to the public if the public chose to attend. It was a tedious process, and occupied several weeks. Under this plan fraud, cheating and unfair play were impossible.

A great many people who drew lots in the new purchase did not themselves settle on them, but sold them to others.

As soon as the preliminaries were over, settlers by hundreds crowded into the newly opened country. A majority of them were already Georgians, coming mainly from the families of the Virginians and North Carolinians who fifteen or twenty years before had emigrated into the new region between the Ogeechee and the Oconee. The elder sons of these families, and in many instances the old folks themselves, now moved into the still newer country between the Oconee and the Ocmulgee, on account of the advantages offered by the still fresher and richer lands. A great many new emigrants also came from other States, mainly again from

Virginia and the Carolinas. A very large proportion of these settlers were people of means, education and refinement, and of the highest character. No new country was ever settled by a better, finer or more capable class of people, with a smaller intermixture of base and inferior elements. Money, brains and character were applied at once with powerful energy to the development of the region. It had not the rough, rude and coarse experiences that usually belong to the pioneer life of a new country; but by a wonderful change, not gradual, but sudden, it passed from the dark night of barbarism into the full light of a high and noble civilization. This was especially true of Putnam, Jasper, Jones, Baldwin, and Morgan counties and measurably true of Twiggs, Wilkinson, Laurens, and Pulaski counties; but Dodge, Telfair, and Montgomery counties, which lay chiefly in the "pine barren" section, had, like all the rest of that strange region, a very slow development; in fact, had scarcely any development until after the Civil War.

From a print of 1841.
Oglethorpe University, Midway, Baldwin County.

All of the forces and influences that go to create a noble civilization and to develop great men were now fully at work in Georgia. The management of public affairs, the administration of law and justice, the development of the new country, the conducting of agri-

The University of Georgia, Athens, Ga.
The Oldest State University in the United States.

culture and commerce, stimulated intellect and aroused ambition. In all professions and callings men of a high order of ability arose, and among them there appeared some men who were pre-eminently great.

Along with territorial expansion came great improvements to the whole State. Churches were built in great numbers, and they were well attended and well supported, and some of them were served by preachers of wonderful eloquence. Ever and anon great religious revivals would sweep over the country exerting a good and lasting influence on the character and the lives of the people. People *felt* religion much more deeply in those days than they do in ours. A "religious revival" meant more then than it does now. Then it was "deep calling unto deep"; now it is usually "shallow calling unto shallow."

Soon after the Revolutionary War, Georgia began to manifest much interest in education. In 1802 the University of Georgia was established. Academies and "old field schools" were quite abundantly distributed over the State, and they were the great educators of the people. The methods of these old-time schools were no doubt crude and faulty, and they are the object of unstinted ridicule and abuse by the self-conceited pedagogue of the present day; but somehow many of the greatest men, the noblest characters and the best-trained intellects that the State of Georgia has ever produced were educated at these old-time schools. "By its fruits shall the tree be judged."

In 1793 Eli Whitney invented the cotton gin.* It

---

*For an interesting account of the invention of the cotton gin, see Joel Chandler Harris's charming little book, "Stories of Georgia."

proved to be one of the most important events in the history of America. This simple contrivance, scarcely bigger than a baby's cradle, made the fortune of our Southland, fixed her destiny, and determined the character of her civilization. Its effects were felt speedily and powerfully, especially in Georgia. By the year 1815 the cultivation of tobacco was almost wholly abandoned in

By courtesy of The Howe Photographic Company, Atlanta, Ga.
Picking Cotton on a Georgia Plantation.

the State, and the raising of cotton was adopted in its stead. The farmers still continued to raise all of their own provisions and supplies, so cotton was "a surplus crop." It proved to be a much more lucrative product than tobacco. Georgia farmers who all along had been making a good living now began to acquire wealth. A stream of emigrants, with their gangs of negroes, came pouring in from Virginia to make money by raising cotton on the fresh soil of Georgia, a power they had lost by raising tobacco on the worn-out lands of the "Old Dominion."

By the year 1818 well-nigh every desirable acre of land in the cotton belt of Georgia from the Savannah to the Ocmulgee River was occupied. The people began to call importunately for more land to raise more cotton to make more money. The time was ripe, conditions were favorable, and the demand imperative for another expansion of Georgia. Again the thing to be done was to make another clearing out of Indians.

IV. THIRD EXPANSION: FROM THE OCMULGEE TO THE FLINT.

In 1821, by another treaty, or purchase, the State of Georgia acquired from the Creek Indians all of the lands lying between the Ocmulgee and the Flint rivers. This region, as a whole, was well adapted, both in soil and climate, to the cultivation of cotton. The lands were distributed among the people by the Land Lottery plan, and the country was settled up very rapidly. The upper part was settled mainly by plain people in moderate circumstances, and without much education, but of sturdy, sterling character. The middle and lower parts were settled very largely by rich planters from the contiguous older counties of Jones, Jasper and Putnam. This was specially true of Monroe, Bibb, Houston and Macon counties, into which sections wealthy settlers came in large numbers, with their gangs of negroes. Here they implanted the high civilization to which they had been accustomed, and in this new soil it flourished like the green bay tree.

A large majority of the settlers of the new region, both rich and poor, devoted themselves to the raising of cotton. Indeed, this had now become the greatest industry of Georgia. King Cotton, in his fleecy robes, was now thoroughly established on his throne, and ruled the State with undisputed sway. He proved one of the most energetic of monarchs and gradually wrought a wonderful change in Georgia's civilization, giving to her customs and modes of life their permanent form. He enabled his subjects to make great fortunes. He built towns and cities, influenced politics and government, and there was scarcely an important business or public enterprise in the State in which he did not take a hand.

Raising cotton was a profitable business in Georgia in those days. The staple brought from twelve to fifteen cents a pound. As the cost of production was small and the farmers still made their provisions and supplies at home, the cotton money was nearly all clear gain. People made fortunes rapidly. Choice lands in the new purchase could be bought for a dollar or two dollars an acre. Often men would pay for a farm or a plantation with one year's crop of cotton. From 1820 to 1840 may be called the money-making period *par excellence* in Georgia's history. The negro population grew enormously during this period. The natural increase among these people was great. From selfish interests as well from humane impulses, masters took good care of their negroes, who rapidly increased in numbers, the birth-rate exceeding the death-rate. Besides, large numbers of new negroes were brought into the State. Though the importations of natives from Africa had been entirely stopped by the Federal Government, many slaves were brought from Virginia and eastern Maryland, which had become congested with negroes. These states contained many more slaves than could be used with profit; so the owners sold off their "surplus stock" to negro speculators, who brought them in great droves to Georgia and sold them at a handsome profit to cotton planters. These "nigger traders" were held in universal contempt by the people; nevertheless they were liberally patronized, and they made money by their traffic. As fast as the planters made money by raising cotton, they spent it in buying more lands and more negroes, to raise more cotton to make more money, so

Expansion of Georgia. 343

that they could buy more land and more negroes. For twenty years or more this increase in wealth and slave population went on. Georgia had now won the title of "Empire State of the South."

Scene on a Cotton Plantation.

During the first part of this period the best people of Georgia lived in the country on their farms and plantations, where the greatest men that Georgia ever produced were born and reared. The brains, character and culture of the State were not concentrated in towns and cities, as is now the tendency, but were to be found in the country.

V. FOURTH EXPANSION: SOUTH GEORGIA AND ITS TARDY DEVELOPMENT.

Until 1814 the Creek Indians remained in possession of an extensive territory in extreme south Georgia. It consisted of a broad zone of country stretching from near the Atlantic Ocean on the east across the State to the Chattahoochee River on the west. In this region was embraced the beautiful "Tallasee Country," so beloved of the Creek Indians, and which, as you remember, had been saved to them by the masterful diplomacy of their great chieftain, Alexander McGillivray, in the Treaty of New York in 1790. At length, however, in the year 1814, the United States Government, acting for the benefit of the State of Georgia, by the Treaty of Fort Jackson forced the Creek Indians to give up the whole of this southern territory. By a subsequent treaty, made in 1816, a small strip lying to the northeast of this territory was added to the cession.

Into the new country thus acquired there was no immediate rush of settlers. It was not considered as a desirable or inviting region. The Indians were expelled from it not mainly to make room for white settlers, but to protect the already settled parts of

Georgia. It seems not even to have been surveyed by the State Government until after 1818, which shows that there was not much demand for the lands. The eastern portion of it was covered very largely by the so-called "pine barrens," which in those days were thought to be worthless for agricultural purposes. The western portion was almost unexplored land; and because it lay next to the hostile Alabama Creeks, who lived on the other side of the Chattahoochee River, it was regarded as dangerous ground. Hence while every other newly opened portion of Georgia was settled up with great eagerness and rapidity, the southern zone of the State lay for a number of years neglected and ignored. It was not until after the year 1825 that any considerable number of people moved into this region. In the meantime it had been discovered that mixed with the "pine barrens" there was a good deal of fertile hummock land lying along the rivers and creeks. These choice spots were bought up by planters living in the old and now nearly worn-out eastern counties. There they settled with great gangs of negroes, and soon brought the soil under fine cultivation. It was discovered also, in the course of time, that the western end of the zone, or what we now call southwest Georgia, was made up very largely of rich and fertile lands, both bottoms and uplands. Wealthy men from middle and western Georgia bought up these tracts in large estates, turning them into cotton plantations, which they peopled with troops of negroes in charge of overseers. It was considered in those days a very undesirable country to live in, on account of malaria and bad water, so the owners of these plantations usually had their homes elsewhere, and visited their places only two or three times a year. Even into the "pine barrens" proper a good many poor people crept (for the lands could be had almost without money and without price), and there established their rude homes, and there lived for generations and generations, in unprogressive simplicity and strange isolation.

It was not until several years after the War between the States that the possibilities and resources of south Georgia were fully realized and that it received its true development.

VI. FIFTH EXPANSION: FROM THE FLINT TO THE CHATTAHOOCHEE.

In the year 1825, by the famous Treaty of Indian Spring, of which you have had a full account in the chapter on "Troup and the Treaty," Georgia acquired from the Creek Indians the rich and beautiful region lying between the Flint and the Chattahoochee rivers.

Expansion of Georgia.

The Creeks had now surrendered to the whites the last foot of land that they owned in Georgia. Two years later they were removed in a body to a reservation set aside for them beyond the Mississippi River.

There was an immediate rush of settlers into the vacated lands. The upper part of the new purchase was settled almost entirely by poor people with few slaves or none. The lands there were generally poor and were not supposed to be adapted to the cultivation of cotton, and hence were exceedingly cheap. The settlers devoted themselves largely to raising cattle. Most of them were from the older parts of Georgia, but there was also considerable emigration from other States. These people, as a rule, were good, honest and industrious, but there was among them a lawless and depraved element that gave much trouble. The middle section of the purchase was by far the best. The richest and most desirable lands (the section now included in Coweta, Troup, Meriwether, Harris, Talbot and Muscogee counties) were settled mainly by wealthy planters from central Georgia. By the careless and wretched system of tilling the soil that then prevailed through the cotton belt of Georgia, these planters had, in the course of fifteen or twenty years, worn out or greatly damaged the fertile uplands of their original places; and now they moved to the fresh, rich lands of western Georgia only to pursue the same land-destroying system of agriculture. They brought with them not only industry and energy, but also wealth, culture and social refinement, which they transplanted with perfect success into the new region; and in a marvelously short time they caused "the wilderness to bloom and

From an old print.
Columbus, Muscogee County, as It Appeared When First Settled.

blossom as the rose." The southern end of the purchase included the upper part of what we now call southwest Georgia. For reasons already given this was at that time considered an undesirable region to live in, though it contained large areas of fertile lands. These were bought up by rich men, who converted them into big cotton plantations, peopled with negro slaves, in charge of white overseers. The owner rarely lived on the place himself, but visited it only occasionally for business purposes. Throughout both the middle and the southern sections there were quantities of poor piny woods lands, which were usually settled by people correspondingly poor, for they sold for a mere trifle.

VII. SIXTH EXPANSION: THE CHEROKEE COUNTRY.

In the northwest corner of Georgia lay that extensive region of country which was still possessed and occupied by the Cherokee Indians. The story of how these Cherokees were finally, in 1837, expelled from Georgia and transported beyond the Mississippi, has been fully told in Chapter XVIII. Thus passed the last red man from the State of Georgia!

The new territory thus acquired was a beautiful region, covered with hills, mountains and interlying valleys, with a bracing and delightful climate. From this region have been formed the counties of Cherokee, Bartow, Gordon, Cobb, Forsyth, Gilmer, Lumpkin, Murray, Paulding, Walker, Chattooga and Floyd. The whole of it was distributed among the people of Georgia by the Land Lottery system, already described. In one part of the territory (the section which is now Lumpkin, Gilmer and Union counties), some gold had been found, and the belief generally prevailed that the whole section thereabouts was extremely rich in the precious metal. Several years before the Cherokees were expelled, many adventurers had gone into this so-called gold country, from which they were driven at the point of a bayonet by the State militia. When the lands were finally distributed among the whites by lottery, those persons who drew lots in the "gold diggings" sold them readily at a high price to capitalists and adventurers. The purchasers moved at once into their possessions and began searching for gold, expecting to acquire princely fortunes in a short time. But almost without an exception they were bitterly disappointed. They found little or no gold, and in the course of a year or two their visions of untold wealth had "gone a-glimmering like a schoolboy's dream." The lands for which they had paid such a high price were for the most part sterile, mountainous and rugged, and of little value for agricultural pursuits. The disappointed owners sold them for a song and moved away, or else abandoned them to the first "squatters" who might come and take possession. Except in a small region around the present town of Dahlonega, in Lumpkin County, gold mining in Georgia has never "panned out" anything worth considering.

After this mountainous, rugged and sterile part of

Georgia was abandoned by the disappointed gold seekers, it was occupied by mountaineers from North Carolina. Their descendants are still in the Georgia mountains; and though rough, they are honest, kind, independent and hospitable.

The hill country below the mountains, including what is now Cobb, Forsyth and Cherokee counties, was more inviting to enterprising settlers than the mountain section just described. Still it was far from being a choice region for agricultural purposes. It was rugged and stony, and the lands were generally more or less sterile. They were very cheap, and for ten or twenty dollars a man could buy a small farm of forty or fifty acres. They were occupied mainly by settlers coming from east and northeast Georgia, especially from Franklin, Hall, Jackson, and Madison counties. They were a sturdy, brave, self-reliant people, but possessed little property and little education. They devoted themselves to the cultivation of corn, wheat, rye and oats, and to cattle raising. They did all of their own work, for there were few slaves among them. They lived very comfortably, but plainly, for they had never known luxury and were independent of it. Most of them had a limited English education, but there was scarcely a classical scholar among them.

The best part of the Cherokee acquisition was what

was then known, and is still known, as the "blue limestone country." The choicest section of this choice region was included in what is now Chattooga, Floyd and Bartow counties. It was a beautiful country, covered with lofty hills and broad, fertile valleys, watered by swift rivers and bold, crystal streams; the scenery was charming and the climate was invigorating and delightful. The region was rapidly settled up, mainly by people of wealth and culture. Many of them were from middle Georgia; many came also from excellent families in South Carolina. They brought their gangs of negro slaves with them, and quickly established large, well-cultivated farms. The broad, fertile valleys lying between the lofty hills were splendidly adapted to the cereals, and abundant crops of corn and wheat were produced. For many years prior to the Civil War and during the Civil War, this section of Georgia was the great granary of the State. By the year 1840 nearly all of this blue limestone region was well settled by a very superior class of people, who soon established churches, good schools and a civilization of refinement and culture.

Georgia had at last spread her civilization to the utmost confines of her present geographical limits; but as yet she had not reached her full development.

CHAPTER XX.

GEORGIA AND GEORGIANS IN 1840.

I. THE MOUNTAINS.

In 1840 Georgia had, according to the United States Census, 691,492 inhabitants, including 407,795 whites and 283,697 negroes.

Let us take a rapid bird's-eye view of Georgia and her people at this time.

The State naturally divided itself into five principal sections, namely: The Mountains, the Up Country, the Cotton Belt, the Sea-Coast, and South Georgia.

The Mountains embraced an irregular zone or belt stretching across the extreme northern part of the State. This section was sparsely inhabited by a peculiar and picturesque type of the Anglo-Saxon race known as mountaineers. They were uneducated and without ambition or aspiration. In personal appearance they were generally tall, raw-boned and muscular, and unshaven, unshorn and unkempt. They spoke with a rapid utterance and a quick, sharp accent; and their language was replete with provincialisms, such as "mam" and "pap," "we uns," "you uns," "yan," and "beyant." They were universally very poor and lived in the rudest fashion. They knew not the common comforts, much less the luxuries of life. Their homes, nestled in the mountain gorges, were rough log cabins, generally with only a single room, in which frequently a family of ten or twelve persons lived. Their food and clothing were correspondingly coarse and meager. The mountain-sides, owing to roughness and steepness, were not arable, so their farming was confined to the narrow and contracted valleys, the lands of which were generally more or less sterile. Their principal crop was corn. This they converted into bread for eating and whiskey for drinking, for they were hard drinkers. Small herds of cattle grazing on the mountain-sides and a few hogs in a pen near the house furnished them with sparse rations of meat. They handled very little money. They would earn a few dollars by now and then selling "a bunch" of cattle, or a barrel of corn whiskey, or a few chickens, or a cart-load of apples, to their better conditioned and more civilized neighbors among the foothills to the south of them. They would have to journey many miles over the worst

From an old print.
Cabin of a Mountain Settler.

Georgia and Georgians in 1840.

A Mountaineer.

of roads to get this produce to market, but these trading expeditions were almost the only contact they had with the great world beyond their mountain peaks. They had no slaves, and there were no negroes among them. Many of them grew almost to manhood and womanhood without ever seeing a black face. Notwithstanding their limitations and deficiencies these people possessed certain sterling virtues that command the respect of all men. They were brave, honest, independent, kind-hearted and hospitable. Though they were great drunkards and fighters, heinous and base crimes, such as murder and theft, were extremely rare among them. In the mountainous regions of northeast Georgia may still be found many specimens of this type of people but little changed after sixty years, or two gen-

Mountaineer Mother and Daughter.

erations. There are many others who have been considerably improved by contact with civilizing influences, but none of the class has ever attained a high plane of civilization and culture.

II. THE UP COUNTRY.

Just below the mountains lay what was generally known in those days as the Up Country, so called because it was in the upper or northern part of the State. It was also sometimes called "the Hill Country," because it lay among the foothills of the Blue Ridge Mountains.

The inhabitants of this region were much more advanced in civilization than the mountaineers above them. Still they were a plain people, with little wealth and little education and with no great pretensions or lofty aspirations. They lived on small farms, which they worked with their own hands, for they owned few negroes or none. By hard labor they managed to dig a fair subsistence out of the stony and not very fertile soil. They usually had the common comforts of life, but were entire strangers to its luxuries. The principal products of the country were corn, wheat, rye, cattle and horses. The people were the shrewdest horse traders in the world. The "horse swapping conventions," held annually or semi-annually in the different towns and villages, were unique meetings and were full of ardor, life and business ability. There were also many distilleries in this region, which manufactured great quantities of corn and rye whiskey. Much of it was shipped and sold in other parts of Georgia, but much of it was also consumed by the people at home. They indulged extensively in hard drinking, which was their chief and most harmful vice. Gambling also was too common among them. Notwithstanding their vices, they were essentially a good and worthy people; and when the temperance reformer, the religious revivalist, and the schoolmaster came among them they yielded readily, and gave up in large measure their wicked ways. These people constituted the true yeomanry of Georgia, and the State had reason to be proud of them. From this stock sprung some of Georgia's ablest and most notable men.

This sketch does not apply to the "blue limestone" section of the hill country in northwest Georgia. As has already been stated, that region was settled from the beginning by people of wealth, culture, and refinement.

III. THE COTTON BELT.

Straight through the middle of Georgia from the Savannah to the Chattahoochee River stretched a broad, irregular zone of country, known as the "Cotton Belt," so called because it was wholly given over to the raising of cotton; and, indeed, at that time it was supposed that the staple could not be successfully cultivated outside of that belt. This was by far the most flourishing part of Georgia. Here King Cotton had reigned supreme and absolute for twenty years. He had brought great prosperity to his domain. He had built several large cities and a number of smaller towns. He had made many of his subjects very rich, and many more comfortable, independent, and well-to-do. He had established as fine a civilization as ever existed on the face of the earth.

From a print of 1831.
City Hall at Augusta.

From a print of 1831.
Medical College, Augusta.

The wealth of this section consisted mainly in lands and negroes. The small farms of twenty or thirty years before had practically disappeared, for they had been bought up by rich men who combined them into large plantations. Many very rich men owned several such plantations and counted their slaves by the hundreds. These princely cotton planters did not generally live on their plantations. Their luxurious homes were usually in some city, or more frequently still in some smaller town, contiguous to their estates, where they could give personal attention to their business. The direct management of the plantations was in the hands of overseers, who lived on the plantations near the negro quarters. These overseers were generally men of energy and of fine judgment and executive ability. They received good salaries, and some of the more thrifty of them accumulated considerable fortunes and, in the course of time, became themselves owners of plantations and negroes.

The management of a great cotton plantation in those days was a good illustration of executive ability. The government was well-nigh perfect. The slaves were divided into gangs of plow hands, hoe hands, axemen, et cetera. There were also carpenters, blacksmiths and other mechanics, all well trained in their various crafts. The discipline was very rigid, but rarely ever cruel or over-severe. Absolute obedience and hard work were required of every slave, and where these were not forthcoming, punishment by flogging with a leather strap was sure to be the penalty. These negro slaves were their owner's most valuable property, and his financial interest, to say nothing of humanity, made him take good care of them. They were well housed, well clothed and well fed. The weekly ration (or "allowance" as it was called) of a field hand was a peck of meal, three and a half pounds of bacon and a pint of molasses. They were also supplied with the common vegetables in their season, such as turnip and collard greens, peas, and sweet potatoes. Their meat diet was varied by fresh beef now and then, and during "hog-killing" time by an abundance of toothsome fresh pork. Each family was allowed a patch of land for a garden, and nearly every one had a hen-house full of chickens. The best-available physicians attended the negroes in sickness, and educated white preachers were employed at good salaries to administer to their spiritual needs. They "enjoyed religion" keenly in an emotional way, but it had little influence on their morals, which were generally slack.

The feeling between master and slave was usually of the happiest nature. They were deeply and warmly attached to each other. With all of the modern talk about the "universal brotherhood of mankind," the world will never again see such genuine love and affection between the high and the low of God's human

A Black Mammy and Her Charge.

creatures as that which existed between the Anglo-Saxon master of the South and his negro slave.

At the period of which we are speaking there were more negroes than whites in the cotton-growing region of Georgia. They were a very superior class of negroes. As stated in a previous chapter, most of them or their parents had been brought to this State from Virginia and Maryland. They were many generations removed from their savage and degraded ancestors who had been brought from Africa a century or two before. During all of these generations they had been in constant and close contact with the best civilization of America, first in Virginia and Maryland and afterwards in Georgia; and they had acquired, for people of their race, remarkable intelligence and a culture which, though purely imitative, was nevertheless very genuine. All of the missionary societies in the world put together have never done as much for low, benighted and degraded peoples as was done for the Africans by the institution of Southern slavery. By that institution they were raised to a higher plane of civilization than they could ever possibly have attained by any other means;

Family Cook.
Type of Middle Georgia Slave.

and under that institution they were, take it all in all, the healthiest and happiest people that ever the sun shone on.

Besides the very wealthy planters above described, there was a much larger number who were not so rich, but still well-to-do, owning a score or two of slaves or less. This class generally lived on their plantations and took direct charge of their affairs without the aid of overseers. There were also still left a number of small farmers, who worked their small places mostly or entirely without slave labor. These generally lived in the "piny woods" sections, where the lands were comparatively sterile and very cheap. Some of these piny woods people were extremely poor and ignorant. The negroes regarded them with great contempt and called

Mulatto House-Maid.
Type of Middle Georgia Slave.

them "piny woods poor white trash." Like the mountaineers of northeast Georgia, they were generally without ambition and hopelessly unprogressive. There are many specimens of them in the piny woods of middle Georgia and south Georgia to-day, little changed from their ancestors of two generations ago.

IV. THE SEA-COAST.

From the City of

A Mountaineer and His Wood Cart.

A Piny Woodsman and His Splinter Cart.

Savannah southward, bordering on the shores of the Atlantic Ocean nearly down to the Florida line, there was a strip of country known as "the sea-coast," or, as it was more commonly called, "the low country." A more appropriate name than either of these would be (to adopt a Virginia phrase) "tide-water Georgia." The section embraced a large part of the present counties of Chatham, Bryan, Liberty, McIntosh, Glynn, and Camden. The most characteristic feature of this region was the great rice plantations that occupied the low, rich, marshy lands along the river banks near the seashore and some of the islands just off the coast.

The owners of these rice plantations were very wealthy men and lived in princely fashion. They usually had two homes, one on the plantation, where they spent the fall and winter, and the other back in the upland piny woods, where they passed the summer to escape the malaria of the marshes. Both establishments were maintained in elegant style. Their owners were high livers. They indulged themselves in every luxury that money could buy in the State of Georgia at that time. Their homes were furnished in mahogany and rosewood, with solid silver service for the dining-room; their tables were supplied with rich viands and choice wines; they wore costly clothes, rode in fine carriages, and were attended by troops of negro slaves. Their hospitality was proverbial. For heartiness and magnificence it was not surpassed or scarcely equaled anywhere in Georgia or in the South. But these rich sea-coast planters were high thinkers as well as high livers. Most of them were men of classical education and literary culture; their homes were supplied with good libraries, and they subscribed for the leading newspapers and magazines both of this country and of England. In political faith they were democrats, but by birth and rearing they were aristocrats in every fiber of their being. They were inclined to draw the social line sharply wherever they went. An illustration of this may be found in the society caste system that prevailed in Savannah before the Civil War, and that exists there to some extent even to this day.

The negroes who worked on these rice plantations were the lowest and most degraded of their race in Georgia. They were either native Africans or the children of native Africans. They had not been in America long enough to become much civilized. In thought, feeling, and mode of living they were still in large measure savages, but most gentle and docile savages, as all Africans are. They were still under the influence of African superstition. Many African words were mingled with their English speech, and their accent was so peculiar that a stranger could scarcely understand them. They came very little in contact with the master and his family. They were in direct charge of white overseers, who maintained over them a rigid but not unduly severe discipline. Their work during three or four months in the year was very hard, but the rest of the time their tasks were exceedingly easy. They outnumbered the whites among whom they lived ten or twenty to one. They might have risen in insurrection and in a single night exterminated the whole white population, but no thought of rebellion or resistance or even of complaint ever entered their minds. They were perfectly content with their lot, as well they might be; for, poor as their condition seemed, it was infinitely better than it ever had been or ever could possibly be in the jungles of Africa. Along the sea-coast of Georgia there are still many unmixed descendants of these lowly Africans of sixty years ago; and, though they are much more civilized, they still preserve in many particulars the characteristics of their ancestors, as is shown especially in their humble and submissive spirit and in the peculiar accent and lilt of their speech.

The sea-coast plantations were not devoted entirely to the cultivation of rice; a number of them were given to raising sea-island or long staple cotton, which brought nearly twice the price of ordinary short staple cotton, and the production of which was an immensely profitable business.

Back from and immediately adjoining the rice plantations were stretches of sterile pine lands, which were occupied, as such lands nearly always were, by poor and ignorant people. They made rather a scanty living by cattle raising and by floating rafts of pine logs down the rivers to the sea to be sold to lumber dealers and shipped to various parts of the world. Between these inhabitants of the piny woods and their neighbors, the rich rice planters, there was almost no intercourse; but it made no odds to the poor woodsman, for he was one of the proudest, most independent and self-sufficient of citizens.

No other part of Georgia has perhaps suffered so great a change since the Civil War as this rice planting, sea-coast region. The great rice plantations and the rich rice planters, with their luxurious homes and magnificent display of wealth, have vanished like a dream. Thousands of acres of rice lands have been abandoned and have gone back to a state of nature, and are now unarable marshes and swamps. Other portions have been drained and converted into prosperous market gardens, conducted by energetic white men; and other portions still are occupied in spots and patches by lazy negroes, who are content to dig a scanty living out of them. There are still left a few large fields cultivated in rice, just as they were more than a hundred years ago. The fine houses that were the homes of the wealthy antebellum planters are now, in some instances, occupied by negroes or very poor white people, and are fast going to rack and ruin.

V. SOUTH GEORGIA.

In Chapter XIX was given, in a general way, a description of that broad zone of country known as south Georgia. The characteristic feature of this section of the State was the immense, unbroken pine forests that with dreary monotony occupied hundreds of thousands of acres of land lying for the most part as level as a parlor floor. These great pine forests were the predominant feature of the country from the Altamaha to the Chattahoochee. They were not confined to the extreme south zone of the State, but covered a considerable portion of what may be called east-middle Georgia, including, especially, Emanuel, Tattnall, Montgomery, and Dodge counties. Much of the land was too wet for culture, much of it a barren sand bed, and very little of it was naturally rich and productive. In the early days of the State the whole region was regarded as hopelessly barren and unfit for agricultural purposes, hence it was settled very slowly.

The first people to move into these "pine barrens," as they were called, was a large colony of Scotch-Irish folk who came directly from North Carolina, where they had been living for several years. About the year 1800 they bought, for a merely nominal price, immense tracts of land in Montgomery and Telfair counties, and moved thither with their families. They were not farmers, but ranchmen or cattle-raisers, in a business that requires plenty of "elbow room." So these settlers spread themselves thinly over a large area of country, thus allowing a wide range for their cattle to feed on the wire grass, a peculiar grass that grows nowhere except in the so-called "pine barrens."

These Scotchmen were a race of brave, sturdy, independent and thrifty people. They attached great importance to education and maintained good schools where their children were well taught. In religion they were Presbyterians, and for many years their religious services were held in the Gaelic language. From this good Scotch-Irish stock of the wire-grass country has sprung a number of Georgians eminent in the professions and in public life. Many descendants of the original settlers still live in Montgomery and Telfair counties; others are widely scattered over the State, and wherever found they nearly all preserve the race characteristics, and are an excellent, energetic, prosperous folk.

Besides these Scotch people, a good many Americans from other parts of Georgia and from the Carolinas began about the year 1820 to move into the wiregrass regions. They were invariably very poor people, who were attracted to this region by the great cheapness of the lands. They were crude and ignorant, but in native abilities, possibilities and modes of life were superior to the mountaineers of north Georgia, already described. They were very thinly scattered over large areas of country. They were cattle rangers and wood rangers. They lived isolated and independent lives in their rude homes, with which they were perfectly content. Many years afterwards their descendants responded readily to the civilizing and refining influences that were introduced among them, and many of them are now well educated people and among the most substantial citizens of Georgia.

This region of Georgia had its tragedies, as well as its life of Arcadian simplicity. In the early part of the nineteenth century, speculators bought up hundreds of thousands of acres of it at a very small price. They had it laid off in lots, had an attractive and lying map made of it, represented the lands as being exceedingly fertile and abounding in oak and hickory timber, and so beguiled many innocent persons in nearly all parts of the United States into buying the lots at prices from ten to fifty times as great as the speculators had paid for them. Furthermore, it turned out that these scoundrels had purposely had the lands falsely surveyed, including in their map many thousands of acres that had no real existence. When the innocent victims came from nearly all parts of the Union to Georgia to claim their property, they discovered that they had been outrageously and cruelly swindled. In many instances they could not even find the parcels of land they had bought, and those that were found proved to be practically worthless. The cheated purchasers sold out for a song, or abandoned their property and allowed it to be sold by the State for taxes. This stupendous swindle is known in Georgia history as "The Pine Barren Speculation."

Again, about the year 1830, a rich company of Maine lumbermen bought a vast tract of pine lands lying in Telfair and Dodge counties, with a view to converting the pine trees into lumber for shipment to all parts of the world. They erected on the streams a number of big sawmills with groups of workmen's shanties near by. But the business proved unprofitable, and after two or three years was abandoned, and the mills and shanties were left to rot down. The Northern owners, however, continued from year to year to *pay taxes on* their lands, and thus kept good their titles to them. But as the years went by, many "squatters" crept in and settled on these deserted lands; also a number of designing scoundrels,—deliberate land thieves,—who took possession of large tracts, laid them off in lots, covered them with bogus titles, and sold them out to innocent purchasers. After many years, nearly a decade after the Civil War, the Northern owners of this property, under the firm name of W. E. Dodge and Company, came to Georgia, showing perfect titles to the lands. They immediately proceeded to oust the intruders, as they had a perfect right to do. There were many lawsuits; but the courts decided in favor of W. E. Dodge and Company, as undoubtedly they should have done. Then followed bloody and tragic times that made a mighty sensation throughout Georgia. The "squatters" and the innocent victims of the bogus titles had been living on these lands so long that they believed, or pretended to believe, that they really belonged to them, and they refused to vacate. Conspiracies were formed against the agents of W. E. Dodge and Company, and several of them were assassinated in cold blood. The murderers were arrested and convicted. One of them was hanged and others were sent to the penitentiary for life. Of course, in the end all of the intruders were evicted (for the arm of the law is strong), and Dodge and Company came into full possession of their own.

Down to the close of the War of Secession and for a number of years afterwards, this so-called "pine barren" region of Georgia was very sparsely inhabited, and mainly by very poor and ignorant people. You could ride from ten to twenty miles in many parts of it without passing a human habitation. By degrees, however, it was discovered that mixed with the pine barrens there were many acres of fertile hummock lands, and that the barrens themselves were not so barren after all. Railroads penetrated the country, and a rapid and wonderful development followed. The great pine forests yielded an enormous output of lumber and naval stores (tar, pitch and turpentine), which made fortunes for many men, and a substantial living for very many more. The hitherto despised lands, under careful cultivation and fertilizing, produced from year to year abundant crops of long staple cotton, Georgia cane syrup, tobacco and early vegetables for the Northern markets. Thus within the past decade south Georgia has forged forward more rapidly than any other part of the State, and its population and wealth have increased enormously. It is to-day in material prosperity one of the most flourishing parts of Georgia.

The proud citizen of this region might say without great exaggeration: "This stone rejected of the builders has become the chief corner stone of the temple!"

INDEX.

Adams, President John Quincy, controversy with Governor Troup, 271-280; attitude toward Cherokee Indians, 292.
Alexander, Samuel, murders Grierson, 155, 156.
Amelia Island, 45, 92.
Andrews, Major T. P., investigates charges against Indian Agent Crowell, 267, 268.
Angus, Mr., British stamp officer for Georgia, 125, 126.
Anne, the, Georgia emigrant ship, 11, 13, 14.
Assassination of Cherokee Indian chiefs, 320.
Augusta, city of, visited by Oglethorpe, 91; occupied and defended by Brown, the Tory, 148-150; siege and capture of by Americans, 160-163.
Baird, Colonel James, 141, 142.
Baldwin County, 336.
Banks County, 339.
Bartow County, 352.
Beaufort (S. C.), town of, 14.
Bibb County, 340.
Big Warrior, Creek Indian chief, 254, 255, 257.
Block-houses, 327.
Bloody Marsh, battle of, 104-106.
Bolzius, Rev. Martin, Salzburg pastor, 59, 65, 67, 69.
Boudinot, Elias, Cherokee Indian chief, 289, 320.
Bowles, William Augustus, 225-231.
Boyd, Colonel, killed at battle of Kettle Creek, 158.
Brewton Hill, Savannah, 138.
Brown, Colonel Thomas, Tory leader, career, 147-151; at siege of Augusta, 160-162.

Brown, Mrs., scene with Alexander McGillivray, 221.
Bryan, Jonathan, 133.
Bull, Colonel William, 14, 15, 16, 19, 25.
Bulloch, Colonel Archibald, President of Georgia, 132, 133.
Cameron, Captain, killed at Savannah, 139.
Campbell, Colonel Archibald, 137, 140, 141, 143, 145, 157, 158, 165.
Campbell, Duncan G., United States Indian Treaty Commissioner, 260.
Caroline, Queen, receives Tomo-chi-chi, 35; wears dress made of Georgia silk, 67.
Castell, Robert, dies in Debtors' Prison, 6.
Chappell, Absalom H., his "Miscellanies of Georgia," 233, 250.
Charter of the Georgia Colony, 8, 9.
Chattooga County, 352.
Cherokee Indians, general account of, 285; relations with Colonial Georgia, 285; in the Revolution, 286; civilization of, 288-291; political claims, 292-294; controversy with State of Georgia, 294-300; suits before United States Supreme Court, 301-308; Treaty of New Echota, 313, 314; expulsion from Georgia, 316, 317; assassination of Treaty chiefs, 320. (See also *Treaties with Cherokee Indians*.)
Cherokee Country, the, 349, 350.
Cherokee County, 351.
Clarke, General Elijah, 148-150, 157-164, 193, 196, 213.
Clarke, John, 159.
Cobb County, 351.
Colonial Congress of 1765, why

378   *Index.*

Georgia not represented at, 121; protest against the Stamp Act, 121.
Colonial Dames of Georgia, erect monument to Tomo-chi-chi, 52; restore old Fort Frederica, 85; project monument to Oglethorpe, 118; erect monument on site of old Fort Augusta, 163.
Colonists, Georgia, character of, 112, 113.
Columbus, city of, 90, 348.
Condition of Georgia at close of Revolutionary War, 322-324.
Cornwallis, Fort, 161.
Cotton, beginning of the cultivation of in Georgia, 339; becomes "King," 341; wealth and civilization produced by, 358; princely planters and management of plantations, 359-361.
Coweta County, 89, 90, 347.
Coweta Town, great council of Creek Nation held at, attended by Oglethorpe, 89, 90; great council of Creek Nation held at, attended by Alexander McGillivray, 208.
Creek Indians, 27-33, 88, 93, 208-234, 251-281. (See also *Treaties with Creek Indians.*)
Crowell, John, United States agent to Creek Indians, 258, 260, 267, 268, 272.
Cumberland, Duke of, his present to Toonahowi, 39.
Cumberland Island, 44, 82.
Curry, James, the traitor, 179, 180.
Darien, town of, settled by Scotch Highlanders, 76.
Daughters of the American Revolution, obtain copy of Georgia Colonial seal from London, 11; mark spot where Oglethorpe crossed Chattahooche River on way to Coweta Town, 90; project monument to Oglethorpe, 117; erect marble memorial fountain at Jasper Spring, 189; purchase Nancy Hart place in Elbert County, 203.

Debtors' prisons in England, 5, 6.
Dodge County, 336, 369, 372.
Dolly, Quash, negro guide to British army at capture of Savannah, 137-141.
Dooly, Colonel John, 158, 197-202.
Ebenezer, Old, settled by Salzburgers, 62-64; abandoned, 65.
Ebenezer, New, settled by Salzburgers, 65, 66; during Revolutionary War, 71, 72; decay of, 72.
Elbert, Colonel Samuel, 133, 137, 138, 143.
Elbert County, 154, 159, 192, 202.
Emanuel County, 332, 369.
Estaing, Count d', at siege of Savannah, 173-183.
Eugene of Savoy, Prince, Oglethorpe serves under, 4, 5.
Extinguishing of Indian land titles, 251, 252, 256, 261.
Florida, 8, 45, 74, 225.
Floyd County, 352.
Forsyth County, 351.
Franklin County, 326, 329, 351.
Frederica, town of, founded by Oglethorpe, 81, 82; progress and decay, 81-85; the "Thermopylæ of Georgia," why so called, 101, 102.
Frederica, Fort, built by Oglethorpe, 82; ruins of, 85; in Spanish War, 102.
French, espouse American cause, 173; army at siege of Savannah, 174-183.
Gaines, General Edmund P., investigation of Creek Indian affairs and controversy with Governor Troup, 269-271.
Gascoigne's Bluff, in Spanish War, 102.
George II., 8, 9, 34, 120.
George III., 122, 131.
Gilmer, Governor, 296, 297, 299, 302, 304.
Girardeau's plantation, landing of British at, 137, 140.
Gold region, the, in Georgia, 298, 299, 349, 350.

Index. 379

Greene County, 329.
Greene, General Nathaniel, 238.
Grierson, Colonel, Tory leader, 155, 156.
Grierson, Fort, 155.
Gronau, Rev. Israel, Salzburg pastor, 59, 65, 67, 69.
Gunn, James, connection with the "Yazoo Fraud," 237-240; death, 247.
Gwinnett, Button, 133.
Habersham, Joseph, 133.
Hall County, 351.
Hall, Lyman, 133, 210.
Hancock County, 210, 247, 329.
Harris County, 347.
Harris, Joel Chandler, his "Stories of Georgia," 202, 215, 238.
Hart County, 203.
Hart, Benjamin, American Partisan captain, 192, 197, 201, 202.
Hart, Nancy, 192-203.
Haslan, William, British deserter, 135.
"Head Right," land title, 327.
Henry, Patrick, speech against Stamp Act, 120.
Highlanders, Scotch, in Georgia, 43, 74-78, 80, 92, 95, 96, 103, 113, 139.
Houston County, 340.
Houston, George, 133.
Howe, General Robert, 137, 138.
Huger, Colonel, 137, 178.
Indian affairs in Georgia in 1823, 251-255.
Indian Spring Treaty, 257-261.
Jackson County, 351.
Jackson, President Andrew, dealings with Cherokee Indian case, 307, 309, 310, 313.
Jackson, James, in the Revolution, 164-172; fight against the Yazoo Fraud, 244-248.
Jasper, Sergeant, in the Revolution, 185-190; monument, 191.
Jekyl Island, 43.
Jerusalem Church of the Salzburgers, 70-72.
Jones, C. C., his "History of Georgia," 84, 107, 133.
Jones County, 336, 340.
Jones, Noble, 133.
Land-claim tragedy, 372, 373.
"Land Lottery," 334, 335, 340.
Laurens County, 282, 336.
Lee, "Light Horse Harry," 160, 166, 167, 168.
Lembke, Rev., Salzburg pastor, 69.
Leopold, Archbishop, persecution of the Salzburgers, 55, 56.
Lexington, Battle of, 131.
Liberty Boys, the, 122, 125, 127.
Lincoln, General, 167, 168, 174, 175, 178, 183.
Little Prince, Creek Indian Chief, 254, 255, 257.
Loyalists (see *Tories*).
Lumpkin, Governor Wilson, 308.
Lynah, Dr. James, 182.
McCall, Colonel, American officer, 160.
McGillivray, Alexander, parentage, 205; education, 206, 207; made chief of the Tribe of the Wind, 207; becomes Supreme Chief of the Creek Nation, 208; in the Revolution, 208-210; connection with Oconee War, 210-225; opposed by William Augustus Bowles, 230; character, 231-233; death and burial, 234.
McGillivray, Lachlan, father of Alexander McGillivray, 204-207, 209.
McGirth, Colonel Daniel, Tory leader, 154, 155.
McIntosh, Chilly, 262, 264, 265.
McIntosh, Lachlan, 133.
McIntosh, William, parentage and character, 253, 254; speech at Broken Arrow, 255; leader at Indian Spring Treaty, 257; murder of, 263-265.
Mackay, Captain, Highland leader, 77, 104, 105.
Macon County, 341.
Madison County, 329, 351.
Maitland, British officer, 174.

Marshall, Chief Justice, decisions in Cherokee Indian cases, 302, 306.
Mathews, Governor George, connection with Yazoo Fraud, 242, 247.
Mayham tower, at siege of Augusta, 161-163.
Milledge, John, 166.
Meriwether County, 347.
Meriwether, J., United States Indian Treaty Commissioner, 257.
Money-making period in Georgia, 342, 343.
Monroe County, 340.
Monroe, President James, 256, 257, 292.
Monteano, General Manuel, in Spanish War, 94, 107.
Montgomery County, 329, 336, 369.
Moosa, Fort, in Spanish War, 95, 96.
Morgan County, 336.
Mountaineers, Georgia, 353-356.
Muscogee County, 17, 23.
Musgrove Creek, Savannah, 143, 178.
Musgrove, Mary, 17, 23.
Negroes, great increase of in Georgia, 342; treatment of by whites, 359, 360; feeling between master and slaves, 361; superiority of cotton-belt negroes, 361, 362; beneficence of Southern slavery, 362, 363, 367; rice plantation negroes, 366, 367.
New Inverness (see *Darien*).
North Carolina emigrants to Georgia, 328, 329, 331, 336.
Oconee War, the, 213-224, 327, 328.
Oglethorpe, James, parentage, education, and early career, 1-5; prison reform measures, 6-8; Georgia Colony enterprise, 8-12; conference with Governor Johnson of South Carolina, 13, 14; finding a location for colony, 15, 16; first meeting with Tomo-chi-chi, 17; reception of Yamacraw visitors, 21-24; treaty with Lower Creek Indians, 30-33; visit to England, 34; expedition down Georgia coast, 40-49; kindness to Salzburgers, 62-65; settles Darien with Scotch Highlanders, 74-77; settles Frederica, 79-83; builds forts down Georgia coast, 82; expedition to Coweta Town, 90, 91; in Spanish War, 92-108; takes final leave of Georgia, 109; closing years of life, 114-117.
Oglethorpe County, 58, 163, 246, 329.
Palmer, Colonel, in Spanish War, 95, 96.
Panton, William, Scotch merchant, 234.
Patriots, 128, 145, 146, 157, 194.
Perceval, Lord, 10.
Pickens, Colonel Andrew, 158.
Pine Barrens, 332, 345, 369.
"Pine Barren Speculation," the, 371, 372.
Piny Woods Folk, 333, 346, 349, 363, 364.
Pitt, William, Earl of Chatham, 128, 129.
Population of Georgia in 1783, 1790, 1800, 333; 1840, 353.
Prevost, General, at siege of Savannah, 174-177.
Products, early agricultural in Georgia, 332.
Pulaski, Count, career, 175; at siege of Savannah, 180; death of, 184; monument to, 184.
Pulaski County, 336.
Putnam County, 336, 340.
Rabenhorst, Salzburg pastor, 68.
Religious revivals, 338.
Rice planters of Georgia, 365-369.
Richards, Major, 43, 48.
Ridge, John, Cherokee Indian Chief, 289, 311, 320.
Ridge, Major, Cherokee Indian Chief, 289, 311.
Ross, John, Cherokee Indian Chief, 289, 301, 311, 318.
Royalists (see *Tories*).
Rum trade, prohibition of by Oglethorpe and trustees, reasons for, 111, 112.

Index.

St. Augustine, siege of by Oglethorpe, 94-98.
St. Simons, Fort, built by Oglethorpe, 98; battle of, 101, 102.
St. Simons Island, 41, 79-82, 98, 99.
Salzburgers, the, persecution in Austria, 54-57; emigration to Georgia, 58-60; settlement and life in Georgia, 61-72; descendants, 73; compared with the Highlanders, 75; lack of enterprise, 113.
Savannah, founding of, 21-25; capture of by British, 133-144; siege of by Americans, 173-183.
Schermerhorn, Mr., United States Indian Treaty Commissioner, 313.
Schools, Old Field, 338.
Scotch-Irish in Georgia, 253, 288, 329, 369-370.
Scott, General Winfield, in Cherokee Indian case, 317.
Sea-coast region, 364-369.
Seal, Georgia Colonial, 10, 11.
Sehoy, Indian mother of Alexander McGillivray, 205, 207, 234.
Senawki, wife of Tomo-chi-chi, 17, 33, 35, 40, 50.
Silk culture in Georgia, 67.
Slavery, prohibition of in Georgia by Oglethorpe and trustees, reason for, 111, 112.
Smith, Captain John, at capture of Savannah, 139.
Sons of Liberty, 122, 126.
South Carolina, 13, 14, 17, 25, 88, 92, 93, 98, 99, 108, 159, 166.
Spain and Spaniards, 8, 14, 42, 45, 48, 72, 77, 87-108, 212, 223, 225, 230.
Speedwell, the, Georgia stamp ship, 124.
Stamp Act in Georgia, 120-130.
States' Rights, 224, 270-281.
Stevens, Rev. W. B., his "History of Georgia," 84, 133.
Talbot County, 347.
Tallassee Country, the, 214, 222, 344.
Tassel, George, Cherokee Indian hanged for murder, 296, 297.

Tattnall County, 332, 369.
Telfair County, 336, 372.
Thunderbolt Road, Savannah, lines of battle across, 138, 139.
Tomo-chi-chi, first meeting with Oglethorpe, 17; visit and speech to Oglethorpe, 21-24; character, aid to Oglethorpe in founding Georgia, 27-49; death and burial, 50-52; monument, 52, 53; unselfish patriotism, 110.
Toonahowi, adopted son of Tomo-chi-chi, 17, 33, 39, 44, 48, 106, 107.
Tories (Loyalists, Royalists), 128, 132, 140, 145-149, 157-171, 194-202, 324.
Treaty, with Cherokee Indians, of Augusta, 210; of 1819, 287; of New Echota, 313, 314.
Treaty, with Creek Indians, of Savannah, 30; of Augusta, 210; of Galphinton, 214; of Shoulderbone Creek, 215; of New York, 222, 223; of Coleraine, 225; of 1802-1804, 333; of 1821, 340; of Fort Jackson, 344; of Indian Spring, 258.
Triebner, Rev. Christopher, Salzburg pastor, 70, 71.
Troup County, 347.
Troup, Governor George M., 225-284.
Trustees of Georgia, 9-11, 57, 110, 111.
Twiggs County, 336.
Twiggs, General John, 172.
Tybee Island, 15, 135.
University of Georgia, founding of, 338.
Up-country folk, 355-356.
Van Buren, President, in Cherokee case, 316.
Vinton, Lieutenant J. R., 277.
Virginia emigrants to Georgia, 328-331, 339.
Von Rek, Baron, leader of Salzburg emigrants, 61, 62, 64.
Walton, Colonel George, 133, 137, 138.

Washington County, 326, 329.
Washington, President George, 218, 222, 225, 236.
Watkins, George, 242.
Wayne, General Anthony, 171.
Weekachumpa, Creek Indian chief, 31.
Wereat, John, 164.
Wesley, Rev. Charles, 83.
Wesley, Rev. John, meetings with Tomo-chi-chi, 40; as Indian missionary, 41; last visit to Tomo-chi-chi, 50.
West Point, town of, 235, 275, 276.
White House, Augusta, used as a fort by Brown, the Tory, 149, 150.
Whitfield, Rev. George, 50.
Whitney, Eli, invents the cotton gin, 338.
Wilkes County, 157, 158, 159.
Wilkinson County, 336.
William, Fort, 98, 99.
Wilson, Judge Henry, connection with Yazoo Fraud, 239, 240.

Worcester, Rev. Samuel A., connection with the Cherokee Indian case, 304-308.
Wright, James, Royal Governor of Georgia, loyalty to English Government, 120; tries to get Georgians to submit to Stamp Act, 121-128; character, 129, 130; flight to England, 131; return to Georgia, 146.
Yamacraw Indian tribe, 16, 27, 28, 53, 106.
Yazoo Fraud, the, the Yazoo country, 235; land speculators, 236; the Yazooists and their corrupt methods, 237-241; passage of the Yazoo Act, 241, 242; sale of lands by the speculators, 243; James Jackson's fight against the Yazoo Act, 244, 245; popular indignation against Yazooists, 246, 247; repeal of the Yazoo Act, 248; public burnings of the Yazoo records, 249; settlement of the Yazoo claims, 250.

CPSIA information can be obtained
at www.ICGtesting.com
Printed in the USA
LVHW082354160521
687618LV00014B/621